LITERATURE
AND
REVOLUTION

JACQUES
EHRMANN

BEACON PRESS   BOSTON

CONTENTS

The Editor

Foreword

In heading this issue "Literature and Revolution" we have resumed Trotsky's title at the risk of appearing presumptuous. Yet if we have taken it up again, it was not in order to take it over, but to echo it and in this way to underline the enduring actuality of this great revolutionary's book. It was also an attempt to reevaluate the problem in function of new data, politico-historical and literary.

Indeed, since the Second World War the urgency and the preeminence acquired by the political scene have become so evident as to obviate any pretense of escape in a world where the slightest conflict, in any spot on the globe, threatens to become fatal to the entire planet. On the other hand, and in contradiction to this situation, literature, at least in the West, seems to have detached itself from politics, retired into itself for lack of a language acceptable at once to both the political and the literary realms. This backing away from commitment is nonetheless the sign of a connection — negative, yet perhaps only temporarily so — between literature and history. Whether this connection be positive or negative, the problem it raises remains as such and will continue to be a problem as long as men are convinced of their power (or their helplessness) to inflect and to reflect the course of history, as long as this power (or helplessness) is manifest in the words which men use.

The power of words over history, of history over words, such is the problem of our own time which begins, in the history of the West, with the questioning, *through words,* of the relationship between man and government in the Age of Enlightenment. It is echoed, *in history,* by the famous refrain: "C'est la faute à Voltaire,/C'est la faute à Rousseau." At first this was the West's own problem, but it has become a world problem since the world has become irreversibly "historical."

To the sound and the fury of the poet's word, for two centuries and with unabating intensity, corresponds the sound and the fury of the silence which political power (regardless of the shade it may assume) imposes more or less openly, stealthily, radically, through censorship, incarceration, or death, upon those heretics of the word, poets. Politics has superseded religion in the governing of men. The heresy may have changed its target but not its form.

Since then, the voice of historical man — the "individual" of our People's or Capitalist democracies — has split in two, built and destroyed by the dialogue between political and poetical powers which speak to him in both parallel and contradictory terms of his freedom.

This issue begins with 1789 and not with the preceding phase which prepared it because we believe that the problem of history — like the problem of literature — could only arise *with* and *after* the first revolution that viewed itself in historicist terms. It was necessary first of all that this historic event take place so that this problem might acquire its fullest meaning and reverberate through literature as a problem. The problem of History — which at moments of acute crisis becomes the problem of revolution — continues to confront us History of humanity lasts — unless the second revolution of our time, the atomic revolution, abruptly interrupts its course. But that too will be our history. And its end.

Even if we do not have the solution, it is fitting to ask whether the space era which we are entering marks the end of the historical era, or whether it is only one of its variants. Perhaps the historical age is already falling behind us, at least in the industrialized countries where revolution — in the sense Western tradition has given to the word, pregnant with the dates of 1789, 1848, 1870, 1917 — has increasingly fewer chances of taking place. Indeed can it not be said that the type of economy toward which these countries are turning is upsetting the kind of power and culture (the arts and literature) that we know, rendering them obsolete and engendering a kind of political and literary discourse bound together by a connection which is still impossible to define, but nonetheless inevitable?

So many questions which can receive only historical answers, and whose answers, in unveiling their meaning, will outdate them both as questions and as meaning. These are questions which in the intervening time we will only be able to resift; questions which we cannot abstain from asking since, as it happens, they are our own.

It becomes apparent then — and this is where we began — how absurd it would have been to limit ourselves to a single national tradition, a single literature, the French, on the pretext that the title of our review mentions it in adjectival form. But how, in 1967, can we understand Sade, Flaubert, Breton, Sartre, and Simon, without becoming aware of the fact that the problem they raise is the same — despite or because of the historical, geographical, sociological, and political differences which separate them — as the one which can be found in Heine, Marx, Mayakovsky, Brecht, Lu Shun, and Gombrowicz? In other words, in order to generalize the problem of the connections tying history to literature, it was necessary to relativize it in function of particular histories and literatures. Thus we had to resign ourselves to being incomplete, to saying nothing about this author or that literature although they are evidently linked to our subject. On the other hand it was necessary, in ensuring a coherent whole, that the concrete analyses and the theoretical ones should serve to illustrate each other and be viewed in varying perspectives. The inevitable gap separating them can lend itself to the personal reflection of the reader.

In closing, I would like to thank my friends: Michel Beaujour for suggesting the topic of this issue, Antonio Regalado for the many conversations we have had together which permitted me to clarify a good number of the subject's points, Michael Holquist for having given me his time so generously and for his advice on the Russian section of this issue, and Peter Brooks for his help on many editorial problems.

September 1967

J. E.

Jacques Ehrmann

On articulation:

The language of history
and
The Terror of language

ar-tic-u-late, *vb*, 1a: to pronounce distinctly, b: to give clear and effective ut-
terance to. 2a: to unite by means of a
joint, b: to form or fit into a systematic
whole.

In approaching the problem — already more than a century old —
of the interrelationship of literature and revolution, I would like to
begin with a very simple definition of revolution: revolution is a political moment of history, situated in History, at which the orientation
of politics changes abruptly and violently, thereby giving a new
direction to history.

This definition lays no claim to being either very original or very
sophisticated; nevertheless, it may be useful insofar as it permits us
to identify three concepts which are often confused: History, history,
and politics.

The capitalization in the initial term, History, will suffice to underline its abstract, global character, marking the course of human
time. Of the two others, politics exists at the level of the isolated historical fact, the event or the limited group of events taken at short
term and in a limited temporal and structural sequence (writing the
history of revolution one might, for example, speak of a politics of
the reign of terror), whereas history falls into a long-term temporal
sequence able to encompass more than one successive politics, and
within which each political event is bound to those which accompany,
precede, and follow it, forming a self-contained structure which embraces them all.

These definitions have nothing absolute about them. They are relative and vary according to the historical sequence one chooses as the entity to be studied (for the historian of the French Revolution there exists a politics of the Reign of Terror; the historian of the Reign of Terror will recognize a politics of Robespierre) and whether the history in question is that of the historian who studies it or of the statesman who makes it. The politician or statesman who has an active hand in making the history of his time can know only its political aspect even though he may appeal rhetorically to history to justify the politics he advocates. Inversely, even when he tries to piece together the various politics of a particular history, the historian has finally at his disposition only a historical knowledge of politics. Thus, politics and history involve and exclude each other in reciprocal fashion.

Politics, for the politician, is closed and unidirectional (the politics he practices is in his eyes the only valid one); it is the stuff of history yet to be made and at the same time a judgment on that history which is itself open, since two politicians having opposed views of history may at a particular junction practice a similar politics. For the historian, on the other hand, politics — the politics of the interval he chooses to study — is open and incomplete (more than one must be considered as having been possible), whereas history, because it is accomplished, is closed, unidirectional — the stuff of politics and judgment on politics (it is one politics which will have prevailed over all the others).

Hopefully these indications, which attempt to distinguish between points of view in the literal sense of observation places and which may appear somewhat oversimplified and schematic to the historian or the student of politics, will uncover their usefulness when the time comes to relate literature and revolution.[1]

Finally, let it be pointed out that in a "normal" (nonrevolution-

---

[1]Without going into the detail of an analysis which would exceed the limits of this study, it should be noted that this distinction between history and politics would resolve the confusion sustained by a number of authors concerning the "historical" role and status of literature. Sartre, for example, in the three essays of *Situations II*, often shifts from one term to the other, either unsystematically or without notifying the reader.

Jacques Ehrmann

ary) period of history, historical continuity is preserved due to the fact that the rhythms of history and of politics are not the same. Thus even if politics changes abruptly these changes take place within a history which assures continuity (for example, the change from Fourth to Fifth Republic in France). On the other hand, when there is a break on the level of history, continuity is ordinarily maintained on the level of politics (for example, the political continuity noticeable between the Third and Fourth Republics despite the historical rupture of the Second World War).

These distinctions made, it is possible to modify in the following way our first definition of revolution: revolution is a violent rift because it occurs *simultaneously* at the levels of politics and of history. The Hungarian uprising of 1956 was not, according to this new definition, a revolution, since the political overthrow it sought to bring about never succeeded in imbedding itself in history. Those who were active in it might have at that moment hoped they were bringing about a revolution; however, it was not until its failure (the moment at which it became *historical*) that it was recognized as merely a revolt.[2] Logically, therefore, it is impossible to say I am or We are bringing about a revolution. Revolution comes about. The true subject of revolution is history.

In order to understand better the links between politics and history — a relationship whose implications for literature will soon occupy our attention — it may be pertinent to review the comparison between language and games proposed by Hjelmslev:

> One might say that a language is put together like a game — chess, for example, or a game of cards. . . . Like different games, different languages have rules that are totally or partially different. These rules govern the way in which one may or may not use a particular element, or piece, or card. They limit to a certain extent the possible combinations but in language, as in

[2]Cf. *Les Temps modernes*, special issue on "La Révolte de Hongrie" (January 1967). Note the inconsistent terminology: "revolt" and "revolution" are used alternately from one article to the next, or even within the same article. It is worth calling attention in this issue to a number of articles pertinent to the present subject which deal with the relationship of intellectuals to the authorities and their role in the uprising.

chess, the number of possible combinations, the number of possible signs that can be formed, is immense. The body of rules governing the number of pieces composing a game and the ways in which each piece may be combined with the others can be called the structure of that game; this structure differs from the actual practice of the game in the same way that the structure of a language differs from its usage. To describe the usage of a game it would be necessary to furnish indications not so much on the way in which one *may* play the game (its structure) as on how the game is *habitually* played or how it has been played up to the present (its usage) — that is, on the patterns sanctioned by convention under certain conditions.[3]

It is permissible at this point to carry the terms "structure" and "usage" of a language or a game over into History and to speak of its structure and usage, keeping in mind that the comparison is of limited validity since it has to undergo some transformation when applied to a different field. Structure corresponds to history, usage to politics. We might thus paraphrase Hjelmslev and say that history can be called the complex of rules governing the status of each of the elements in the structure of power and the way in which each can combine with the others. To describe politics would require indications concerning not so much the manner in which one *may* practice politics (which would be history) but rather the way in which politics has been practiced *habitually* (which is politics itself).

This comparison of the structure and usage of a game to history and politics has the advantage of pointing up the play and interplay *(jeu)* inherent to History — the slack between combinations, usages, the politics which have actually solidified into facts, as well as those in whose name these last were conceived (the politician's point of view on his own politics) or those which might have been possible (the historian's point of view on the politics of a given period). Into this space, into this interplay slip the two extreme visions of the world, one — the revolutionary's — future-oriented (see Blanchard's

[3]Hjelmslev, *Le Langage* (Editions de Minuit, 1966), pp. 66-67.

Jacques Ehrmann

remarks on Saint-Just), the other — the counterrevolutionary's — past-oriented (Regalado on Donoso Cortés).[4]

With this possibility of and necessity for leeway *(jeu)* in our history we reach the crucial juncture of the problem of revolution. This kind of free play *(jeu)* is the gap through which violence may burst at any moment, the flaw in the armor which admits the sword-point. Thanks to this flaw in History, after all, and through it, our historical civilization could be born. (To speak of a flaw is perhaps not strictly accurate here; without it, without the provision for free play *(jeu)* in the armor, the armor would be rigid but would no longer be armor.)

Thus the possibility of free play points up the need for articulation. The very latitude *(jeu)* necessitated by a joint is at once the weakness of an articulation and its essence. We shall choose the locus of this articulation to articulate our own observations on the relationship between history and revolution, between revolution and literature, pursuing our analysis of this articulation which the dictionary gives to understand in three ways at the same time: as joint, pronunciation, and forming of a systematic whole.

Revolution, then, is situated at the juncture of two histories, appearing as the moment when the relationships between politics and history become disjointed for lack of a suitable language to articulate these relationships, and also for lack of a language (that is, a symbolic conceptual system) fit to articulate reality.

At the oncoming of revolution the rules of the game which codified a certain political and institutional order become inapplicable con-

[4]The play in History between history and politics will be found also on the level of institutions and laws. Thus to the three operational concepts that we have already identified (History, history, politics) correspond three other concepts which cover and complete them: the Laws, laws, justice.

By the Law is meant the bio-sociological organization of human societies. It is less easy to know than to postulate. This encourages systematization and has the advantage of providing a theoretical framework within which individual anthropological discoveries come to roost. The framework is scientific insofar as this biological organization *could* be observed in all human societies, metaphysical to the degree that hypotheses still unverified by any biological discovery are involved. (These furnish the philosophical foundation for the anthropology of Lévi-Strauss in particular.)

The term "laws" refers to the structural aggregate of a society's institutions as they exist in codified form. This term has a function equivalent to the terms "history," "structure" (of a language), and "rules" (of a game) examined previously.

Justice, finally, as it is rendered in court, is the usage of laws. If politics is waged in the name of history, justice is dealt in the name of the law. The practice of justice is inevitably the object of a constant reinterpretation at the level of language, the object of an arbitration necessary for the continuation and intelligibility of law as well as for the maintaining of order.

cretely and inadmissible ideologically — repugnant, in a word, because paradoxically they appear so arbitrary. Far from feeling itself articulated by these rules, society finds itself gagged and paralyzed by them. Violence is the only means of overcoming this paralysis. The institutions which sanctioned the play *(jeu)* of history are overturned. With the old game and the old rules invalidated, the rules of a new game and a new order await articulation (that is, pronouncement). The difference between these two orders and systems of laws (pre- and post-revolutionary) is clearly illustrated in the passage from Victor Serge's novel analyzed here by Richard Greeman, particularly the phrase "The laws are burning," with its symbolic value.

In the interval between the two orders, however, anything goes. Theoretically all orders are possible in an interjacent situation of disorder — the vacuum, the dead joint of history to which corresponds the furious struggle of revolutionary factions, from the most moderate to the most extreme, a battle whose inevitable outcome is the reign of terror, inescapably linked to "the intermediate phase of revolutions" as Sebag puts it, and whose own role is to purge the revolution of its impurities, to "cleanse" it, even at the price of physical extermination pure and simple. Literally, the reign of terror may be considered as the purest, most utopian phase of revolution.

But the all-too-evident disorder and confusion, beneficial in the context of the "order" of the past whose strictures were felt to be paralyzing, cannot continue indefinitely. The reign of terror is harmful to society for two contradictory reasons: the ironclad rules for self-purification it imposes on society quickly become so oppressive that society is paralyzed by them; inversely, seen by society as disorder, chaos, breakdown of rules, and absence of restraints, it paralyzes society by its very lack of restraint. The essential thing at that point is to articulate, to pronounce immediately new rules and new laws which restore society's flexibility (that is, its possibilities of articulation) and which permit the articulation of a new politics on a new history.

And on a new literature, perhaps. In its terrorist phase, given

Jacques Ehrmann

the urgent nature of the political problems to be solved, revolution cannot bother with literature. As Trotsky aptly remarks, "the moments of great tension — those at which our revolutionary age finds its highest expression — do not favorise literature and artistic creation in general. When the cannon thunders the muses are stilled. We had to be able to breathe more easily before literature could be reborn. Literature here is beginning to revive with the N.E.P." ("Le parti et les artistes," in *Les Lettres Nouvelles* [May-June 1967], p. 119). In effect, the N.E.P. opens the constructive phase of the Russian Revolution; the stated wish and the warnings of Trotsky and of numerous artists notwithstanding, however, it is clear that for literature it opens the destructive phase as well, since it is precisely at that moment that literary order begins to find the new political order constricting. The constraint is already discernible in Victor Serge's article "Is a proletarian literature possible?" written in the Soviet Union in 1925 and directed at French readers. Can the proletarian political order engender a proletarian literary order? In other words, can politico-economic structures reflect literary structures, and vice-versa? — the Marxist's question to which neither Marx nor Engels replied directly or systematically, as Edmund Wilson shows perceptively in his essay "Marxism and Literature" (in *The Triple Thinkers* [rev. ed. Oxford University Press], 1948).

Trotsky, the first Marxist theorist to have faced the question directly, gave a somewhat reserved answer which the following sentence may be said to summarize: "One cannot approach art in the same way one approaches politics . . . because [artistic creation] has its rules and methods, its own laws of development" ("Le parti et les artistes," p. 115). Few were the politicians and, often, the artists who subscribed to these remarks *of a Marxist,* thoughts whose accuracy and implications are only just beginning to be appreciated, thanks to the development of structural methods of analysis applied to history and to literature. The impossibility foreseen by Trotsky of superimposing term for term (via mechanical, not dialectical, analogy) bourgeois culture and proletarian culture, politics and artistic creation was to be proven thirty years later by Roland Barthes in his *Degré zéro de l'écriture,* from which the chapter "Writing and revolution" will be found reproduced here.[5]

It does not seem exaggerated to say that this question of the relationship between literature and politics has been *the* major question of the period between the two world wars and has given to this period its most deeply seated unity. Anyone who has not had direct experience of this and has the curiosity to look will find tangible evidence of its importance on every page of back issues of liberal and leftist journals, continental and American, such as *Partisan Review, New Masses, The Monthly Review, International Literature, Clarté, Commune, Le Surréalisme au service de la révolution, Europe,* and so on.

This question is also at the heart of the dispute between Surrealists and Communists, which is the subject of the highly informative essay by Robert S. Short, "The Politics of Surrealism, 1920-36,"[6] prefaced by a revealing epigraph taken from André Breton: " 'Transform the world,' said Marx; 'Change life,' said Rimbaud; for us these two rallying-cries are but one." But for Breton and the Surrealists, who are poets above all, changing the world and life means planting poetry in life like a bomb (the bomb of a language pushed to the farthest limits of the utterable) whose continuous explosions would make the revolution "permanent." Thus for them it was less a question of engineering a revolution than of living it. It is not surprising therefore that most Surrealists chose to remain faithful to the poet rather than to the political thinker.

In the Soviet Union the question crystallizes in the thirties, more precisely in 1934 at the First Soviet Writers' Congress[7] concerning the problem of socialist realism. J.-P. Morel shows in this connection that the relationship between ideology and reality presupposes a

---

[5]See also the immensely useful and important article by Roman Jakobson on the ideological nature of realism, "Du réalisme artistique," translated from the Russian in *Tel Quel,* No. 24 (Winter 1966). This article dates from 1922, which says a great deal about the genius of this critic and about the witlessness or unawareness of so many others who continue imperturbably to wield this term, hardly guessing that the use of tongs in the form of quotation marks might help them avoid burning their fingers.

[6]In *The Left-Wing Intellectuals between the Wars, 1919-1939,* ed. Walter Laqueur and George L. Mosse (Harper and Row, 1966). Published in the *Journal of Contemporary History,* Vol. 1, No. 2 (1966).

[7]Cf. *Problems of Soviet Literature,* Reports and Speeches at the First Soviet Writers' Congress, A. Zhdanov, M. Gorky, N. Bukharin, K. Radek, A. Stetsky (New York, International Publishers, n.d. [1934?]).

Jacques Ehrmann

theory of the mirror-image infinitely more complex than the apostles of socialist realism were ready to admit, bound as they were by political imperatives.

These imperatives made themselves felt beginning in the twenties. Many of those who preferred not to submit to them or who, in their conscience as writers, socialist or otherwise, could not bring themselves to do so gave in to despair. "A lost generation" was Jakobson's somewhat bitter epitaph in his article after the death of Mayakovsky, excerpts from which will be found in this issue, translated from the Russian. To the somber tally of suicides must be added the expatriates and those who were reduced to silence (a euphemism, alas) by Stalin.[8]

A lost generation — perhaps, but not for everyone. Particularly not for the state, which did not hesitate to utilize Mayakovsky, making him into a hero whose proportions were idealized and conventionalized by the socialist realist technique of the same official art to which he had been unable to submit. Nothing speaks more eloquently of this than the collage of photographs and texts assembled by Michael Holquist. These juxtapositions alone suffice to expose the ideological contradictions contained in the various judgments made on this poet.

The Soviet example of ideological contradictions stemming from the encounter and the resulting clash between literature and politics is undoubtedly the most extreme and the most gratingly ironic because of the number of human lives involved, but it is not the only one. The same ideological blindness, the same impoverishment of art subjected to the dictates of politics are denounced in postwar Poland by Gombrowicz in the passages from his *Journal* translated here and constitute one of the themes of his most recent play, *Operetta,* of which we print here the hitherto unpublished "Commentary."

But no single camp has a monopoly on obtuseness. The mask that Gombrowicz hangs on his characters would hardly seem out of place in a right-wing dictatorship or, for that matter, in a liberal democracy. There is a fine and voluminous anthology to be compiled

[8]See also *Dissonant Voices in Soviet Literature,* ed. Patricia Blake and Max Hayward (Pantheon Books, 1962).

17

by juxtaposing texts of all types on Gide before and after the *Retour de l'URSS,* on the art of Romain Rolland, Barbusse, Malraux, Céline, Brasillach, Pound, and others, judged according to their political stands. Of course neither these authors nor their critics could be acquitted.

This brings us back inevitably to the three questions which our civilization has asked for more than two centuries. Briefly, they are:

(1) Is there a relationship between literature and politics? The answer is twofold and is furnished by history itself. Yes, because so many writers have borne its costs, at times at the price of their lives; no, because there is no example of a work of literature (poem, novel, play) which has had a direct and immediate influence on the course of history (see Claude Simon, "Littérature: Tradition et révolution," in *La Quinzaine littéraire,* No. 27 [May 1-15, 1967]).

(2) Are words weapons? They are insofar as revolutionary rhetoric stirs up crowds and insofar as they inform us of certain political situations. But what we expect to find in these cases is not art. No, words are not weapons, since we continue to read authors independently of their ideology. Lenin read Pushkin. Furthermore, when used by "true" artists, words reveal to us precisely the other side of political ideologies, as we will try to show further on. After all, what good would literary language be if it only recapitulated political language?

(3) May literature, *must* literature play an educative role in a revolutionary society? If the answer to this question has been affirmative for so long without ever being sufficiently qualified, it is because it is founded on the myth of education inherited from the philosophers of the Enlightenment. Born at the same moment, the concepts of (social) education and history are probably congenitally linked. Our historicist civilization may therefore be said to be a civilization of education as well. Without taking this idea any further — pages would be necessary to establish it and give it dimension — let us say that it is not by chance that Sartre saw in the eighteenth century a writer's paradise. This same problem of the education of a writer's public haunts the pages of *Qu'est-ce que la littérature?* in

Jacques Ehrmann

the form of the triple question placed at the beginning of the book and which forms its three parts: "What is writing? Why does one write? For whom?" To which he adds, "it seems in fact that no one has ever been moved to ask" (*Situations II* [Gallimard, 1948], p. 58). It is hard not to be surprised by this statement; I find it difficult to believe that all during his youth and the early part of his adult life Sartre never opened *Europe, Commune,* or any of the reviews mentioned earlier in which these same questions are studied from every conceivable angle. As a matter of fact, exactly these questions were asked by Mao Tse-tung in 1942, in his "Talks at the Yenan Forum on literature and art."[9]

It is evident that a writer writes for a certain public, but that he does not choose this public, as Barthes quite correctly points out. The writer can write only for people who can read, who know how to read. To speak of the problem of education by literature thus makes sense only at the sociological level, not at the literary level. When a revolution storms a country and is fomented by and to the advantage of the least educated class, those who direct it must guide it through two successive stages: the first, political, must raise the level of instruction of the masses. Clearly this problem did not exist for France in the same way it existed for the U.S.S.R. in 1917 or for China in 1942 or today. These historical, sociological, and cultural differences are stressed by the studies of Spence and Chisolm devoted to the latter country.

The second, literary, stage is the province of the artists of the new society, whose job it is to create a new art. Trotsky understood perfectly that these two stages were distinct when he wrote: "The principal task [of the party] in the domain of literature and culture is to develop the instruction . . . of the working masses and to create thereby the basis for a new art" ("Le parti et les artistes," p. 20).

To jumble these planes and these imperatives, to subordinate literature to politics under the pretext that it is dependent on history (within limits which will be defined) is to distort both poetic lan-

[9]In *Selected Works*, Vol. 3 (Peking), pp. 69-98. One may well be perplexed when certain Marxist theorists reproach Sartre for the idealism of his question "What is literature?" He shares the shortcoming with Mao.

guage and history. This we now know. Our certainty is recent, however. It appears that not until revolution proved to be impossible in the occidental world (in other words, once the question ceases to be one) were we able to understand this question beyond a doubt. The article by Michel Beaujour is capital in this respect: it destroys all traces of self-illusion that might linger on.

But if this particular question (concerning the relation of poetic to political language) ceases to be such for the poet — and for the politician of good faith — the question of the relationship of literature to history remains a question for the critic and the historian. What is most important is to specify the vantage point from which one speaks of literature or of history. This has been ignored for too long, which is why it seemed essential to distinguish carefully from the very beginning of this essay the points of view of the politician and the historian. Their perspectives on history and on politics may under no circumstances be interchanged or superimposed. The same precautions should be observed when treating the relationship between history and literature.

The error of the politician, or for that matter of anyone who examines literature from a political vantage point (obviously this applies above all to contemporary literature in the broad sense of the term), lies in judging it from the point of view of a history already part of the past. In other words, he leaps over his own time and, posing as his own posterity, mutters anathemas against any work unfortunate enough not to conform to his own political beliefs. We can only applaud when J.-M. Blanchard and Ludovic Janvier find common ground to write, respectively, "to history, literature can make only irrelevant contributions" and "literature that is not naive passes through the refusal to write under the dedication of history." The history they speak of is open, history-in-the-making; a history which is a projection of politics and therefore ideological.

But there is still the other history — closed, history-after-the-fact, seen by the critic-historian who tries to understand how men of past ages invented their history, hoping thereby to understand better how his own era invents and constructs its own history. However, this double understanding does not duplicate itself. There still remains the play between the two, the margin of interpretation through which seeps away the meaning of things known. We do not even have a choice. For us, historians in a historicist civilization, the question of the intersection of literature with history, of literature *and* history, remains open indeed.

To consider it, let us come back to the reign of terror, a moment suspended in history, a moment bereft of meaning, where meaning begins to find articulation. This reign of terror is the blind joint which dictates our vision, the theater at once "ideal" and void of the total drama (*jeu*) in which history and literature, disarticulated, become confused in excessive rationalism or in pure literalism.

At its extreme limit (never actually reached, since it would be the outer edge of limitlessness itself) the reign of terror represents the moment at which the very language which names and organizes the world flows out in an uninterrupted tide intent on wiping out the boundaries of the world as established by law (the law of language) — the "major impropriety" of Sade as Blanchot so admirably puts it. To say everything (*Tout dire*): such is the motive for writing formulated by Sade and which pushes reason to its extremes. His motivation (or his madness) corresponds to the freedom to write everything. In Blanchot's words,

> With Sade — and at a very high point of paradoxical truth — we have the first example (but was there ever a second?) of the way in which writing, the freedom to write, may coincide with the action of true freedom, when such freedom is in a state of crisis and provokes a break from history. *A coincidence that is not identification.* And Sade's motives were not those which set the revolutionary power in motion. They even contradicted them. (italics mine)

It is understandable that the Surrealists found a precursor in Sade, because for him too language had an explosive value. Not just any language — only poetic language enjoys this privilege. Thus it is that in our civilization the Word was made twofold. The Word was Law. But if its ideal objective is to say everything, it fathers violence, disorder, chaos. In breaking through prohibitions it breaks the Law. This anarchic purpose coincides with the revolutionary purpose (the revolutionary too breaks the Law) but contradicts it (the revolutionary's goal is the setting up of other laws). Thus the "law" of poetic language — which consists in maintaining the world "open" through the sheer force of words (breach in the laws which permits communication with the "other side" of the laws) — is finally incompatible with political language, which consists in "closing," in delimiting the world through laws in order better to define "this side" of the laws.

If poetic language can pass through the boundless sea of "saying everything" it can also express itself in the form of an immediate language where it is no longer necessary to say anything at all. J.-M. Blanchard, Michel Beaujour, and Naomi Greene each establish this, in the language of Saint-Just and in the theater and poetry of the French Revolution, in poetic language in general (particularly in certain extreme cubo-futurist experiments), and in the work of Antonin Artaud, respectively.

What these critics focus on, at different moments in our history and through different types of language and of literary forms, is the same dazzling literalness of the word, the same instantaneousness branching out into two modes of communication situated at extreme opposite poles. In the case of the theater during the Reign of Terror, the message is transparent — the audience has no trouble identifying the political situation to which it alludes. In the case of Artaud and the cubo-futurists the message is fused into the language itself, which refers back to nothing other than itself; literalness is onomatopoeic, pure vocalization. However, the language of each is transparent; it is given no density. It is therefore not surprising that in their exacting analyses Beaujour and Blanchard should come to the same conclusion: that poetic language is suspension of action.

Thus the counterpart of Sade's "saying everything" (which ends up saying everything endlessly in an uninterrupted flood of words) becomes, at the other end of poetic language, the cry into which all words are distilled and in which they drown. Infinite, these are the flood and the cry of naked Desire: birth and death united by the ecstasy of an affirmation-negation of the world-language. This inarticulate flood and cry (the apparent pleonasm and paradox are no more than apparent) call simultaneously to our attention the utopia and the tragedy, the origin and the end of language. Everything, in other words; in other words, nothing.

It is easier now to see how the confusion developed between poetic language and political language. In the prerevolutionary phase both seem to seek the same thing, to be in agreement on the urgent need to destroy the old order; they even go so far as to merge in the terrorist phase of revolution, although this is never more than the illusion of a common cause.

Trotsky warns against this illusion from a political point of view in the chapter of *Literature and Revolution* devoted to "Prerevolutionary art." In "Avant-garde and politics," translated here, R. Poggioli shows from a sociological point of view that literary and artistic avant-gardes are ideologically unstable and that they can turn quite as easily to Communism as to Fascism — which from the point of view of politics is clearly inadmissible.

But the illusion of speaking a common language disappears quickly when the terrorist phase of the revolution is over and the task is to create a new political order. This is an unhappy awakening for literature, which cannot function governed by the passwords of authority without seeing itself reduced to idle chatter or to silence; passwords (*mots d'ordre*), principles of order (*mots de l'ordre*) incompatible with the pursuit of disorder and freedom at any price which has been literature's for two centuries.

This is not to say that politics and literature seek to express two different things. On the contrary, it seems to me that both seek to express the same thing: history, or liberty, since both claim to "liberate" men. But if their ways of putting history contradict each other to such a degree it is because they do not describe it from the same vantage point. What literature says originates in language and the possibilities of language. What politics says originates in the world and its possibilities. World and language thus limit each other reciprocally.

Politics and literature scrap for the privilege of annexing history and giving, exclusively, a "true" picture of it. Each tries in its own way to bring the world into its descriptions. Yet for politics, to make history is to use language to represent the world-to-be-won, reality-to-be-realized. Political language is thus realistic in the only acceptable sense of the word: that which subordinates reality to an ideology. It is therefore a means. Through it laws are made and carried out, and (world) order established.

For literature, on the contrary, to historicize is to use the world to conquer language; it is the attempt to inject man (the world, reality) into his language. Poetic language is thus the "elsewhere" of the world. From this point of view, and in spite of traces of "realism" (that is, of ideology, whose mark language inevitably bears) which do enable the historian to situate it in history, poetic language is utopian.

It is not surprising then to discover that the key concepts which temper the question of literature and revolutionary politics are realism (the quotes may be put aside now that we know who is uttering the word and from what standpoint) and utopia. Realism of political intention, accusing poetic language of irrealism (were the Surrealists not irrealists in the Communist view?); realism of poetic intention too, which presumes that reality is to be found in language. And utopia: of political intention, which aims to dominate reality; of poetic intention, which aims to dominate language. A double illusion which Baudelaire foils through irony, as Richard Klein shows perceptively.

We might say, then, that history is built up along a double system of contradictory and complimentary descriptions. Based on a double language, history appears to the historian as a double desire (the mastery of world and language). It is thus a double absence revealed by the very presence of a double which it rejects.

If literature and politics contend for reality — that is, history —

each is bound to consider the other as utopian. To say that the judgment made on one or the other depends on the viewpoint of the judge is no longer a banality but a capital precaution. This can easily be seen by substituting for the word "real" various synonyms: "true," present, here, inside; and for the word "utopian": "false," absent, elsewhere, outside.

But this is not all. In spite of their longing for "purity," for immediacy (particularly evident in revolutionary periods), or because of it, politics and literature are each other's tragedy as well, insofar as each remains unfaithful to the origin and to the end it proclaims. Suffice it to say without further elaboration that literature's tragedy is to be at the mercy of the world, imprisoned in the flesh of reality; the tragedy of politics is to be at the mercy of words, disembodied.

Politics and literature, the agencies which articulate history and are in turn articulated on it, are thus linked by a threefold association. The language which expresses them is realistic-utopian-tragic to degrees that are variable and relative and which must be determined in each individual case, *taking care to identify the standpoint one adopts to speak it, and the object in question.*

It remains, finally, to ask an important methodological question from which it may be possible to draw theoretical conclusions, a question whose answer might shed a new light both on the problem of history and on our own situation as we confront this problem. Can our analysis, which has taken the reign of terror (the moment at which different historical languages tend to become blurred, and beginning with which they become distinguishable) for its point of departure, remain valid in a society, our own, where revolution (in the sense the word takes on from 1789 to 1917) is difficult if not impossible to imagine, as we have presumed above?

If our conjecture is right, if revolution is unthinkable in our industrial society, then the reign of terror which was its pith is automatically excluded both as a historical possibility (pure, poetic moment in history) and as an archeo-teleological ideal of poetic language (history as the origin and end of poetry). We are forced, therefore, to move our inquiry toward the prosaic and indeterminate site of a history without a center (without a terror) and which never either culminates or peters out at any moment of its duration; a history without poetry — that is, without truth; a history in the course of which the various languages which normally give it expression would no longer be able to merge, whose laws would be both historically determined and determinable, but at the same time irreducible to some sort of Law of History.

This essential hesitation, this room for play, brings us back naturally to the distinctions established at the beginning of this essay between politics and history, usage and structure of a language, a game. (At the price of leaving it unused for a time — the time needed to isolate two different types of language — it was perhaps wise to build this framework at the outset and to use it thereafter as the scaffolding for our construct.)

We have seen that the structure of a game (or of history) must be studied within the system of usages which characterize that game (or that history). The several languages which articulate history and which compose it (principally political and poetic languages) may be considered as different usages which allow the historian (of history or of literature) to lay bare the structures of that history.

For the historian, history is made of language, but of a composite language made of different usages (each of which offers contradictory and complementary interpretations of history) whose mechanism (*jeu*) and structures are to be found. Furthermore, each of these languages taken separately is made up in turn of a certain number of usages and interpretations (for political language, each political "discourse"; for literary language, each "work") which combine to form the structure of political or literary activity (*jeu*).

Thus the complex of these usages, these interpretations, these articulations of the play and interplay (*jeu*) of history permit the historian to isolate the rules (structural laws) of history. In turn, these rules constitute the articulation (in the sense of interpretation as well as in the sense of joint), the point of intersection of this history with the *facts* which it embodies.

Jacques Ehrmann

But in enunciating, articulating the structural laws of history, the historian has no choice but to force each usage in the historical complex (*jeu*) into an overall structure which deprived history of its flexibility, its freedom of movement (*jeu*). Thus the historian runs the risk of reducing history to its structures heedless of both the autonomy of the different languages he is studying and the fact that he himself needs language in order to articulate them (in other words, that he is himself in the position of an interpreter). The more the laws he formulates are rigorous (in the double sense of exact and inflexible), the more he will reduce his subject to the algebra of a terse, direct language which we recognize to be that of the reign of terror itself.

It is therefore more important than ever to preserve the rights and duties of interpretation. Not that any so-called autonomy or immunity from the action (*jeu*) of history is to be given to the subject who interprets it; on the contrary, to maintain interpretation it is necessary to involve the interpreter in this action, to include him in it in order to preserve its flexibility and to preserve the freedom of movement (*jeu*) of the structure.

Here we are convinced that the study of literature may and should play a privileged role, insofar as literary language, in its function as the freedom of history and as the conditions for its functioning (*jeu*), offers a prime example of the leeway (*jeu*) inherent in historical activity (*jeu*). If the reign of terror as point of departure and horizon of our knowledge of history has been set aside for a moment, it reappears here as the grounds for that knowledge and as a warning of its limits and limitations. It must thus be reinstated, no longer as goal of the game, ideal purity of an immediate order, but as its (negative) guarantee, continuing possibility of historical interplay, presence of disorder in and of order.

In other words, the reign of terror is no longer the principle of meaning it was to the poet and revolutionary, meaninglessness (*nonsens*) outside meaning (*sens*); rather, integrated into meaning, it embodies the presence of meaninglessness in meaning.

Our concrete historical situation can be said to justify this view of things. If it was possible, formerly, to see in revolution the unique and privileged moment which could, in changing the course of history, carry to men the release of hope, all this has changed. Violence and terrorism have become a part of our daily life: outside, in Vietnam; inside, in Watts and Detroit. It is to be hoped that such violence will be short-lived and localized. But there is another violence — continuous, generalized, directly threatening us all: the violence born of the atomic revolution. Might this not be the reign of terror that is a permanent, inherent fact of our history, following its uncertain course, articulating it and finding articulation on it?

Translated by Barry Lydgate

Michel Beaujour

Flight out of time: poetic language and the revolution

> In harmony, one of the first procedures will
> be to convoke an assembly of grammarians and
> naturalists to devise a unitary language, whose
> system will be regulated on the analogy with
> animal cries and other natural documents.
>
> — Charles Fourier, *Le Nouveau
> monde industriel et sociétaire*

The study of the relations which can exist — and which have repeatedly been said to exist — between revolution and poetry swirls almost immediately into contradictions and confusions. These two expressions of the desire to create another world seem to coincide only on the level where a link can be made between the ideological content of a poem and the economic, political aspirations of an oppressed group or the watchwords of a revolutionary party. At this superficial level — where many poets and critics come to rest — aesthetic investigation is impossible. There the poem figures as one of the elements of a sociological and historical situation, as a kind of emotion condenser which serves a specific rhetorical function in a potential or actual mass demonstration. Written for the occasion, the poem can crystallize an emotion, channel it, and give it form. Widely known, it has its meaning en bloc: a few words, a line, a verse will arouse a whole complex of predictable and desired emotions. Snatches of the poem may serve to evoke its entirety, which under the right conditions assumes a more inclusive meaning: that is why this kind of revolutionary poetry flourishes only with the complicity of the recitant (not necessarily the author) and the audience, and why it measures the full extent of its power in the mass participation of song.[1]

But complicity, at this level, rests on a misunderstanding which

---

[1]The separation of words and music in the modern poetry of the West is, from an anthropological point of view, an aberration which tends to be overcome by recitation, declamation, or group chanting as soon as the poem is recited in a collective situation.

derives from the very structure of poetic language. It is this fertile and inevitable misunderstanding which stirs the collective need for poetry in certain historical periods (the German occupation of France, for example,) and in certain social situations (at rallies and demonstrations) when the group wants both to manifest and to structure its unity, its demands, and its enthusiasm. The demonstration is in fact an aberrant form of action; it accomplishes nothing by itself as long as it is not transformed into a destructive mob. It signifies a desire for action and agreement on the intended objectives. It calls on the participants to acknowledge their number, their strength, and their common faith. But paradoxically, its festive character masks its real impotence, and the demonstration is often a playful substitute for real action. The unity, strength, and fellowship which the demonstration proclaims are only fleeting utopian forms of that unity, strength, and action which, one day, may actually be achieved somewhere in reality. The demonstration therefore needs poetry and song; their words and music also create a kind of fleeting utopia, an evanescent harmony. But if the political demonstration does not revolutionize society, neither does poetry establish or legitimize a new language. Both are only promises: by making *present* what is beside and beyond, their absence is concealed and revealed only to analysis. Demonstrations and poetry try to wrap themselves in their utopias, without ever entirely succeeding. The social order with its obstacles and frustrations continues to exist; so does ordinary language, pledged to its task of patient, difficult communication.

These utopias and illusions are at the crux of the misunderstanding which prevails between poetry and revolution; they are best observed and analyzed in the refrains of publicly known poems. The homeliness of the examples (and their renown) will clear the way for subtler and historically better defined analyses.

Example 1:

Allons, enfants de la patrie
Le jour de gloire est arrivé . . .

Aux armes citoyens . . .
Marchons, marchons . . .

Michel Beaujour

Example 2:
C'est la lutte finale
Groupons et demain
L'Internationale
Fera le genre humain

These poems (we will avoid for the moment any value judgments) are derived from two distinct phases of the French revolutionary movement — one bourgeois and national, the other proletarian and international. However, in ordinary practice, these poems can be sung in the course of the same demonstration. Sometimes, depending on the aim and composition of the meeting, they may be mutually exclusive. Note, however, that their effectiveness, logically in the case of the Internationale, and for complex historical reasons surrounding the Marseillaise, is not limited to French assemblies. If universal revolutionary poetry can be said to exist, it must exist here in these poems, which have spread throughout Europe and the world, which have resounded in the streets, in the factory yards, and in the prisons. To reflect on their extraordinary fortune is to be convinced that there does exist effective poetry, poetry which invites action, poetry which is already a revolutionary act. When the crowd sings the Marseillaise or the Internationale it declares its unity, its common aim, and its impatience to seize power.

But now we notice that these refrains are constructed around imperatives: "Allons! . . . aux armes! . . . formez!" and "Groupons-nous! (Debout les damnés de la terre)." At first glance then these poems do not refer back to themselves, to their own verbal universe, but, in the form of *commands,* they prepare for — and designate — some action in society, since they are addressed directly to those who sing them and who thus express through them their collective will.[2] The idea of preparing for action — and, consequently, of opening a future which is oriented and teleologically organized — is confirmed by the future tenses ("L'Internationale fera"; "Le jour de gloire *est* arrivé": here the present tense is in reality a future to

---

[2]The analysis of first- and second-person plural imperatives, "Allons/partez; Groupons-nous," could be refined. We would see that the people are fictitiously addressing themselves; the authority which gives the order is not exterior to the group which receives it.

31

the extent that glory, while not yet achieved, is the necessary consequence of anticipated future action). These poems are commands, endowed with all the authority of the mass singing in unison. Nothing could be clearer: "Allons! Groupons-nous! Debout!"

These revolutionary poems (in a political sense) are by no means written in revolutionary poetic language (in an aesthetic sense), whose most visible characteristics are ellipses and semantic instability. On the contrary, nothing could be more conservative, more logical, and more clear than these declarative statements which call for action in given circumstances: "Allons, [parce que] le jour de gloire est arrivé"; or "C'est la lutte finale, groupons-nous [afin que] demain l'Internationale [fasse] le genre humain." The ellipsis of cause and effect conjunction (parce que, afin que) could be easily filled in by a child. Political revolution uses the same language as naïve piety:

C'est le mois de Marie
C'est le mois le plus beau
A la vierge chérie
Chantons ce chant nouveau.[3]

Revolutionary violence, provoked and channeled by these poems, does no more violence to language than rose-petal showers in the month of Mary: a wholesome, clear, and direct language is the fulcrum to move the mass or to sanctify it.

If we look a little closer, not at syntax, but at meaning, we immediately become aware of a phantasmagoria. It is not necessary to push analysis very far in order to notice the imprecision of "enfants de la patrie," "jour de gloire," "lutte finale," "demain," and so on. The sharpness of commands like "allons" and "groupons-nous" begins to blur: these orders have no specific content. Go where? Join together how? In what kind of group? Revolutionary enthusiasm marks time in a lyrical chorus, "Marchons! Marchons!" and with

[3]The structural analogies between this pious verse and revolutionary verses are striking: declarative formulas specifying the circumstances in which the song has its meaning, "mois de Marie," "lutte finale," "jour de gloire"; collective exhortation by an expression assigned to the singers, "chantons," "groupons-nous," "marchons." Notice however that the canticle reduces the distance between the reality of the situation and the utopia, to the extent that it belongs to an institution: the month of May *is* the month devoted to Mary in the Catholic Church and a fair-weather month in Europe. But a very clear divergence exists between the religious exhortation and the revolutionary imperatives: the song is addressed to an individual (the Blessed Virgin) who hovers above the crowd of the faithful.

Michel Beaujour

liturgical invocations rallies working-class solidarity. The poem cannot direct the demonstrators: it is addressed to all people in "all times and all places." It is thus addressed to no one and can serve only as a catalyst. Instructions (if there are any — if the song has not degenerated into a simple ritual of solidarity, into an alibi for inaction) have already been distributed or will be later. The song interrupts action. It delimits and consecrates a moment out of time, which suspends and delays the return of the time for action; like prayer, it invokes the eternity of essences — nation, glory, unity, the human race — rather than the specificity of existents.

Poetry is negativity: even that poetry which appeared at first to be the most effective derives its powers (and especially the virtual power it has, as long as it is understood, to move its audience) from the status of poetic language, which, in essence, stands diametrically opposed to the language of action. If the poem can address itself to all men, it is evidently because it cannot command any specific action.

"Debout les damnés de la terre," says the Internationale, a symbolic appeal crowded with connotations and echos: the mythical uprising of the Titans, the romantic conception of Satan, the religious tinge of the class struggle — the whole cosmic and metaphysical revolution as Hugo conceives it. It skirts the promises and defeats of the present to seek refuge in an anti-world. The poem is infested with utopias; it announces for the thousandth time an absent apocalypse, "the day of glory," "tomorrow," "the final struggle," while in the present, men sing. Revolutionary poetry encourages forbearance, enflames minds and hearts, then cools them off; a political demonstration, whose verbal analogue is this poetry, does the same. It procures for the mass a utopian dream, the flash of catharsis, a holiday: it serves the authorities all too well!

Unlike the demonstration which is a dated historical event and a non-reoccurring one (unless it is institutionalized and thus defused), the poem survives. Within certain temporal limits, it is trans-historical. If a Spartacist song were to have come down to us, it would still be endowed with the emotive power common to poetry. Unlike the language of action which is specific and which vanishes as soon as it has fulfilled its communicative function, the poem survives by virtue of those features which render it politically powerless and designate it as a poem: its utopias (metaphors and other tropes), its disregard for the present, the density of its linguistic structure. The poem persists as a linguistic object endowed with an aberrant organization which allows it to connote more than it denotes.

Indeed, what distinguishes the poem from the rallying cry or slogan (historically anchored in a context) is its multiple meanings, its flight from specificity, the distance which it keeps from the referent. It is predisposed to all social tasks. The poem can prove to be politically "good" or "bad" from a revolutionary point of view. Without going into detail, it is worth remembering that one can sing Fascist Marseillaises and anti-proletarian Internationales: like all poetry, to different degrees, the revolutionary poem is capricious.

If revolution is a violent attempt to make relations between men more rational and to make man's transformation of nature more efficient, is the misunderstanding between revolution and poetry inevitable? And the divorce unavoidable? Is it the destiny of all poetic language to have equivocal ties to rationality, that is, to the sanctioned use of language for communication between men and for the conquest of the world? From the perspective of these initial inquiries, the answer would seem to be yes. Further analysis will confirm this intuition, but before proceeding, we must answer a serious objection: is not the poet a kind of linguistic hygienist? If the poet contributes to semantic health, if he gives "un sens plus pur aux mots de la tribu," from which reason can only profit, is he not, in the sphere of language, the analogue of the revolutionary in the social sphere? And, consequently, are not poet and revolutionary, perhaps unwittingly, the twin instruments of enlightenment's progress in the world?

This objection is heard everywhere: it underlies all the formulas which join together revolution and poetry and is so often repeated that it has lent the equation a kind of legitimacy which passes, among certain people, for certainty. But let us examine it in a critic whose political beliefs dispel any suspicion of deliberate obscurantism. What remains is a naïve confusion, hence, a revealing one.

Because it subverts language, and because it tempted him with the promise of salvation, Sartre distrusts poetry. Or rather, he hates it, with a hate which takes its energy from the love and fascination he has determined to repress. But he imagined at a certain moment that the poetry of Francis Ponge might have escaped the curse of poetic language: the miracle was that *Le Parti-pris des choses* put language back on its feet and could thus pass for an authentically revolutionary gesture, the very opposite of Surrealistic "quietism."

In "L'Homme et les choses,"[4] the famous essay on *Le Parti-pris des choses,* Sartre comments on this passage taken from the early writings of Ponge:

> these governments of businessmen and merchants might be tolerable if we were not obliged to participate in them . . . . Alas, the greatest horror is that, within ourselves, the same sordid system speaks, because we do not have at our disposal any other words or any other abstractions (or sentences, that is, other ideas) except those prostituted since eternity by daily use in this vulgar world. (Ponge)

> One can see, it is not really language which he attacks, but language "as it is spoken." Thus he never considered remaining silent. As a poet, he envisages poetry as a general undertaking to *cleanse* language, just as the revolutionary, so to speak, can envisage cleansing society. Besides, for Ponge, it comes to the same thing: "I will rise up only in the pose of a revolutionary or poet." (Sartre)

Sartre's commentary is as ambiguous as possible: it is, therefore, typical of the vagueness which operates in the realm of relations between revolution and poetic language.

Ponge postulates a homology between the "sordid" social order and the "prostituted" order of language, as well as a cause and effect relation between these two forms of degradation. But is the prostitution confined to the language "that everyone speaks," the victim of society's corruption? Does there exist a language other than the

---

[4]Jean-Paul Sartre, *Situations I,* pp. 249-50.

one we all speak? Can the individual, in the privacy of his consciousness, in the particularity of his own speech, hold himself aloof from this order? Ponge does not seem to think so. The individual and his speech are alienated to the degree that society and language are. There is no private garden, no authentic speech miraculously preserved: "within ourselves, the same sordid system speaks." However, Sartre expresses concisely what the whole work of Ponge implies: certain individuals, poets and revolutionaries, succeed in pulling free of the social and linguistic trap and in apprehending the prescribed order so as to overthrow it. How does one grasp and *speak* a truth which departs from the order of the world and escapes it, if man is condemned for all eternity to prostitution? Sartre — and Ponge — sidestep the difficulty which their homology between revolution and poetry entails by endowing their closed system with an escape hatch. It opens onto an Adamic language whose fabulous existence is secured by our nostalgia and which preceded "eternity": a pure and integral language whose original virginity is implicit in the notion of prostitution. The words of Ponge, "ordinary use," "vulgar world," belong to poetic language. The postulation, through negation, of a *special use* of language (only on Sunday, in eternity?) in a *refined world* (an ethereal one? ideal? particularly elegant?) lays claim to no philosophic or scientific status. It is a utopia inseparable from poetic language. At the same time, Ponge's entire poetic work attests admirably to the power of man to deal with words. His powerlessness to overthrow society is no less striking.

This dichotomy cannot satisfy Sartre as an apologist for socially effective poetry. Hence, he introduces a distinction in order to justify the freedom of Ponge qua poet. This distinction, which differs from the implicit primitivism of Ponge, is no less illusory, and without benefit of the same poetic alibi, Ponge does not "really" attack language, but rather language "as it is spoken." If the opposition between "spoken language" and "language — period" has meaning, clearly it must be sought in the normative distinction which our culture makes between *spoken* and *written,* between what is legitimate and what is illegitimate. Without realizing it, Sartre does not ground his judgment on the opposition between "bourgeois language" and the "language of proletarian revolution," but on one which distinguishes great-writer language from the vulgar language of newspapers and socialites. This vulgar language is parasitic; it befouls and deforms without completely obliterating the contour of an eternal essence: authentic language. The poet needs only to "cleanse" it for it to recover its original brilliance, its suppleness and rigor, for it to become the beautiful material of critical and poetic creation. But here we confront the difficulty hidden under the adverbial expression "so to speak," lodged in the crucial sentence where Sartre seemed to establish irrefutably the identity of poet and revolutionary: the poet cleanses language "just as the revolutionary, *so to speak,* can envisage cleansing society." The discomfort one feels here resembles the feeling one gets reading the avant-garde manifestos of the last hundred years: Can the Word have magical power? Can its action be analogical and substantial? Is it enough, as Confucians claim, to speak rigorously in order to remake (to cleanse) society? Or rather does the *like* (the revolutionary *like* the poet) also have a purely metaphorical value? Can one say, without draining the word "revolution" of all content, that the revolutionary limits his ambition to wanting merely to *cleanse society?* "Besides, for Ponge, it comes to the same thing . . . ." No! This move is inadmissible. If the poet can imagine he is polishing a tarnished essence, the revolutionary is engaged in preparing a future which by definition is unknown and which remains to be made.[5]

We have been observing a bizarre series of quick changes: the sense of the word "revolution," in the context of a discussion of poetic language, is precisely the inverse of the one it acquires in a social and political context (as long as one admits that the modern revolutionary is not so Rousseauistic as to conceive the revolution as the unveiling of a primordial golden age, always virtually intact under the filth deposited by society and history). Viewed more

---

[5]I realize that tactical imperatives exist, that the revolutionary can appeal to nostalgia to deceive others and himself. I concede that concepts like "negritude" or "Arabism" can serve to constitute an anti-imperialist ideology. But I would also remark that the Leninist revolution was not based on pan-Slavism, nor the Chinese revolution on "sinitude." The complexity of a revolutionary movement can include — to the detriment of its ends — "reactionary" elements.

closely, the action of the poet on language — whether one conceives it as purification or more drastically — is the inverse of the revolutionary in society. Every poetic revolution is a utopian attempt to return to the origin of words, radical in the literal sense of seeking "the fundamental elements of the root, the spelling of primitive words which pass into derivatives" (Littré). The poetic revolution, because it is poetry and can deal only with the specificity of poetic language, is an old utopia, a mythical dream in which every poet imagines himself to be Adam in the terrestrial paradise.

Even in its utilitarian function of information and exchange, language is a magical abbreviation, since it allows the world (the referent) to be designated and acted upon in its absence. Nothing in its pocket, nothing up its sleeve: the transaction uses the arbitrary currency of phonemes. But this miracle has always seemed contemptible to certain men impatient with the duration to which all linguistic communication subscribes. They would like to abbreviate even more the temporal (syntacmatic) linearity of spoken or written language in order to make it instantaneous. To this enmity of the constitutive duration of discursive speech must be added their refusal of the obstacles which the diversity of languages throws up between minds avid for transparency.

Gestures, cries, tears, or laughter present us with the image of what universal, immediate transparency could be. To the extent that the poem tends toward the status of a "pur sanglot" or a punch in the face, it lends special weight to whatever in language can pass for instantaneous magic — onomatopoeia, sound effects — which escapes the arbitrariness of phonemes. But the poet makes this choice to the detriment of all those features which linguistics has taught us to discern in language as a function of a symbolic system of exchanges: duration and arbitrary and systematic organization are its fundamental characteristics. To escape duration and arbitrariness is not so much to break the chains of language as to break out into the void of non-language. It fosters the illusion of escaping the human condition.

Michel Beaujour

Revolutionary poetry (as it has been defined by *literary* history) claims to be a destructive undertaking (perhaps a cleansing one?) or a resurgence of antiquated poetic languages, or it claims to be a prefiguration, if not an incarnation, of the unalienated language of a world to come: a transparent language of devastating concision, freed from the scourge of time. It is often difficult to distinguish these two divergent assertions, one focused on the origin, the other on the end of time. Directly confronted with non-meaning, the listener is at a loss to know if what he hears is an assault against the alienated language of discourse (the negative phase of destruction) or the unprecedented babbling of the "new man" (in the positive phase of de-alienation). The meaning of the anti-language is always a refusal of present language: above all it signifies No! (This is often its only function, that is, its only meaning.) But it can also mean *somewhere else. Anywhere out of the world.*[6] In this case it offers itself as an indecipherable utopia. At the very least, to the extent that language and society are inseparable, these anti-languages anticipate the abolition of the relations which at present exist within society. We are confronted by an anarchic utopia which eludes all determination and duration: it is a full-blown apocalypse right here and now, the universal holiday, time off forever.

We are far from the sober revolutionary poems (as defined by *political* history) analyzed above. And yet we have noticed that, insofar as the Marseillaise and the Internationale are poems, they are uneasy with the present, overflowing it on every side. They bear the mark of all literary language which poetry only aggravates. The study of radical poetic experiments (which, by seeking to escape the limitations of poetry, emphasize and exacerbate them) may thus indicate more clearly the nature of the relations between poetic revolution and political revolution. The key to their inherent incompatibility can be found in their diametrically opposed way of envisaging time, both as history and duration — and that in spite of appearances.

[6]Baudelaire's English.

Two examples chosen for their historical importance and ideological confusion will suffice to illustrate this argument.[7] In the poetic production of Russian Cubofuturism and German Dadaism the limits of radicalism were immediately attained. Among the Futurists, some were revolutionaries from the first (Mayakovsky), and others rallied to the Soviet revolution shortly thereafter. The German Dadaists, pacifists during the war, found themselves at the side of the Communists during the aborted German revolution. We aim to show that their extreme productions (that is, their most typical ones, since we are dealing after all with extremist movements) barely disguise an infatuation with edenism or apocalypse. In any case, as Trotsky shows with his customary vigor in his study of the difference between Futurists and Communists, we are inevitably dealing with a rejection of time and of history:

> A Bohemian nihilism exists in the exaggerated Futurist rejection of the past, but not a proletarian revolutionism. We Marxists live in tradition, and we have not stopped being revolutionists on account of it.[8]

The limit of the Cubofuturist undertaking, which consists first in emphasizing the *word,* is the creation of a transparent language (and as a result, given the characteristic perversity of language when one tries to transcend it, an *unintelligible* language). To quote Angelo Ripellino:

> The cubofuturists, by dint of testing and decomposing words, arrived at what they called a transmental language (zaumnyi jazyk),[9] which appeared as aimless succession of meaningless

---

[7]It would require a book to analyze in detail the ideology of these movements and their poetic practice. We have restricted ourselves to a few examples and a few generalizations. For further discussion consult the following works.

    Russian Cubofuturism:
        Victor Erlich, *Russian Formalism* (The Hague, 1965), pp. 41-50.
        Angelo Ripellino, *Maiakovski et le théâtre russe d'avant-garde* (Paris, 1965), pp. 11-50.
        Leon Trotsky, *Literature and Revolution* (New York, n.d.), pp. 126-61.
    German Dadaism:
        Raoul Hausmann, *Courrier Dada* (Paris, 1958), pp. 51-68.
        Hans Richter, *Dada — art et anti-art* (Brussels, 1965), pp. 112-15 (following Hausmann).
        Alfred Liede, *Dichtung als Spiel,* Studien zur Unsinnpoesie an der Grenzen der Sprache (2 vols. Berlin, 1963).
[8]Trotsky, p. 131.
[9]Erlich, p. 45, translates these words by "trans-sense language." He adds: "The most extreme proponents of this language were Kručěnyx and Kamenskij. They tried to write verse composed solely of arbitrary combinations of sounds, and they advertised their accomplishments as vastly superior in expressiveness to Puškin's and Lermontov's 'effeminate' poetry."

Michel Beaujour

terms, a confused progression of raw sounds and arbitrary combinations. Kroutchonykh gave us a first example, in December 1912, when he published these grating, meaningless lines:

Dyr-boul-chtchul
Oubechtchour
Skoum
vy-so-bou
r-l-ez.

The following April he published the *Declaration of the Word as Such,* where one can read in particular: "Words die but the world is eternally young. The artist sees the world in a new way, and like Adam, he gives everything a name. The lily is beautiful, but the word *lilia* (lily) is ugly, worn out, "raped." That is why I call the lily *eouy* and thus restore its original purity." On August 31, 1913, Khlebnikov wrote to Kroutchonykh that it was a great find: "Eouy fits the flower. The rapid succession of sounds expresses perfectly the stiff petals (of the closed flower)."[10]

One sees the flagrant contradictions in this linguistic conception: they derive from the rejection of language's arbitrariness. As a result, the arbitrariness will either be exacerbated (as in the poem quoted or in the decision to rebaptise the lily) or negated purely and simply, as in the response of Khlebnikov, who finds a substantial identity between the appearance of the lily and the phonemes invented by Kroutchonykh to denote it. The key to this confusion lies in the manifesto we cited: the artist is a new Adam. But its author forgets—if one concedes that Adam invented language — that he was also the only man not bound by social convention, and that, further, function of language is infinitely more complex than mere naming or designating.

The poetics of Khlebnikov are more complicated, but they too rest on a dream of origins. They incarnate the desire to flee out of time.

[10]Ripellino, pp. 37-38.

The basic unit of Khlebnikov's bizarre idiom is not the individual sound, nor the syllable, but the morpheme; the latter, be it a root or an affix, is bound to have a certain, at least, a potential meaning. Khlebnikov's avowed, though obviously unattainable goal, was to "find, without breaking out of the bewitched circle of the roots, the philosopher's stone of the mutual transformations of Slavic words." . . . One of Khlebnikov's poems, "Incantation by Laughter," is based on an astoundingly ingenious play with formants; it consists almost entirely of newly coined derivatives from the root *smex* (Russian for "laughter").[11]

Here, the myth of origin appears in the desire to preserve the roots, which then refer to some prehistory of language, to a linguistic "nature" of which every natural articulated language is only a distorted reflection, the very sign of its fall into temporality and fragmentation.[12] The reference to a "common Slavic" pertains to a particular form of pan-Slavic primitivism and needs hardly detain us: the radical break (a "revolutionary" one on the level of language) conceals a bizarre return to origins whose reactionary character cannot be mistaken. And too, it seems illogical to limit the temporal regression at the stage of a common Slavic tongue; recourse to etymologies, especially if accompanied by a latent "nominalism,"[13] must eventually lead the poet to Indo-European, and from there, to infinity, to the common birth of all languages. In the end, Adam alone possesses authentic language. It is true that he is equally free of any necessity to communicate.

Although the Cubofuturists reject the "correspondences" of symbolism[14] as being too submissive to ordinary discursive language, their dream of universalism, of purity and immediacy, dictates a mythology which in fact differs only slightly from the mystical, analogical beliefs of the symbolists. The desire for unmediated communication (ex-

---

[11]Erlich, pp. 45-46.
[12]Cf. this striking parallel in a German Dadaist: "indo-european language has an avenging spirit, and itself returns to its sources, to the point where it still had no plural, nor pronoun and where thought (that is, seeing-hearing-speaking) was *categorizing*, super-individual. It is this language, this speaking, which seeks a new meaning for a new use" (Hausmann, pp. 61-62).
[13]See the linguistic, etymological tradition of the Middle Ages.
[14]Erlich, p. 43.

pressed as a transmental language, a kind of utopia of nonverbal communication) is revealed first through the attempt to compress the message into root words, which would tend to accelerate its coding and decoding on the mistakenly conceived analogy of telegraphic language.[15] Their whole aim is to destroy grammar, to supplant it with the flash of "extrasensory" communication. Thus the Cubofuturists fall back on the old dream of perfectly transparent minds, paradoxically attained through the opacity of an atomized message whose linguistic material is stripped as much as possible of its denotations, reduced to suggesting affective connotations. Mediation between minds is entrusted to onomatopoeic morphemes (ultimately replaced by "real noises": the din of machines or the "cacophony of wars and revolutions"[16]). Finally, the Cubofuturists in their impatience with ordinary language can only hope for an apocalypse: at that extreme, time is abolished and all minds erupt in the shattering of the cosmic cataclysm. At that instant, which is identical with eternity, the peal of the divine Word crashes down on chaos. We are poles away from the Leninist revolution, modestly based on the power of the Soviets and electrification.

The "revolution of the word" finds its demented prophet in Jean-Pierre Brisset. He is known principally through the proselytizing efforts of André Breton. His work, which appeared between 1883 and 1913, seems close in many respects to Khlebnikov's. In his *Anthologie de l'humour noir*[17] Breton wrote that Brisset

formulates a doctrine which passes for the infallible key to the book of life. Brisset does not hide his own astonishment at being able to grant men the brilliant prospect of divine omnipotence. The only predecessors he recognizes are Moses and the prophets, Jesus and the apostles. He declares himself to be the seventh angel of the Apocalypse and the archangel of the resurrection.

The cabalistic and totally untranslatable work of Brisset is not strictly speaking poetic. Unlike Khlebnikov's, for example, it claims to be

---

[15]A confusion between the rapidity of transmission and the compression of the text which is based purely on economic imperatives.
[16]Mayakovsky, quoted by Erlich, p. 43, n. 41.
[17]André Breton, *Anthologie de l'humour noir*, Revised Edition (Paris, 1966), p. 309.

objective and scientific. Although it cultivates none of the *differentia* which characterizes poetic language, it approximates it to the degree that it swarms with utopias. And these utopias are all variations on the Adamic, apocalyptic utopia observed in the Cubofuturists. Breton writes about them: "Brisset's fundamental idea is the following: 'The word which is God has preserved within its folds the history of the human race since creation, and in each idiom, the history of every nation, with a sureness and irrefutability which confounds the wise and the simple alike.' "[18]

The deification of language, the "revolution of the word," or the emphasis on the "word as such," does not stand up to objective analysis. It can acquire a semblance of legitimacy only at the heart of a myth which denies the very ground of modern linguistics, namely, the arbitrary and systematic character of all natural language.

Thus for the German Dadaists, who proclaimed the advent of the *Lautgedichte* (the phonetic poem), the rejection of all system, or of structure, must be compensated for by the negation of all arbitrariness. These free syllables (or letters), these rhythms quoted by Raoul Hausmann,[19] indicate once again the determination to find one's way back to the origin. In this poem of Hugo Ball's (which exists in several versions)[20] one catches echoes of nonsense rhymes, pig latin, "parler nègre," and counting rhymes:

> Gadji beri bimba
>
> glandriri lauli lonni cadori
>
> gadjama bim beri glassala
>
> Glandradi glassla tuffm i zimbrabim
>
> blassa galassasa tuffm i zimbrabim.

All the commentaries of the period, those reported by Richter and Hausmann, and especially those of Ball, confirm that we are dealing here with an attempt at radical primitivism, in a period when "nègre" and "primitive" are practically synonymous. No doubt this "primitive" pseudo-language must have seemed closer to some primordial outflow

---

[18]Ibid.
[19]Hausmann, pp. 54-63.
[20]Quoted in his book *Die Flucht aus der Zeit* (*Flight Out of Time*), whose title is significant. It refers to a poem recited for the first time on the 14th of July, 1916, in Zurich (Richter, p. 38).

Michel Beaujour

than the utilitarian discourse of bourgeois Bavarians. But even this poetic revolution locks itself in a negative phase: in order to purify language, it hastens to destroy it by postulating a form of "verbal alchemy" which leads at last to the disappearance of all language. Hugo Ball himself declared in preface to the first reading of the above poem: "With these sonorous poems we wish to renounce the language which has been devastated and made impossible by journalism. We must retreat to the most profound alchemy of words, perhaps even abandon the word, thereby preserving for poetry its most sacred realm."[21] Whether Ball is using the word "alchemy" in the same way that Khlebnikov understood "transmutations," or whether he is simply echoing the symbolist tradition to which he remains indebted, the similarity is no less striking. This cannot be accidental: given the nature of Western civilization against which the Futurists and Dadaists revolted, and their joint efforts to *save* language by uprooting it from its vulgar functions in practical communication, the only ground on which they can legitimize their transgression is sharply limited to the Bible and to the esoteric tradition. It is a curious revolution which permits Hugo Ball to write: "We have charged the word with forces and energies which permit us to rediscover the evangelical concept of the *word* (logos) as a magical complex of images."[22]

Is it not in an evangelical concept of logos that our civilization, in spite of its revolts and disavowals, seeks to establish language, when reason becomes too burdensome, science "inhuman," and when action in the world of men seems futile? Is this not precisely that vision of History's mythical moment in which eternity is swallowed up, the moment when the Word becomes flesh and so unburdens us of our humanity with the promise of Time's extinction? For it is time which weighs heavily upon us. We will not be delivered from it by revolution.

At this stage of our reflection, we have seen that the poetic revolution, unlike proletarian revolution, merely repeats a symptom, repeats it and marks time, for it has no hold on reality. Revolutionary

[21]Quoted by Hausmann, p. 56.
[22]Hugo Ball, quoted by Hausmann, p. 61.

poetry, under cover of innumerable metaphors and utopias, designates, as it disguises, a "primitive scene." For us who live in spite of everything in a Christian world, this scene belongs to primitive Christianity for whom the Kingdom of God was at hand. Saint Paul bears witness to this folly.

In the fourteenth chapter of the first *Epistle to the Corinthians,* Saint Paul contends against the invasion of the church by glossolalia ("speaking in tongues") — a language of prayer and of "communication with God" in which man so to speak is *spoken through* by the Holy Spirit. In verse 18 Paul confirms his own gifts in this area and seems to accept the possibility of interpreting this "language" (verse 5). The apostle opposes these "tongues" with the language of preaching:

> he that prophesieth edifieth the church. (verse 4).

> If therefore the whole church be come together into one place, and all speak with tongues, and there come in those that are unlearned, or unbelievers, will they not say that you are mad? But if all prophesy, and there come in one that believeth not, or one unlearned, he is convinced of all, he is judged of all. (verses 23-24).

Thus, glossolalia, which in certain respects is superior to discursive language, encourages outsiders to deride the church. It is easily mistaken for madness. It is therefore negotiable only within the group (as a sign of the Spirit's presence), within the church where it has meaning. In spite of its aberrant semantic value, this "tongue" surpasses all possible meanings of ordinary language. It reflects, by its meaninglessness, an infinite abundance of meaning. And in certain conditions (of grace) it is susceptible to at least partial translation into other natural languages. God, who is incomprehensible and speaks mysteriously (verse 2), ensures its meaning: a source and a receptacle of all meaning.

But within the framework of Christian mythology, which establishes and consecrates this provisional meaninglessness, Paul seeks to establish a hierarchy of requirements for the benefit of the missionary

Michel Beaujour

task and with a view to solidly establishing the church *on earth*. For this super-language serves only individual salvation and its practice engenders what could be called a "quietist" attitude. When the individual speaks to God and allows the spirit to speak through him, he imagines that human time has been suspended; he rejects the slow, shuffling duration of social action in order to seek refuge in a present which he mistakes for eternity.[23] Those who practice glossolalia are, so to speak, already installed in the Kingdom whose coming they believe to be imminent. Their utopia, like all utopias, is incarnated in language: they reenact the apathy of the first Galilean communities in Jerusalem which turned their backs on all earthly values, on all projects and prospects, judging that the present moment was only a minute pause before the Last Judgment and the Kingdom of Heaven. Perverted language signifies here an inversion of revolutionary spirit: the desire for another world, incomparably superior to this one, breaks out in passivity. Glossolalia is the immediate miraculous substitute for an unalienated world. Outsiders are not wrong in calling it *madness*.

In preferring the language of preaching, which teaches and converts, Paul vividly calls into question the status and the significance of language deprived of meaning. Situated out of society and time, this language is unfit for action, and it denies History. It destroys the ground of all projects and planning in order to give exclusive sanction to the *moment of the word*. But this moment is a false one, since it seeks to identify itself with the moment of origin and with the moment of absolute end: this prattling moment is a utopia of eternity.

This detour leads us back once more to the origin, the source of the insurmountable opposition between poetic revolutions and political revolutions. The revolution is not an apocalypse. As Trotsky reminded us, revolution makes history and is immersed in history. This hardly needs elaboration.

But then how are we to explain the unbounded radicalism of poets, their utopianism which refuses all compromise? The first explanation which offers itself quickly reveals its limitations: poets are

[23]One might recall the American expression which describes this aberration: Turn on, tune in, drop out.

bourgeois who never see beyond the destruction of their class and its (corrupted, filthy, rational, discursive) language. Explosion, dispersion, and violence: for them revolution is only the negation and, consequently, the destruction of language, an oscillation between a primordial or an ultimate chaos. To abolish reason, to get out of time, is the fervent wish of Rimbaud:

"A une raison"

> Un coup de ton doigt sur le tambour décharge tous les sons et commence la nouvelle harmonie.
>
> "Change nos lots, crible les fléaux, à commencer par le temps," te chantent ces enfants. "Elève n'importe où la substance de nos fortunes et de nos voeux" on t'en prie.
>
> Arrivée de toujours qui t'en iras partout.[24]

But evoking Rimbaud immediately suggests another explanation. For in studying the lengths to which the Cubofuturists and Dadaists have gone, we have lost sight of poetry, or rather it appeared meager and barely viable. We have been examining poetry which pushes its radicalism to the point of destroying itself or of freezing itself in its own impossibility. By forbidding language to unfold all the richness of its morphology and syntax, this poetry simply forgets that no poetry, to the extent that it too turns away from history and communication, is revolutionary. On the contrary, poetry is the incarnation of man's permanent aspiration as a speaking being to a *beyond* which only language, whose code is shaken by the poet, can offer him.

We have thus been considering a false problem. But on the way we have seen how and why this false problem is engendered and perpetuated within our civilization. The period from 1910 to 1920, particularly rich in historical cataclysms, also produced the most extreme pronouncements, and the intoxication of upheaval led poets to seize upon the language of militancy without fully understanding its function. In the relative calm of the twenties, Surrealism, emerging from the gravest confusions, put poets back *in their place,* which is not first

---

[24]Arthur Rimbaud, *Illuminations,* ed. H. de Bouillane de Lacoste (Paris, 1949), p. 79.

place where politics are concerned. It was then that *The Surrealist Revolution* became *Surrealism in the Service of Revolution.*

The nostalgia for a language which is free of all individual, temporal, or geographical determinations is not dead. The dream, current among contemporary "structuralists," of identifying language with the world, of making it the subject of all authentic speech, can perhaps be compared, in its rejection of history, and in spite of its rejection of mythology, to the efforts of the poets we have studied: as world or chaos, language raised to the status of a subject will deliver us from the human condition. And once more the dream of *Unity,* which has always enticed the poets, temporarily triumphs over the patient determination to incarnate *Totality.* That, however, is the only goal to which a revolutionary project can conceivably aspire.

Translated by Richard Klein

Maurice Blanchot

The main impropriety* (excerpts)

. . .

3. Reason is excessive.

. . . Writing was Sade's particular madness. Such madness is not
to be sought in the oddity of his habits, which he himself saw as
simply the effect of his particular constitution or, more strikingly, as
the sign of his freedom, the very sign which, by putting him in a class
apart, freed him from the prejudices of his society to the point of
his asserting that the day his society stopped opposing his madness,
he would passionately give it up. A remarkable statement. Very
quickly — as he said and repeated — he identified them with his
prison, and it was from that buried solitude which was repugnant to
him (doubly so: in itself and through the punishment that it meant to
him) that — the repugnance of it reversing into an attraction — his
irrepressible need for writing, a terrifying power of the word, which
was never to abate, originated and took wing. Everything must be
said. The first of all freedoms is the freedom to say everything. That
is how he interpreted the basic requirement — in the form of a demand which, for him, was henceforth inseparable from a true republic.
But note that the "everything" involved in this freedom to say everything is no longer merely the universality of encyclopedic knowledge
(including the knowledge of our perverse possibilities) or even the
totality of an experience in which meaning is achieved by way of the
movement of a negation carried to its extreme — a circular discourse
which is thus the closed and completed affirmation of the mastery of
everything. Sade's *everything that must be said* — the everything that
is understood, in his books, as the stupendous repetition of an eternal
word, eternally clear, eternally empty — goes even further. It is no
longer every possibility which they convey and express. Nor is it, as

*Translated from "L'incovenance majeure," preface to de Sade's *Français, encore un
effort* . . . (Editions J.-J. Pauvert, 1965). We also refer the reader to Maurice Blanchot's
Lautréamont et Sade (Editions de Minuit, 1963).

50

has been too readily believed, the whole body of values which a religion, a society, and an ethics forbid us to express. The prohibition, of course, plays its part, as a limit to transcend, in this movement of unlimitedness. But it is in no way the ultimate limit. And Sade may well have taken pleasure — a simple and wholesome pleasure — in the strong scenes that he imagined and in which all the truths of his time are flouted, in which he says what should not be said and recommends horror. Having to blaspheme, to exalt evil, to support the passions of crime, none of that mattered much to him, and while he did not deprive himself of doing so, there was no question of his being satisfied with it. Something more violent comes to light in this rage for writing, a violence that did not manage to exhaust or allay all the excesses of a superb or wild imagination, but that was always less powerful than the transport of a language which could not bear to stop any more than it could imagine a limit. A violence all the stronger in that it is simple, asserted by means of an unambiguous word, which is devoid of any ulterior motive, is always expressed unpretentiously, and leaves nothing to the imagination, thus speaking purely — a violence pure, indeed, with which the majestic emotions of Chateaubriand were soon to muddle language, without being punished by any law. Here, the main impropriety is entrusted to the power of simple repetition — the impropriety of a narration that meets with no prohibition, because there is none left (this entire ultimate-work conveys it to us through the monotony of its terrifying murmur) but the time of *entre-dire* [interval of silence between words], that pure stop which can be attained only if speaking never ceases.

4. Writing was Sade's particular madness. Freedom did not rid him of that madness — acquired from prison or at least caused by prison to be what it was, an underground and forever clandestine power — but rather combined it with another type of madness, which made him believe that it could be affirmed in broad daylight, like the reservoir or the future of common possibilities. Thus for a moment, at the time when revolution and philosophy in irons[1] were to meet,

[1]The expression comes from Sade, who applied it to himself: "Fortunate Frenchmen, you felt it when you were pulverizing those monuments of horror, those unspeakable prisons from which philosophy in irons cried this out to you, before being aware of the energy that made you break the chains by which its voice was stifled."

two gaps in history coincided — gaps that were certainly very different, one marking an era and opening history, the other on which history was always prone to close. I shall not go into an investigation of Sade's political behavior during the years when — to the great embarrassment of the Revolution's righteous and to the great satisfaction of the counter-Revolution's righteous — he was an "active citizen," spoke and wrote against the king, spoke and wrote in honor of Marat, appeared at the Convention, where he also took the floor, presided over the Pikemen's section (that of Robespierre), suggested a form of worship without gods, upheld his own particular ideas on the notion of sovereignty and had them adopted, gave revolutionary names to the streets of Paris, and was even — to his not inconsiderable delight — an indictment juror. Whether or not his feelings were, sincerely or hypocritically, in keeping with his behavior and his public statements is a matter for tireless discussion. I do not believe there is any great mystery about it. He himself changed his mind. This was true for everyone, even for Saint-Just and Robespierre, who were not the first to ask for the fall of the monarchy — simply because the truth of events always preceded the thoughts about them. Cautious he was, but without true caution and always less cautious than unstable — that kind of instability which meant fidelity to the swiftness of historical becoming. Had he been really cautious, nothing would have kept him from remaining in the background or from trying to flee: he could have. Even if all the other reasons that induced him to remain in Paris were taken into account, there is little doubt that he took the keenest interest in what was happening and that a whole part of himself acknowledged it. What part? That obscure (extravagant) part which, without managing to make him into a true, socially plausible writer, doomed him to writing without stop. I think the word "coincidence" is the most accurate of all. With Sade — and at a very high point of paradoxical truth — we have the first example (but was there ever a second?) of the way in which writing, the freedom to write, may coincide with the action of true freedom, when such freedom is in a state of crisis and provokes a break from history. A coincidence that is not identification. And Sade's motives were not those which set the revolutionary power in motion. They even contradicted them. And yet, without them, without the mad excess represented by Sade's name, life, and truth, the Revolution would have been deprived of part of its Reason.

5. In order to get some idea of Sade's political concepts, I think it will be enough to quote just a few of his texts. The very title of his little treatise [*Français, encore un effort . . .*], characterized by invisible irony, speaks to us rather clearly. It says that to be a republican it is not enough to live in a republic; nor is a constitution enough to make a republic; nor, finally, is having laws enough for that creative power, the constituent act, to persist and keep us in a state of permanent constitution. An effort must be made, and yet another effort, always — there lies the invisible irony. Whence the conclusion — barely hinted at — that the revolutionary era is just beginning. But what kind of effort will have to be made? Who will ask us to make it? Sade calls it *insurrection,* which is *the permanent state of the republic.* In other words the republic can never possibly be a state, but only a movement — and, to that extent, identical with nature. Such perpetual perturbation is necessary, because, to begin with, the republican government is surrounded by enemy governments that hate it or are envious of it (hypothesis of encircling): the end of peace for the man who has awakened just one single time; revolutionary vigilance excludes all tranquillity, and consequently the only way to preserve oneself is never to be conservative — that is to say, never at rest — a situation that Sade deemed incompatible with ordinary morality, which is no more than inertia and sleep:

> The moral state of a man is a state of peace and tranquillity, whereas his *immoral* state is a state of perpetual motion drawing him toward the state of necessary insurrection in which a republican must always keep the government to which he belongs.

There we have the first reason, but there is another that is given us as a result of *very bold* reflection: all the nations today that want to have a republican government are not only threatened by outer violence; they themselves, because of their pasts, are already violent within or, according to the terminology of the times, criminal and corrupt; how would they overcome this dismal, inherited violence except through an even stronger violence and one that is more terrible as well because of being without tradition and, as it were, original? The virtue that legislators consider the principle of the Republic would be suitable for the Republic only if we could achieve it without a past, outside history itself, and by beginning history with it. But whoever is already in history is also already in crime and will not emerge from it without going it even one better in violence and crime. (A hypothesis that we perfectly well acknowledge and which it is pointless to be shocked at, calling it Hegelian so as to keep it from being true.) Yet will we ever emerge from it? And what will the difference be? What will we have gained? First of all, a change in vocabulary: what used to be called crime will be called energy — an insignificant change, but one of great consequence. The world of the future will not be a world of values. Neither good nor evil will be its poles, neither virtue nor vice, but the relationship to which affirmation and negation, carried to the extreme, correspond, by becoming identified with it. When Sade writes: "Everything is good when it is excessive," such excess — which is different from the state of effervescence and goes through phases of what Dolmancé calls *apathy,* a state of high tension and clear insensibility — indicates the only morality of the energetic man and also indicates the sovereignty to which he may lay claim, in this movement of freedom within which, even when wrapped up in himself, he no longer feels separate from the disintegration which is the common characteristic of the whole. Excess, energy, disintegration — these are the key words of the new era.[2]

6. . . . Was it Sade or Saint-Just who wrote: "Nothing resembles virtue so much as a great crime?" And the following statement, which is more enigmatic than it seems: "In times of anarchy virtue espouses crime" — and the following recommendation, which was meant to have a harsh reverberation in the Jacobins' club: "Arm virtue with

---

[2]Rather than immediately thinking of Nietzsche, let us recall Blake: "Energy is the only life . . . . Energy is Eternal Delight," and even Van Gogh: "There is something good in any energetic movement," for energy is thought (the intensity, density, and sweetness of thought carried to an extreme).

the dexterity of crime, against crime." All we need do, in a spirit of frankness, is substitute "violence" for "dexterity" (How could the honsty of the act here be anything other than violent?) and we have the essence of Sade. Finally, when in his first speech Saint-Just praised energy, saying: "Energy is not strength," he was saying something that all of Sade's works were also trying to say more passionately. I recall the final morality of *Justine* and *Juliette*: *people's* happiness or unhappiness depends not on more or less virtue or vice but on the energy they give proof of, for "happiness is bound up with the energy of principles; he who constantly floats could never experience it.") Let us read Saint-Just again: "The solution lies in the effective insurrection of minds." And Sade: "Insurrection . . . must be the permanent state of the republic." What differentiates, I shan't say these two men, who are as unrelated as two close contemporaries can be, but these two equally absolute judgments? It is clear. For Sade, insurrection must apply to customs as well as to ideas; it must affect the whole man and the whole of man; and even more: being both permanent and excessive, subversion would constitute the only permanent feature of our lives, constantly carried to its highest point — that is, constantly as close as possible to its attainment — since, wherever there is energy, the reservoir of strength, there is energy, the consumer of strength, an affirmation that can be realized only by way of the greatest negation. I expect that here one will uncover the trace of utopia and the danger of utopia (which has at least the advantage of not being merely the utopia of evil). Let us suspend judgment.

7. A third text should be of help in directing our interpretation. I am taking it from the fourth volume of *L'Histoire de Juliette:*

The reign of laws is vicious; it is lower than that of anarchy; the greatest proof of this statement is the government's obligation to transform itself into a state of anarchy when it wants to remake its constitution. In order to repeal its former laws, it is obliged to set up a revolutionary regime in which there are no laws: in the end, new laws are created by the regime, but this second state is necessarily less pure than the first, since it derives from it, since it had to effect that first state, anarchy, in order to achieve the second, a state constitution.

An apparently very clear text and one further clarified by many others, in which we hear Sade state that there is not one single free government in existence — and why? Because everywhere man is and will be the victim of laws. Laws are capable of an injustice that makes them ever more dangerous than any individual impulse. The dangerous passion of one sole man may injure me, but only to the extent that my own passion will allow. However, there is no recourse against the law, which restrains one everywhere: the law wills that I be forever deprived of myself, forever passionless — that is to say, mediocre and soon stupid. Whence the following criticisms, which recur in every possible form: the law is unjust because it is in control of the power and usurps the sovereignty, which must never be delegated for what is essential; the law, which was invented to control the passions of my neighbor, perhaps protects me from him, but gives me no guarantee against the assertions of the law itself, which are the most corrupt and the cruelest, because they never represent anything free, since they represent no more than a cold strength, without freedom; finally, they weaken and deform the proper relationships of man, whether with nature or with the future of knowledge:

> Without laws and religions, one can hardly imagine how glorious and grand human knowledge today would be; it is incredible how these shameful brakes have hindered progress . . . . People dare to inveigh against passions; they dare to curb them by laws . . . . The invention and wonders of the arts are due only to strong passions . . . . Individuals who are not moved by strong passions are no more than mediocre beings; one becomes stupid as soon as one is no longer passionate."[3]

A series of convictions that ends with this impressive statement: "Great actions blaze out only during the short moment when laws are silent," but since it is clear that such a statement will never have any far-reaching effect, it is wiser to settle for a compromise conclu-

---

[3] The same formula is found in Helvetius: "One becomes stupid as soon as one stops being passionate."

sion: if laws must exist, they must be few in number and must be gentle; if they must "punish" those whom others persist in calling guilty, they must not have the pretension of improving them; finally, never should they encroach upon life itself — and no compromises here — for if a people cannot transmit its right to sovereignty, how could it delegate its right to exist — that is, ultimately, its right to die? "However much Jean-Jacques Rousseau's authority inspires me with veneration, I do not forgive you, O great man, for having justified capital punishment." A call that, in truth, comes not from Sade but, once again, from Saint-Just. Which does not mean that Saint-Just went along with the demand for anarchy. Nothing would have been more repulsive to him. The word "law," when he pronounces it, has, it would seem to me, from his lips, the same strange resonance and the same purity as the word "crime" has from the lips of Sade. However, precisely because the law is always above laws and is always degraded by precepts, Saint-Just, too, demanded that they be few in number ("wherever there are that many, the people are slaves"), and he claimed that long laws are public calamities, and he refused everything which, in the name of the law, would happen to sanctify the power of civil repression. As he said, with his sublime severity: "I personally will not consent to submit to any law which implies that I am ungrateful and corrupted." And elsewhere, in a concise sentence which expresses almost everything: "To begin with, a citizen has dealings only with his conscience and with morality; if he forgets them, he has dealings with the law; if he holds the law in contempt, he is no longer a citizen: at that point commence his dealings with the power that be." In other words, the law is merely the beginning of a long process of degradation, at the end of which the ruling authority, which has become oppressive, will be drowned in laws, as happened under the monarchy. "To obey laws, that's not clear." "Too many laws, too few civil institutions." "If you want to establish a Republic, take away the least power possible from the people." "If you want to give man his freedom, make laws only for him; do not crush him under the weight of power." Under the monarchy, "the law made the purest inclinations into a crime" [*"la loi faisait un crime*

des penchants les plus purs"] — a judgment in the form of an alexandrine, which Sade was always ready to welcome, just as he would
always have admitted that "tyranny is interested in the flabbiness of
people," for the very good reason that tyranny is fortified only by a
decline in energy, which alone is capable of restricting it and which
is the only true principle, in the eyes of Sade.

8. Thus what Sade calls a *revolutionary regime* is the pure time
during which suspended history marks an era, that time of between-
times during which, between the former laws and the new laws,
reigns the silence of the absence of laws, that interval which corresponds precisely to *l'entre-dire,* or between-saying, where everything
ceases and everything stops, including the eternal speaking propul-
sion, because at that point there is no longer any *interdit,* or prohibition. A moment of excess, disintegration, and energy, during which
(a few years later, Hegel was to say it) being is no longer any more
than the movement of infinity which does away with itself and is
unceasingly born as it disappears, "an orgy of truth in which no one
would be able to stay sober." That moment of silent frenzy is also
the one when man, during a suspension in which he asserts himself,
attains his true sovereignty, since he is no longer only himself, since
he is no longer only nature — the natural man — but something that
nature never is: the consciousness of the infinite power of destruction
— that is, negation — by which nature unceasingly makes itself and
unmakes itself. This is the extreme point of Sade's thinking — a point
at which he does not always remain, but toward which he aims and
which he reaches more especially in Volumes VII and IX of *La
Nouvelle Justine,* when Juliette, in admirable outbursts, puts no less
strength into rejecting nature than she had put into rejecting laws,
morality, and religion. Nature, she says, is no more a truth than God
himself: "Ah! you bitch, you are perhaps misleading me, just as I
was once misled by the infamous chimera of God, to which you were
said to be obedient; we are no more dependent on you than on him
. . . . Yes, my friend, yes, I loathe nature." Thus, for a moment, that
moment of phenomenal suspense for which Sade reserves the word
revolutionary, laws keep silent — social laws, moral laws, and natural

laws — and make way not for the tranquillity of some nothingness — that, for example, of prebirth — but for that power of disintegration that man bears within himself as his future and which is the joy of outrage (nothing gloomy ultimately, only something superb and smiling in this approach of the supreme stormy moment), a need for transcendency which is the heart of reason — dangerous, certainly, and terrifying, in fact, strictly speaking, terror itself, but with nothing baneful to be expected, on one condition, however: "never to lack the strength necessary for going beyond the last bounds." Just as Saint-Just said, in a phrase so terse that it vibrates: "The principle of a republican government is virtue; if not, terror."

9. Liberated in April 1790 and arrested as a suspect in December 1793, Sade, for almost four years, participated in· the advent of the republic and, for sixteen months, took part in the Revolution. He played not a prominent but nonetheless a public role, spoke in the name of the people, and fulfilled important duties. This cannot be forgotten. Something of Sade belongs to the Terror, just as something of the Terror belongs to Sade. One is reminded of the famous text that is so similar to an *image d'Epinal*:

> It is said that when Robespierre, and when Couthon, Saint-Just, and Collot, his ministers, were tired of murders and convictions, when some small remorse penetrated those hearts of steel, and when, at the sight of the numerous judgments they had to sign, the pen fell from their fingers, they went and read a few pages of *Justine* and came back to sign.

This text, written by Villers in 1797, was not meant to denounce Sade as a merely immoral writer but to compromise him by making him an accomplice of the masters of the Revolution. Yet this text, in all its foolishness, does say something accurate to the extent that men who were opposed to one another find themselves united by the same element of excess in their free actions and by the common conviction that the experience of freedom must always have its extreme moment: anyone who doesn't know this knows nothing of freedom. What, then, differentiates these men, who are all considered to be infamous? At first it would seem obvious. When Saint-Just went up to the tribune of the Assembly for the last time, before the 9th of Thermidor, he sketched, with unshakable maxims, a portrait of the revolutionary man: a revolutionary is an inflexible man, he is sensible, he is frugal, he is simple, he is the irreconcilable enemy of any and all lies, indulgence, and affection, he is a hero of good sense and integrity. This moral portrait[4] in no way resembles the portrait one might sketch of the whole man, except for the inflexibility of principles — and, for all that, so are the great masters of debauchery sober out of surfeit, cold out of an excess of sensibility, austere out of an overdose of pleasure, and simple, having rid themselves of any hypocrisy. When Saint-Just accused Desmoulins and reproached him for having said: honor is ridiculous, glory and posterity are foolishness — his reproach would also apply to Sade, but in my opinion it rather sings his praises; for this word "glory," which is found in all the speeches of the times and which was also on the lips of Jean-Paul Marat, is almost never encountered in the writings of Sade, who considered posterity no more than sheer imposture[5] (and, even so, it is necessary to make clear that Saint-Just's reproach was aimed at the agreeable skeptic in Desmoulins, whereas in Sade it was the horror of prejudice, what was later to be called the demand of critical reason — that is, pure negative passion — which did not allow him to be satisfied with such easily accepted values). When, finally, Saint-Just[6] denounced the corruption of morals by the spirit of atheism, it is perhaps on this point that we would find the most solid difference between the two philosophies — if not between the two men — and here again, we must venture to say, to Sade's advantage.

> We have been flooded with unnatural writings: they are deifying intolerant and fanatic atheism; one would think that the priest had become an atheist and that the atheist had become a priest. We must say no more about it! We need energy; and delirium and weakness are what are proposed to us.

[4]In another speech Saint-Just again said: "Simple good sense, energy of the soul, coldness of mind, the fire of a fervent and pure heart, austerity, selflessness — this is the character of a patriot."
[5]In his silent speech, that of the 9th of Thermidor, Saint-Just was to think much the same thing: "Renown is a vain fuss. Were we to lend an ear to the centuries that have passed, we would no longer hear anything."
[6]In one of his finest speeches, in which we find the words: "Those who half-make revolutions have merely dug their own graves."

Maurice Blanchot

An accusation aimed at suspects who had already been jailed, among whom, and on that very date, was the Marquis de Sade. It is doubtless true and most probable that he had been arrested for many of his connections in 1791 or because of his opposition to measures he deemed too radical (for example, the establishing of a revolutionary army in Paris, a kind of Praetorian guard which, according to him, might well have become a resource for the ambitious and for usurpers; another time, he refused, as president of his section, to go along with the votes on "a horror," "an inhuman gesture") or merely because, as an aristocrat and an incautious man, he constantly provoked denunciations. But I would willingly believe that he also incurred suspicion because of his atheistic fanaticism: just three weeks before being arrested, he took the floor at the Convention to uphold the plan for a cult of virtues that would have been observed, with hymns and the fumes of incense, at the secularized altars of Catholicism — and in what terms? In terms that, almost openly, spoke of himself:

> For a long time the Philosopher had been secretly laughing at the antics of Catholicism; but if he dared to raise his voice, he was soon in the dungeons of the Bastille, where ministerial despotism would force him into silence. Well, of course! How would the Tyranny have not supported superstition?

And somewhat earlier:

> The reign of philosophy has just, finally, annihilated that of imposture; finally, a man is becoming enlightened and, as he destroys the frivolous toys of an absurd religion with one hand, he is erecting an altar to the dearest Divinity of his heart with the other. Reason is replacing Mary in our temples.

This plan for an unmistakable atheism (since at no time was any allusion ever made to a supreme Being) received honorable mention, but it did not fail to attract the hostile attention of those in control of the government, who were almost all deists and who, in addition, feared that, since this kind of idolatrous cult would irritate the body of population that had remained Catholic, it would serve as a pretext for counterrevolutionary initiatives. A man is always brought to ruin by what is strongest in him. This must have been true for Sade.

Atheism was his fundamental conviction, his passion, his measure of freedom. While he was a prisoner in the Bastille, Madame de Sade begged him to hide his feelings; he answered that he preferred to die a thousand deaths rather than pretend to be other than what he was, even in personal letters, and his first written work was the well-known *Dialogue d'un prêtre et d'un moribond,* in which he expressed in the strongest terms possible that which he was always to maintain, right to the end: the certainty of nothingness. "It has never terrified me and I consider it as nothing but consoling and simple; all the others [systems] are the work of pride; this one alone is the work of reason." A statement to which must be added that of one of his characters: "If atheism wants martyrs, let it say so, and my blood is quite ready," as well as the following, which is one of Sade's most decisive statements and one of the keys to the system: "The idea of God is the only wrong I can never forgive man." God, the original sin, the sin which explains that one cannot *govern* innocently.

10. Sade's head was saved from the guillotine by very little — and by a mistake at that. Had it not, the Terror would indeed have presented us with the martyr of atheism — but, true, because of another misunderstanding. Liberated in the month of October 1794 — after an investigation and a testimonial from the Pikemen's section, which had at first overwhelmed him with accusations (at the time of Robespierre), reproaching him then for having said that a democratic form of government was impracticable in France,[7] but now, praising his good citizenship and his principles as a good patriot — he began his last existence as a free man. But what did he do? Everything necessary to destroy that freedom he so valued. Not that he behaved badly: having been separated since 1790 from the austere Renée de Sade — who, once briefly liberated by him from her virtue, relapsed into frigidity — he lived conjugally with a sweet and sensitive young woman, who was never to leave him. His demon was not lust. It was

[7]In all probability, Sade did say something to that effect. It shows his sincerity and lack of caution. The text reads: "constantly, in his personal conversations, making comparisons drawn from Greek and Roman history in order to prove the impossibility of establishing a democratic and republican form of government in France." Impossible, "without making an effort and yet another effort"; it is the theme of this short treatise [*Français, encore un effort* . . .]; it was not a crime; it was being said everywhere. It was also the opinion of Saint-Just, who believed that after every Lycurgus come oppressors who destroy his work; "sad truths."

more dangerous. It was Socrates' demon — the demon against which Socrates always held out and to which Plato would have preferred not to give in: the madness of writing, an infinite, interminable, incessant, and continuous movement. It was long believed that, when Sade was arrested in 1801, it was for having defied Bonaparte in an anonymous lampoon. Gilbert Lely made short work of that allegorical tradition.[8] A prisoner in Vincennes and in the Bastille under the royal tyranny, and jailed at Saint-Lazare and at Picpus in the prisons of the Regime of Liberty, it is true that he was sent to Sainte-Pélagie, Bicêtre, and Charenton by the despotism of a general, who was soon to be crowned, but one must say — and I find it remarkable — that rather than a political adversary, it was only the author of *Justine* whom the high morality of the first consul — that is, of the whole of society — condemned to confinement for life. For indeed here lies the truth of Sade: a truth all the more dangerous in that it is clear, lucidly proposed, and expressed with simplicity — specifically, on the last page of *Prospérités du vice* and in the most readable form: "HOWEVER MUCH MEN MAY SHUDDER, PHILOSOPHY MUST SAY EVERYTHING." Say everything. That one line would have been enough to make him a suspect, that plan enough to have him convicted, and its fulfillment enough to have him confined. And Bonaparte is not the only one to be held responsible. We are still living under a first consul, and Sade is still being prosecuted, and because of the same exigency: saying everything; everything must be said; freedom is the freedom to say everything — that unlimited movement which is the temptation of reason, its secret wish, its madness.

Translated by June Guicharnaud

---

[8]*Vie du Marquis de Sade, 2*. G. Lely shows that this lampoon cannot have been written by Sade. Must we recall here everything we owe to the notable works of G. Lely, who is continuing those of Maurice Heine?

J. M. E. Blanchard

The French revolution: a political line or a language circle?

> Nous avons révolutionné le gouvernement,
> les lois, les usages, les moeurs, les cou-
> tumes, le commerce et la pensée même,
> révolutionnons donc aussi la langue qui est
> leur instrument.
> — Barère, *Discours sur l'état de la langue
> française*
>
> Je pense que nous devons être exaltés.
> — Saint-Just, *Discours sur les institutions
> républicaines*

Understanding what happened to France between 1789 and 1794 is fairly easy if one assumes that revolutions are subject only to the historian's investigation. Facts can always be arranged or rearranged to suit the exigencies of a logical mind. But when one tries to evaluate the importance of language and literature during that troubled period, one may well wonder whether to certain people revolution was not actually a game of trying to match the unavoidable classic flourish of language with complete straightforwardness in action. Revolution was still in the making. It imposed itself on energetic minds as a new totality of things, still in the future, yet looming up more clearly with each passing word; still a chaos of passions and ideas, but a chaos soon to be straightened out with the help of dedicated men looking forward to new achievements. Nothing could be left untried; nothing could be rejected before being tried: there was a new world to realize far from the old one. Already the future had prevailed over the present; already the revolutionary felt sucked into this future from which nothing could be dropped. And ascertaining these truths made the orators of the revolution try with unending passion to shape this utopia on the parched grounds of the old regime. Pretty soon they would find themselves caught up in this process of acting with words only and, eventually, imprisoned in the circles they had drawn with

J. M. E. Blanchard

growing sophistication. Language would become an entity per se, alienated from the real world they always lived in, as well as from the other world they wanted so much to promote, the world of their dreams.

These problems would, of course, become more acute with the development of revolutionary passions, and, to be sure, impatient as they were for the birth of a new language to fit the actual process of revolution or, more simply, for their own words to become facts of history, these men tried to burst open the passive chaos of the dreaming philosophers, to organize it, i.e. to make ideas march down the paths of action. The travailing mind was simply denied time for gestation, and creation was expected to spring up. A new feeling was to be no sooner felt than expressed, no sooner expressed than regulating the world. Passion carried every single constitutional password. The revolution was in the making, and everything had to come into action at first sight: a *fiat lux*.

But perhaps it was just another dream closing in on itself, while the actual path of history went its own way. Because they had tried to bend the line so much, these revolutionaries had contrived circles and made their own closed-circuit revolution. They had desperately tried to forge a new language to explain a new era, but the whole story (and much of it still told in the old way) may well have been that of a fantastic conundrum.

On some famous words of Saint-Just

There was a new world to build, but nobody would wait for it to be wholly structured. Everybody wanted that future now, instantly.

And what conflicts most with the complete hypothetical liberty given anyone to deliver an instant devastating speech[1] is a symbolic and equally full desire for construction. Here reason, constructive reason, must come first. It cannot help, and in fact delights in, making

[1] The fact that every single orator of the French Revolution, except perhaps (and yet to what extent?) Mirabeau, Danton, and Marat, are known to have prepared their thundering speeches carefully is somewhat puzzling to anyone who would link extemporizing with devastating, flood-like orations and who has visions of heaving crowds electrified by self-styled leaders. But that is a minor problem. What counts is not how these speeches were prepared, but what they were meant to signify.

its way through endless sums of knowledge and of vocabulary; not categories of logic, since there is only one thing that prevails, and that is having a goal firmly set for every action. Reason is purely the tool of finality, as we can see in Saint-Just's *Esprit de la révolution*: "On a le droit d'être audacieux, inébranlable, inflexible, lorsqu'on veut le bien." It then becomes quite clear, as we go a bit further, that language can serve only as a proof of what liberty there is in political life, and that feeling of liberty in turn reactivates a passion that is bound to spread, lest it grow extinct.

In Saint-Just's flamboyant assertion we find a very negative attitude toward objective reason. We note, first, the support the orator draws from the addition of carefully graded stage directions that will eventually petrify the hero of the revolution into a very formal, if not a ritual, figure. The word "le bien," whatever it may entail, be it the death of Louis XVI on the block or the all-or-nothing recommendations for dealing with the enemies of the Republic made to the generals and representatives in the field, has in the first place a logical impact. It is the general premise that underlies any minor factual conclusion, for is not the common good the sesame of the revolutionary world? But very soon it carries the speaker away to the point where rhetoric assumes the power of logic and settles all questions or problems that may arise.[2] Thus the series, "audacieux, inébranlable, inflexible": "audacieux" sounds like a breach of the law; "inébranlable" resumes an appearance of legality; and lastly "inflexible" implies the reincarnation of law in a new society. All this, as a matter of principle! Action, or the image of action, underlies the speech, which in turn purports to be a justification for action, and not just the action in question, but of any revolutionary action. This is a trick of rhetoric, not a logical process. With this trick the orator leaps into his own revolutionary world.

We have here not only a basis for future generalizations: "Quand tous les hommes seront libres, ils seront égaux. Quand ils

[2]It is difficult to isolate a purely logical process in texts of this kind. By purely logical, we mean a series of arguments that do not rely on any debatable assumption (like the assumption here that the common good actually has an immediate significance for everyone concerned) or a series of statements that are not being used, as is the case here, to condone future violence or radicalism.

seront égaux, ils seront justes. Ce qui est honnête suit de soi-
même."[3] We are confronted as well with a rhetorical buildup, due
in part to the orator's fascination with the four-beat rhythm in
each of the words. Rhetoric reinforces, and then blocks, common
expression. What is there after "inflexible"? One would be inclined
to question the usefulness of roared questions and repetitions, of
careful gradations of speech, nay, of the whole decorum of the revolutionary orator, if all that he appears to attain is in essence the
wordy reflection of his deep-seated antagonism to the past he wishes
to destroy. "Inflexible" is something like a statement of complete
estrangement from reality. Saint-Just needs to cut off from "his"
world all that is not his own self, or related to himself, so as to preserve the totality of the revolution. By doing so, he claims this reality
for himself. ("Avons-nous le droit d'avoir une volonté générale et
une sagesse différente de la raison universelle?" "Tout homme qui
n'a pas le sens droit dans le jugement de ses semblables est un
fripon.")

The world of the revolutionary is that of the future, and the
only coherent one, as we have seen. But in order to maintain its
coherence, it needs its permanent counterpart in the past, the world
of chaos,[4] the old regime. On the one hand, it is true that the revolution
is in its principle strongly antithetical to the past: whatever it posits
and establishes amounts to a rejection of the old structure. "Quoi
que vous fassiez, vous ne pourrez jamais contenter les ennemis du
peuple, à moins que vous ne rétablissiez la tyrannie. J'en conclus

---

[3]See Michelet's famous definition at the beginning of his *Histoire de la Révolution Française*:
"Je définis la Révolution l'avènement de la loi, la résurrection du Droit, la réaction de la
Justice." Saint-Just's statement may be upheld as a direct consequence of the achievement
of liberty in a fully rational world. In other words, "I feel that I crave freedom; I shall
destroy the structure that subordinates me to a tyrant and coordinates me with thousands
of others into a world of slavery. I shall feel free because of the freedom of others, while
others will feel free because of my own freedom." In view of this interrelation, morality is
simply obvious, something like the biological law of the community. Men will have to be
just and honest, since once they are set free no other life will be possible for them than
the one set by community standards. Being "honnête" in relation to oneself is the inner
face of justice. We see here a growing sophistication: life as a biological principle is
applied to the morals of a practical society and, eventually, to the ethics of a conscious
individual. As a matter of fact, for the revolutionary philosopher of 1789, from society as
an establishment to the revolutionary as troubleshooter who strives to reshape it, the
world remains a unified vision, beyond the actions of the day. He is more than ever
before concerned with the future, which he would like to see already pitted against the
past. The present as such is unknown, except for the formal duration of the speech, a
mere period of induction.
[4]This clear-cut classification provides another important "logical" support for terrorist
action: the enemies who may be plotting against the Revolution belong in the past, literally
and figuratively; they must be exterminated as persistent bad memories.

qu'il faut qu'ils périssent." "Qu'ils [those who pledge tyranny] soient superbe ailleurs, on ne peut être ici que citoyen." By leveling the site of past iniquities, Saint-Just makes the preservation of the revolution imperative: it can go only forward, and no one can be given permission to step backward. On the other hand, the revolutionary gradually becomes more estranged from the world he used to belong to, and one can safely predict when the other world of old will fade into a ghostly structure just visible enough to be used as a foil or perhaps a bugaboo. Totality means exclusion.

One detects here a painful desire to bring revolution to a point of near-perfection, while expressing the reality of a new world in so definite a form that it precludes any other meaning. In fact, any other meaning would imply the annihilation of the revolution.[5] Language (words, metaphors) would remain in this case of self-indictment, but it would no longer supply a correct prism for reality. Since language is not an initiator but a medium between two worlds, between two segments of time, the use of rhetoric may help to fill a gap, actually, the great chasm of desire.

Language is an empty construction, but it may mean great reassurance: in fact all the "fripons" have already been punished and did vacate their places, so that nothing should prevent the bringing-about of the revolution. More than a warning, the words prove to be the equivalent of what is wanted, namely, a world without "fripons." Thus Saint-Just acts on behalf of a hypothetical society which supposedly is kept from operating well until such drastic measures have been taken. "It is them or us, him or me." No compromise can be arranged. Language is already one, and that is more than enough. Hence the enormous number of aphorisms, more, indeed, than a few quips.

Clearly Saint-Just is trying to seal his world off, which he cannot do altogether. He cannot help wishing to. Thus he strives to accumulate words, to add up antinomies. Yet it is what he does not say that betrays him. He may eventually manage to cut himself off from everything, but he is still looking for a reflection — in fact,

---

[5]We recall Camus' way out of nothingness: "Je me révolte, donc nous sommes."

J. M. E. Blanchard

paradoxically, a proof — of what he is building with his speeches and what is being derived from them. The brave speaker finds himself alone and searches frantically for an echo, since his words are no longer clearly objectified (the "fripons" have merely some kind of rhetorical existence). What the man is trying to detect is the sound of his own life.[6] As for life itself . . . . Hence something very close to logomachy and raving, a furious longing for words, for the word, buttressed with its negative opposite: "Liberté, égalité, ou la mort"; "La République n'échange avec ses ennemies que du plomb"; "Un gouvernement républicain a la vertu pour principe, sinon la terreur. Que veulent ceux qui ne veulent ni vertu ni terreur?" Saint-Just argues with himself, and the argument very soon becomes religious or even mystical.[7] Fear and dread: man afraid of his work?

The revolutionary drama and its new vocabulary

Playwrights, at least, were not afraid of the work of their elders. The revolution could be handled safely onstage.

If drama is considered purely as the vehicle of fiction, the use of rhetoric is a game. There is no anxiety possible, not even the sign of it, no fear as to the outcome of the plays in the years 1892 to 1894. Revolution always wins. Besides, rhetoric as a game is not only the rule, but a rule corroborated by other rules: there is only one given revolutionary condition, and there is only one way to express it. Otherwise the audience might hiss and boo the unfortunate writer into jail. Thus Corneille would have been assigned a very specific task, considering what was actually done to *Le Cid,* the characters being altered and the plot reshaped to erase all traces of the old regime.

The magic power of the word was sufficient, then, to arouse the

[6]See Michel Foucault's conclusion to the section "Echanger," in his "Archéologie des sciences humaines," entitled *Les Mots et Les Choses,* on the end of the eighteenth century: "Le langage n'est que la représentation des êtres; le besoin n'est que la représentation du besoin . . . . L'esprit obscur mais entêté d'un peuple qui parle, la violence et l'effort incessant de la vie, la force sourde des besoins échapperont au mode d'être de la représentation. Et celle-ci sera doublée, limitée, bordée, mystifiée peut-être, régie en tous cas de l'extérieur par l'énorme poussée d'une liberté ou d'un désir, ou d'une volonté qui se donne comme l'envers d'une metáphysique de la conscience" (p. 222).
[7]Here we overtake the eternal Marxian critic who points out the famous absence of a solid (proletarian) basis for the revolution to develop along modern lines. Saint-Just is actually too concerned with the making of the revolution to be dedicated to the revolution itself. But we can see that he tried hard.

wild enthusiasm recorded on certain nights, when the "citoyens" would jump onto the stage to embrace the frail but victorious heroine while the accursed noble was first pummeled and then ousted with boos. So great was the belief in the "real" world framed by the industrious playwright that there was perhaps no difference between the utopia of Saint-Just and any of the elaborate creations on the stage, really too good to be true except that they happened graphically: the last king on earth could not escape immolation. The compound of words and gestures could have meant nothing except exorcism in a perfect ritual. What in religion had been desecrated through the plundering of the Church and the profanations of the monasteries was reintegrated on the stage into a mockery of the Inquisition. Language had gained universal power, although it had well nigh lost its ability to adjust, its faculty to intimate, its talent for proposing and cajoling, in short, its subtleties. If anything was worth hearing, it was to be imposed.

As Saint-Just needed his "fripons," the theater needs its villains.[8] A mass of villains will therefore bow as the original freedom-fighter swashbuckles his way through. It does not mean that the gallant hero is much of an individual either, but he is vested with all the sacred powers in order to defeat a multifarious, yet purely functional, devil. One can, of course, question the interest of a study of literature of this type, since to us everything appears to be merely a reflection of something else. (As we have seen, the revolutionary makes revolution in his own private new world, where he can see and identify himself.) Yet one thing is certain: it is a fascinating experience to watch the perfect mechanism of the revolution unwind safely. With no motivations of their own, imbued with those from a stock of revolutionary types, characters are expected to move always in the correct direction. When they do not the public riots, because it sees it will have to compromise, that (and here is the core of the revolutionary naïveté) language is not revolution, but only a reflecting mirror, and this it refuses to believe.

---

[8]See Plancher-Valcour, *Réflexions sur les Spectacles,* aimed at antiquated genres, where there still may be found a few villains who retain a human aspect.

J. M. E. Blanchard

No, language *is* revolution and remains it in much the same way as religion keeps mystery anew each year or each day of the year. And it is to language itself that audiences are invited to pay their respects. What was but the chitchat of inner circles has been branded as profanity, and ex-Catholics may learn, at their own expense, to be blasphemous no longer.[9] What testifies to the fact that the change is in the vocabulary and not in the feelings is the permanent ground swell of religious sentimentality, which is better accommodated with lavish phrases and a general profuseness of speech than with precise, meaningful, to-the-point definitions. Thus far, as we evaluated the snappy sentences of Saint-Just, it appeared that rhetoric alone was to blame for the excess of cold-blooded logic. Now it becomes clear that a playwright cannot afford to articulate endless series of syllogisms onstage, lest he bore an audience craving for the action-word. To this problem an institutionalized vocabulary brings the easy solution of a raving conformity. Representatives, well-off, well-bred, cultivated men, lawyers acquainted with the procedures, if not the tricks, of debating and, furthermore, experts in talking other parties down, rivaled one another in wit and eloquence to win their revolution, although, to be sure, every speech belonged to the same category, perhaps somewhat powerless in the end, of a talk before a legislative or executive committee. Theatergoers, however, were largely *peuple,* to whom an abstract debate in the circle of rhetoric would seem another sellout to the enemy. There was only one way to be pedantic. No one would draw from the old classical stock the words with which the orators fashioned their metaphors. The pressure of parliamentary standards, however slight it may have proved to be on some of the more excited members (we recall for instance Marat), had to be relieved. The endless passion of Saint-Just for incontestable indictments or rousing prophecies would have been intolerable onstage, where acting could make up for any reduction in the power of language or any impropriety and immediately illustrate the implications of a few words. Thus, no brain-muddling plot, no Gordian knot, no

---

[9]See Lesur's "comic opera without music," *La Veuve d'un Républicain, ou, Le Calomniateur:* "La bonté des tyrans est toujours une injure"; also, "Tyrannicide auguste, il sert l'humanité."

intricacies: any character will do, providing that he utters a couple of choice phrases. And rightly so, for what good is philosophizing to people who know all the answers? Desire, unsatisfied desire, no longer aches, and the heart-gripping, blood-pounding silence of Saint-Just is filled with a few easy-sounding words amid shouts of joy. The people call for easy solutions, so the playwright must trim things that way. The most incredible adventures are calmly set forth, and enthusiasm awaits the definitive word of victory, usually on the order of "A bas les tyrans!" or something similar.[10] Indeed, the tyrant is well taken care of.

We note here the importance of acting. An orator speaking from his rostrum has only words to inspire fear. A playwright has no difficulty implementing his laws, even *manu militari;* he has actors.

The change in situations is not even a transfer of actions but a change in usage. What La Martelière did with Schiller's *Die Raüber* bears this out: Robert, who in Schiller's play is but a noble highwayman, becomes with La Martelière an underrated Republican patriot proving his "bonne foi." In short what counts is not what is done but what is said. This is where the ground rules of logic, the apparatus of rhetoric, are most easily laid aside. Since most events actually occur onstage as duplicates of historical events rather than as creations of the writer, one may have the feeling that words have gained only in repetitive power, that they are a substitute for some extra gestures that would take too long to act out. But if we take a look at *La Folie de George,* a "comedy" by Lebrun-Rossa, in which King George of England resembles King Lear, we see that cries and roars convey something of a magic power.[11] "Although the story is supposed to relate a crisis of major importance (the English military buildup against France), we may well doubt its historical accuracy: it is in fact related in such a fashion as to make us doubt it has ever been acceptable to any audience. Lebrun pushes the absurd to the point of making

---

[10]See Sylvain Maréchal's *Le Jugement Dernier des Rois,* in which all the kings of Europe are exiled to one tiny island in the Pacific, where an old man, miraculously still alive, welcomes the friendly revolutionary jailers the more heartily when he learns the word "king" has been blotted from the French language.
[11]George, dressed in a kind of kimono, playing with a whip, goes mad suddenly and starts howling, "Taiaut, taiaut, forcez la bête! La voilà, la voilà! Il était beau ce cerf. Toulon pris et repris en douze heures; c'est incroyable . . . il nous ont tué beaucoup de monde, selon toute apparence . . . lâchez la meute!"

the English people sing "Vive la nation!" and turning England into a republic. Yet if no one at the time would really have denied that England was a kingdom, the revolution made it necessary to say, to repeat, and eventually to believe that England could not achieve a fruitful political existence as long as it chose to remain a kingdom. In one of the warnings issued by Fox, the prime minister, we read, "Si le Roi vient à recouvrer la raison, je serai le premier à demander qu'il meure!" At the time there was no question of reading between the lines. The word "revolution" had become a universal fixture. Situations were determined by it alone. To that word was attached a long string of synonyms as well as antonyms to fit all hazards or, if the scene had already passed into history, hazards overcome; in short, a preselected vocabulary.

Using revolutionary words, and before long it is easy to know which words are revolutionary, enables anyone to concentrate a long series of events into a few phrases, which is what Cizos means when, in *Les Peuples et Les Rois* (we note once more the ready-made title and script), he wants to summarize "en deux heures de temps tous les évènements de la Révolution et les motifs qui la rendirent légitime et indispensable." Focusing on concrete experiences, drama demonstrates a relation between morality and action by way of a transfer of vocabulary patterns. It is the practical side of the revolution.

Yet drama symbolizes more than an ever present group of Cesarean words. The people have obviously acquired the tools with which they feel they can master fatality. If Saint-Just wielded his deadly sword with an exasperation that was probably the sign of his inability to make words speak for his innermost self, it was because he found himself dedicated to organizing death without ever questioning its principle. Fighting in the dark he strove to illuminate it with a flash of lightning, and his "et maintenant il s'agit de vaincre" was crashing thunder. But a king who was dragged onstage to reassure an audience that it might be proud of itself was a recognition: it really indicated the dawn of liberty. It was no wonder that Voltaire's *Brutus* was a mandatory part of the repertory (about one in three performances at Le Théâtre de La Nation at one point). People would feel so good seeing each time anew the republican hero deliver his speech and make liberty dawn over Rome . . . . That feeling of power was to remain, ineradicable, for years to come, until Napoleon extinguished it for his own benefit. It seemed that words could seal destiny . . . . And now the Revolution needed nothing more but a few songs to march by.

Poetry: the revolutionary march

Here, in the poetry of the Revolution, we see every revolutionary phase close in on itself and terminate its cycle. Nothing can be added to a mass protest already in motion. Words, then, are superimposed. Again they populate silence, but this time in excess. Every revolutionary aspiration to kill the enemy, despoil the noble, exterminate the foreign spy, and maintain the Terror is already filled to the brim. It is merely an expanse of irresponsible feelings to which the poet wishes to give a proper rhythmical form. This time we have not an echo to some inner preoccupation but a mere poetization of destiny, of the forceful present that was somewhat denied us by the impatient Saint-Just. Hence many imperatives and present indicatives to enliven a dull, empty word too widely used to be provocative. Well-balanced verses could not be a reflection or an image; they were the heartbeat of revolution, the very sound of its life, the very proof of its existence. A song (for most of the poems were to be sung with an already publicized melody) is the next best thing to an effective action, and at any rate the most concrete way to live one. Read from this angle all the "poésies revolutionnaires" appear to have been paeans to anyone who would sing them while marching down the line. It is worth remembering that when the Greeks shrieked for Apollo, it meant that they were fighting victory into their hands. Thus *Le Cri de Mort Contre les Rois,* uttered in 1793 by Th. Rousseau:

> Foulez aux pieds les couronnes
> De ces trop coupables rois
> Et que le plus beau des trônes
> Soit pour vous celui des lois.

Often it sounds as though rhetorical questions were being put to an invisible audience. These one-way expressions raise a feeling shared by the multitude; they are voiced as though conveying raw feelings. At times very coarse, they stop just short of a rousing ejaculation, of one enormous cry, the pure, transparent sound of language revolving into itself. They bear no meaning to our minds, yet they are loaded with so much that we in our turn feel we would like to carry a part of this load and perhaps begin to chant them.

A cette barbare idée,
Qui de nous, saisi d'horreur.
N'a pas l'âme possédée
D'une bouillante fureur?

To an entire world of literary expression, revolution means a circle of progressive and endless phrases. To reestablish one's identity, one needs to break it up, for otherwise one feels absorbed by it, sucked into a fatal process. While history develops along a straight line, language, whatever the original disposition of its elements, moves from circle to circle. Taken separately or gathered up into one of these three elements, rhetoric in the oratory, drama in the theater, and poetry on the march, the circles are nothing more than a pause: language is the slackener of action. In its various forms it serves to strike the consciousness and possibly to promote reflection. The lines quoted above are evidence of this: no one doubted their meaning, but everyone felt obliged to enunciate them, to produce them as the body produces sweat.

Life must be lived, so first it is ordered out of nothingness (recall the rousing speeches of Saint-Just), then it is vicariously acted onstage (in the revolutionary drama), and finally it is lived; it emerges as its own poetry, the "poetry of life and action."

Les Français, peuple de braves,
Seul appui de l'univers,
De vingt nations esclaves
A déjà brisé les fers.

The illusion is complete, for life never stops pouring forth. So much so that we are never quite satisfied with the abrupt endings of the marches. There is a refrain, and it is repeated many times: this preserves the illusion. Still, with the numerous repetitions, one falls back into purely rhetorical figures that must eventually be sustained with acting, just as the figure of the Madelon seems always to be leading an assault of "poilus." Thus a student of the literature of the revolution finds himself caught up in an endless reel, if he wishes to draw literature along the path of history.

It is all very well for men like Andre Chenier[12] to stick to personal views and to sketch original portraits, but it should be understood that this kind of writer does not contribute to the history of his period. And it may well be added that the predicament either of choosing to express what is happening and what is bound to happen, and thereby missing the facts, or of leaving one's own age and seeking to revive it elsewhere in history is what ails any "litterature engagée."

Whether it represents a magnified reflection of one age and is generally restricted to the ornamenting and decorating of what is already there with style, rhythm, and rhymes, at the expense of achieving something really new, or whether it is a poor substitute for action, a pure deceit, an endeavor to sell impossible impulses to the world, it seems that ready-made literature can hardly fit history in the making.

Psychological exposures and personal crack-ups are rife throughout the period of the French Revolution. They are problems of language. To history, literature can make only irrelevant contributions. The orator tries to objectify it, the playwright to reproduce it with the aid of the actor, the poet to glorify it. But where is "La Révolution"? It has gone by, while language revolves upon itself. Still the illusion remains.

[12]The same applies to writers of comedy: history is not an alexandrine ode or an Italian farce.

Roland Barthes

Writing and revolution*

The triumph and breakup of bourgeois writing

The diversity of genres and the movement of styles within the classical dogma are aesthetic, not structural, facts; neither the one nor the other should create any illusions. Indeed, during the period when bourgeois ideology conquered and triumphed, French society had at its disposal one sole type of writing, both instrumental and ornamental: instrumental, since form is presumably in the service of substance, as an algebraic equation is in the service of some particular operation; ornamental, since the instrument was decorated with accidental elements outside its function, which was shamelessly borrowed from Tradition — that is to say, bourgeois writing, as picked up by different writers, never provoked the disgust of its heredity, since it was no more than an effective decor against which the act of thought stood out. Doubtless classical writers were also acquainted with the problematics of form, but the discussion had absolutely nothing to do with the variety and meaning of styles of writing and even less to do with the structure of language; rhetoric alone was involved — that is, the order of the thought-out discourse with a view to persuasion. A plurality of rhetorical systems thus corresponded to the singularity of bourgeois writing; inversely, at the very time when rhetorical treatises had lost their interest, around the middle of the nineteenth century, classical writing lost its universality and modern styles of writing originated.

Classical writing was obviously class writing. Having originated in the seventeenth century within the group that was directly bound up with authority, formed by a series of dogmatic decisions, quickly purged of all the grammatical principles that had been developed by

*Reprinted from *Le Degré zéro de l'écriture* (Paris, Editions du Seuil, 1956).

the spontaneous subjectivity of the common man, and set up, on the contrary, for the task of definition, bourgeois writing was considered, with the usual cynicism of early political triumphs, to be the language of a minority and privileged class. In 1647 Vaugelas recommended classical writing as de facto, not de jure; clarity was still not customary except in Court. In 1660, however — in the grammar of Port-Royal, for example — classical language was invested with the characteristics of universality, and clarity became a value. In fact, clarity is a purely rhetorical attribute; it is not a general quality of language, possible in all periods and in all places, but merely the ideal supplement of a certain type of discourse — the very type that must constantly be meant to persuade. Since the prebourgeoisie of monarchical periods and the bourgeoisie of postrevolutionary periods, in using the same style of writing, had developed an essentialist mythology of man, classical writing, one and universal, forsook all hesitation in favor of a continuum made up entirely of *choice* — that is, the complete elimination of everything possible in language. Political authority, dogmatism of the Mind, and the unity of classical language are thus representations of the same historical movement.

Therefore it is no wonder that the Revolution changed nothing in bourgeois writing, and that there is but a slight difference between the writing of a Fénelon and that of a Mérimée. Bourgeois ideology lasted, free from any cracks, until 1848, without wavering in the least throughout a Revolution that gave the bourgeoisie political and social power, but by no means intellectual power, which it had already possessed for a long time. From Laclos to Stendhal, bourgeois writing had only to be revived and to continue over and above the short break created by political disturbances. And the Romantic revolution — which, in name, was so intent on disturbing form — prudently retained the writing of its ideology. The little ballast thrown in during the mixing of genres and words made it possible to preserve the basic substance of classical language — its instrumentality: an instrument that doubtless took on more and more "presence" (especially in Chateaubriand) but actually was used without arrogance and overlooking the entire solitude of language. Only Hugo, by drawing a verbal thematics from the carnal dimensions of his duration and space — a thematics that could no longer be read in the perspective of tradition, but only with reference to the other and formidable side of its own existence — was able, by the weight of his style, to put pressure on classical writing and bring it to the verge of bursting. Therefore contempt for Hugo still guarantees the same formal mythology, which still shelters the same eighteenth-century writing, a witness to bourgeois triumphs — writing that remains the norm for sterling French, that very shut-in language, separated from society by all the density of the literary myth, a kind of sacred writing picked up indifferently by the most different writers in the name of an austere rule or greedy pleasure, a tabernacle of that wondrous mystery: French Literature.

The years around 1850 led to the conjunction of three great new historical facts: the upsetting of European demography; the change-over from the textile industry to the metallurgic industry — that is, the birth of modern capitalism; and the division (achieved in the days of June 1848) of French society into three withdrawn enemy classes — the final destruction of liberalism. This combination of circumstances threw the bourgeoisie into a new historical situation. Up until then the standards of the bourgeois ideology defined the universal, fulfilling it without question; the bourgeois writer, who was the sole judge of other men's unhappiness — since, facing him, there were no others to look at him — was not torn between his social situation and his intellectual vocation. Henceforth this ideology no longer seemed to be one among other possible ideologies; the universal eluded it; it could transcend itself only by condemning itself; the writer became the prey of ambiguity, since his conscience no longer corresponded precisely to his condition. Thus a tragedy of Literature was born.

It was then that styles of writing began to multiply. Thereafter each one — the well-wrought style, the populist style, the neutral style, the spoken style — was to be the initial act by which the writer assumed or loathed his bourgeois condition. Each one was an attempt to answer the Orphean problematics of modern Form — writers without Literature. For one hundred years Flaubert, Mallarmé, Rimbaud, the Goncourts, the Surrealists, Queneau, Sartre, Blanchot, and Camus had plotted — are still plotting — certain courses toward the integration, the explosion, or the naturalization of literary language, but the stakes are not some adventure in form, some achievement in rhetoric, or some bold invention in vocabulary. Every time the writer outlines a complex of words, the very existence of Literature is brought into question; the reading that modernity has furnished in the plurality of its writing styles is the dead end of its own history.

Writing and revolution
Craftsmanship of style produced a type of subwriting, derived from Flaubert but adapted to the designs of the naturalist school. This style of writing — that of Maupassant, Zola, and Daudet — which one might call realistic writing, is a combination of the formal signs of Literature (the past definite, the indirect style, written rhythm) and the no less formal signs of realism (fragments brought in from the vernacular, strong language, dialectical words), so that no language is more artificial than that which claims to faithfully portray Nature. Doubtless the failure is on the level not only of form but also of theory. In naturalist aesthetics there was a conscious creation of writing. The paradox is that the mortification of the subject matter in no way led to an abandonment of Form. Neutral writing was a late development; it was not invented until well after realism, by writers such as Camus, and less as the result of an aesthetics of refuge than of the search for a style of writing that was finally innocent. Realistic writing is far from being neutral; on the contrary, it is filled with the most spectacular signs of conscious creation.

Thus, by degrading itself, by forsaking the requirements of a verbal Nature which is frankly foreign to the real, without, however, claiming to have rediscovered the language of social Nature — as Queneau was to do — the naturalist school paradoxically produced a mechanical art that became a sign of literary convention with an ostentation hitherto unknown. Flaubert's style of writing gradually created a spell; it is still possible to lose oneself in reading Flaubert, as in a nature full of subordinate voices, where signs are more persuasive than expressive. Realistic writing, on the other hand, can never convince; it is doomed to do nothing but portray, by virtue of the dualistic dogma which demands that there never be more than one highest form to "express" an inert reality as an object, over which the writer would have no power but his art of arranging signs.

These "styleless" writers — Maupassant, Zola, Daudet, and their followers — practiced a style of writing which, for them, was the refuge and the show of the workings of craftsmanship, from which they thought they had rid a purely passive aesthetics. We know Maupassant's statements on the work of form, and all the naïve devices of the School, thanks to which the natural sentence is transformed into an artificial sentence meant to testify to its purely literary finality — in other words, here, to all the work it involved. We know that in Maupassant's stylistics the artistic purpose is reserved for syntax, and vocabulary should remain this side of Literature. Writing well — which, from that time on, was the only sign of the literary act — meant naïvely shifting a complement around or "enhancing" a word in the belief that it was a way to achieve an "expressive" rhythm. But expressiveness is a myth: it is merely the convention of expressiveness.

This type of conventional writing has always been a favorite source for scholarly critics, who judge the value of a text on the amount of work that obviously went into it. Nothing is more spectacular than trying out combinations of complements, like a worker putting a delicate fragment into place. What academics admire in the writings of a Maupassant or a Daudet is a literary sign that is finally detached from its content, unambiguously establishing Literature as a category that has no relation to other languages and, in this way, setting up an ideal intelligibility of things. Between a proletariat devoid of any culture and an intelligentsia that has already begun to question Literature itself, the average group that attends primary or secondary school — roughly, the petty bourgeoisie — is thus going to find in artistico-realistic writing (which now constitutes most commercial novels) the privileged image of a Literature that has all the striking and intelligible signs of its own identity. In this case the writer's function is not so much to create a Work as to produce Literature that is recognizable from miles away.

This petty-bourgeois writing has been picked up by the Communist writers because, for the time being, the artistic norms of the proletariat cannot be different from those of the petty bourgeoisie (actually, a fact consistent with the doctrine), and because the very dogma of socialist realism necessarily insists upon conventional writing, which is meant to draw attention very conspicuously to a content that does not have the power to command recognition without a form that identifies it. The paradox of Communist writing multiplying the coarsest signs of Literature is thus understandable, and far from breaking with what is, on the whole, a typically bourgeois form — at least, was in the past — it continues unreservedly to assume the formal concerns of the petty-bourgeois art of writing (which, as a matter of fact, is sanctioned in Communist milieus by the compositions in primary school).

French socialist realism thus picked up the writing of bourgeois realism, freely mechanizing all the intentional signs of the art. Here, for example, are a few lines from a novel by Garaudy: "bending over, hurling himself at the keyboard of the Linotype . . . joy sang in his muscles, his fingers danced, light and powerful . . . the poisonous steam of the antimony . . . made his temples throb and his arteries thump, adding fire to his strength, his anger, and his exaltation." Clearly, nothing is described here without a metaphor, for the reader must ponderously be made to realize that "it is well written" (in other words, that what he is consuming is Literature). Such metaphors, which overwhelm any verb at all, are by no means the intentional result of a Mood seeking to convey the special quality of a sensation, but merely a literary mark that situates language, just as a tag gives a price.

"To type," "to throb" (in speaking of blood), or "to be happy for the first time" is real language, not realistic language; in order to

Roland Barthes

make Literature, one must write: "strum" on the Linotype, "his arteries thumped," or "he embraced the first happy moment of his life." Thus realistic writing can result only in Preciosity. Garaudy writes: "After each line, the slender arm of the Linotype lifted its pinch of dancing slugs"; or, "Every caress of his fingers awakens and quickens the merry chimes of the copper slugs that fall into the grooves like a shower of sharp notes." Such jargon is that of Cathos and Magdelon.

Obviously, allowances must be made for mediocrity, which, in the case of Garaudy, is tremendous. In André Stil one finds devices that are far more discreet but which nevertheless do not escape from the rules of artistico-realistic writing. In Stil the metaphor does not aspire to be more than a cliché almost completely integrated into real language, calling attention to Literature without much effort: "clear as spring water," "hands shriveled by the cold," and so on. Preciosity is forced back from the vocabulary into the syntax, and Literature is imposed, as in Maupassant, by an artificial cutting up of complements ("with one hand, she raised her knees, bent in two" [*d'une main, elle soulève les genoux, pliée en deux*]). In this language, saturated with convention, the real is given only in quotation marks: it throws populist words and slipshod phrasing into the middle of purely literary syntax: "True, it's really kicking up a storm, the wind" [*C'est vrai, il chahute drôlement, le vent*]; or even better, "Out in the wind, berets and caps shaking over their eyes, they looked at one another with quite a lot of curiosity" [*En plein vent, bérets et casquettes secoués au-dessus des yeux, ils se regardent avec pas mal de curiosité*] (the familiar *"pas mal de"* follows an absolute participial clause, which is a form never used in spoken language). Of course, Aragon is a case apart, for his literary heredity is quite different, and he preferred to give realistic writing a light eighteenth-century tint by mixing a bit of Laclos with Zola.

Perhaps, in this prudent writing of revolutionaries, there is the helpless feeling of being unable to create a free style of writing at present. Perhaps it is also true that only the bourgeois writers are able to sense the compromise of bourgeois writing: the explosion of literary language was a fact of consciousness, not of revolution. There is no doubt that the Stalinist ideology frightens one away from any problematics — even and especially revolutionary problematics: bourgeois writing is judged, on the whole, as less dangerous as it exists than if it were put on trial. Therefore the Communist writers are the only ones who imperturbably uphold a bourgeois style of writing which the bourgeois writers themselves condemned long ago, the very day that they sensed it was compromised by the deceit of their own ideology — the very day that Marxism came to be justified.

Translated by June Guicharnaud

Richard J. Klein

Baudelaire and revolution: some notes

In March 1852, Baudelaire announced to Mme. Aupick his firm resolve to break with Jeanne Duval and to devote himself to the exclusive pursuit of his poetic career. In a letter which was intended to mark a turning point in his life, Baudelaire does not neglect to mention the political events that, since February 1848, had profoundly engaged his attention: "About political events and the devastating influences they had on me, I'll speak to you another day." If Baudelaire ever did, no record of that conversation survives. The characteristic evasiveness of the note suggests that the silence of the documents is no accident. In order to describe those influences, critics have been obliged to hunt for passages scattered throughout his works, to focus mainly on the private journals where politics is a recurring, almost obsessive theme. Almost obsessive, because despite their repetition and frequency, the remarks are for the most part tantalizingly brief, fragmentary or aphoristic, obscure or ironic, as if he were determined to grant them only the most allusive language, a language whose form most closely resembled the promise to speak another day.

In their eagerness to circumvent Baudelaire's reticence, critics have turned lately to documenting his bizarre political career.[1] In 1848, between February and October, if one can credit the very circumstantial evidence, Baudelaire twice supported the popular uprisings and twice edited reactionary newspapers which denounced them. The evidence suggests that we should understand quite literally the brief passage in the journals where he undertakes to describe "My intoxication in 1848." The morning-after came brutally, as it always did for Baudelaire, with the coup d'etat in 1851. From that moment on, Baudelaire insisted that he was "physically depoliticized," in the

[1]Jules Mouquet and W. T. Bandy, *Baudelaire en 1848*, ed. Emile-Paul Frères (Paris, 1948).

sense that literary activity, which had become his exclusive concern, was no longer felt to be compatible with any form of political activity — a renunciation strictly analogous to his rejection of all forms of persistent intoxication, wine, hashish, and opium, whose powers to stir his imagination represent the most intensely felt temptation and the most devastating threat to his poetic project. Intoxication is always followed by spleen, the hangover which comes with the de-intoxication, the demystification of poetic illusions. But in Baudelaire, the renunciation is never definitive; just as he constantly succumbs to the consolation of drugs, he writes in 1853 to Ancelle: "I have persuaded myself twenty times that I would no longer interest myself in politics, and, with each grave question, I am seized again with curiosity and passion."

But despite his occasional weakness, Baudelaire is very clear about what he intends. After 1852, it is no longer a question of affirming, as he did earlier, that "the time is not far off when it will be understood that any literature which refuses to march fraternally between science and philosophy is a homicidal, suicidal literature." On the contrary, he lashes out in his journals with full fury against his own metaphors, as if to avenge himself on the very language which aimed to engage his work in the social revolution sweeping Europe.

> Poètes de combat
> Les littérateurs d'avant garde
> This repeated use of military metaphors denotes minds not militant, but made for discipline, that is, for conformity, minds born to serve [nés domestique], Belgian minds who can only think in groups [en société].

The critical problem is not to discover Baudelaire's "real" political convictions as they fluctuated with each grave event, but rather to explain his reluctance to describe them and, more importantly, his active and persistent refusal to engage his art in any political perspective, not even in revolution. For Baudelaire's increasing revulsion with bourgeois society would seem to predispose him in its favor. At the end of his life, living miserably in Belgium — the nation which epitomized the bourgeois soul of France — Baudelaire cannot prevent himself from speaking seriously of revolution which he understands and embraces for its pure nihilism. Let it be added that when one speaks seriously of revolution, they are terrified . . . . But I am not a dupe, I have never been a dupe. I say *Vive la Révolution!* as I would say *Vive la Déstruction! Vive l'Expiation! Vive le Châtiment! Vive la Mort!* In *Mon Coeur Mis à Nu*, he ascribes his intoxication in 1848 to a taste for destruction, a taste for vengeance. The melancholy record of his correspondence reveals how much he had reason to seek revenge on a society which had made his life an interminable financial struggle.

Baudelaire's refusal to march fraternally with revolution exposes him to serious attack by socially minded critics. Either they denounce his reactionary sentiments and then implicitly indict his poetry, or they seek to save the poetry by refusing to take seriously his insistence that poetry fulfills its authentic function only when it has disengaged itself from politics. Sartre's condemnation of Baudelaire illustrates the first tendency.[2] At the risk of drastic oversimplification his argument may be summarized as follows. Baudelaire, he says, was unwilling to choose any form of revolutionary engagement to the extent that he accepted the values of bourgeois society under the self-deceiving guise of denouncing them. His protest against those values illustrates the characteristic bad faith of all rebellion.

The rebel is careful to maintain intact the abuses from which he suffers in order to rebel against them . . . . He wants neither to destroy, nor transcend, but only to stand up against the order of things. The more he attacks it, the more he secretly respects it; the rights that he openly contests, he preserves intact in the depths of his heart.

As Sartre says later, the bourgeois defines himself precisely insofar as he rebels against the ideology of his own class. Baudelaire's reactionary politics are, for Sartre, one more confirmation of the bad faith of his personal project. Unwilling to distinguish Baudelaire's personal

[2]Jean-Paul Sartre, *Baudelaire* (New York, New Directions Paperbook 225, 1967).

dereliction from his poetic accomplishment (what Maurice Blanchot has called the failure of his life and the success of his poetry[3]) Sartre makes a literary judgment which he only reluctantly admits. For if Baudelaire's refusal of revolution shares in the bad faith of his personal project, then his poetry, which illustrates that bad faith, which denounces the values of society but refuses any radical perspectives, is itself in bad faith. And poetry which is in bad faith is bad poetry; it mystifies its relation to the world at the very moment it claims to be authentically revealing it. Implicitly Sartre must claim that Baudelaire's poetry would have been better if it had been more radically engaged. In fact, he is quite consistent in preferring Rimbaud, who, he says, denied absolutely the values proclaimed by bourgeois ideology. If, on the other hand, one assumes, as this writer does, that Baudelaire's poetry is immensely successful, then its success demands that one take seriously its resolute disengagement. For Baudelaire the disengagement of poetry is not an indifferent factor in its achievement; he is very clear in affirming that it is its absolute precondition.

Other critics — one thinks of Adorno or Walter Benjamin[4] — might be willing to accept this assertion but object mildly to the word "absolute." They might point out that Baudelaire's rejection of politics came in 1852 after the coup d'etat of Louis-Napoleon. Revolution had become impossible; political life in France was absolutely bankrupt. Under these conditions, Baudelaire's retreat from politics could be considered the only possible means of preserving his artistic integrity. To preserve the radical content of philosophic and poetic language, it may become necessary to wage the struggle exclusively in the mind, when the historical situation denies all possibility of fulfilling that content and when society is actively engaged in suppressing it. Or, to invert the thesis of Marx, when there is no point in trying to change the world, poets can only interpret it in various ways. Unable to understand his situation historically, Baudelaire, it might be

[3]Maurice Blanchot, "L'échec de Baudelaire," in *La Part du Feu* (Gallimard, 1949).
[4]This dialogue with Adorno and Benjamin is purely hypothetical. Adorno, to my knowledge, has never written on Baudelaire, although I believe I am accurately representing his general position. Benjamin, whose essay on Baudelaire is the most penetrating critical study of that author I have ever read, never explicitly raises the question. His great subtlety makes me affirm rather uneasily that I am representing the general thrust of his argument.

argued, uses an a-historical vocabulary to express a contingent truth, namely, that in certain periods of reaction all commerce with politics is complicity. To sustain this argument, it becomes necessary once again to deny that Baudelaire understood the full extent of his poetic enterprise; the critic must assume the awesome responsibility of revealing to the poet the truth of his own poetry.

At least the critic should have clearly in view the dangers of that audacity. Either he must admit that he is merely casting an oblique light on the poetry in order to illustrate some psychological or sociological structure, thereby renouncing any claim to understanding the work's immanent intention.[5] Or, if the critic aims to seize that intention, he must avoid the tendency to falsify his reading in favor of the concept by which he will later judge the work. Benjamin is very conscious of the peril. His article offers to discuss "some motifs" in Baudelaire; it is not designed to comprehend the totality of his work. Benjamin can afford to ignore the question of Baudelaire's politics because, at his most brilliant, he tends implicitly to use Baudelaire to confirm on a psychological level certain insights of Marx into the fragmentation of nineteenth-century experience. Benjamin goes farther than any critic in illuminating certain central themes at the price of being partial, of reductively using the poetry to illustrate a certain historical concept which precedes and supersedes the poetry. Whether it is ever possible to avoid this kind of reduction is a question which can be answered only after the critic has considered seriously the claims of poetry itself. That is not to say that the critic can, by some sentimental act of faith, simply exalt poetry beyond the reach of those who try to understand it most fully. Baudelaire's language does not pretend to lie outside history or beyond psychology; it claims to understand history and the self in a way fundamentally different from the conceptions of these critics.

It is clear that Baudelaire denied any ultimate value to revolu-

---

[5]By aim and intention I do not mean of course the thoughts which crossed the mind of Baudelaire, for example, the day he wrote "Le Cygne." I am speaking of the aim, the general intention of the whole work, particularly as that intention can be apprehended through the analysis of form, of the particular form of particular works. Hence, to take an obvious example, the correspondence of Baudelaire is not irrelevant to the intention but it can serve only to support our analysis of the poetry. For the most incisive discussion of intentionality, particularly as it can be distinguished from the bugaboo of "new criticism," one must turn to the indispensable article of Paul DeMan in *Preuves* (October 1966).

tion and that he claimed for literature a higher prerogative than that to which any political act can aspire. Whatever sympathy he lends to the revolutions of his time derives from the energy with which they sought to destroy the existing forms of society. Baudelaire assigns the taste for violence to a "natural taste for destruction," but he by no means values modern civilization as absolutely preferable to more natural expressions of human activity. He writes in his journals: "Nomads, shepherds, hunters, farmers, and even cannibals, all of them can be superior, by their personal dignity, to our Western races." Michel Butor, in a book which contains the best discussion of Baudelaire's politics,[6] cites several passages like this one in order to conclude that for Baudelaire the reign of bourgeois society was so intolerable that "even if the revolution must end in failure, it is preferable to the status quo."

Revolution that arises out of a natural desire for destruction is conceived as a legitimate exercise of human energy against a civilization which stifles it. But insofar as that desire is natural, it is incapable of understanding its own limitations. It aims to be pure negativity — "Vive la Déstruction! Vive la Mort!" — but ultimately it cannot escape the power of that which it wishes to destroy. The old society, washed away by revolution, revenges itself on its victors and returns disguised in the new forms which society creates: "The Revolution and the Cult of Reason prove the idea of sacrifice . . . . The Revolution, through sacrifice, confirms superstition." The sacrificial blood of the revolution is not shed as the price for creating a new life; it is, rather, a kind of ritual purification by which society divests itself of its shabby institutions in order to allow the old content of superstition to flourish. The Cult of Reason is a mystified form of those institutions which possessed at least the virtue of their hypocrisy. In his notes on *Les Liaisons Dangereuses,* Baudelaire discusses "How one made love under the ancien régime . . . . It was still a lie, but one didn't worship one's fellowman. One *deceived* him, but one did not deceive oneself." It is by virtue of its somewhat greater self-consciousness that Baudelaire will often insist that "Superstition is the reservoir of all truths"

[6]Michel Butor, *Histoire Extraordinaire, essai sur un rêve de Baudelaire* (Gallimard, 1961).

and "Nothing on earth is interesting except religions." Just as Baudelaire persists in preferring, in certain crucial respects, the society of natural man to the corrupted, deluded society of the West, in the same way he values superstition above the delusions of revolutionaries, whose vision of human progress is only a beclouded version of the old myths. In their original form, however, surrounded with sentimentality and irrationality, the old myths speak of certain veiled truths more clearly than the new.

Caught between two kinds of mystification, one more opaque than the other, Baudelaire feels obliged to say, "I have no convictions, as the men of my century understand it, because I have no ambition . . . . However, I do have some convictions in a more elevated sense, and which cannot be understood by the people of my time." The poet between two myths can have no ambition in the sense of any real hope to change the world, even to reveal to his contemporaries the truth of their illusions or their illusions of truth. He feels rather like the musician in a room full of hashish eaters, whose attempts to speak sense are derided by his intoxicated friends. The only language possible in a society bent on self-delusion is an ironic one, a language which reveals that it knows the extent of its inevitable misunderstanding and somehow makes use of its predestined failure.

In "Perte d'Auréole," the poet crossing the street in great haste loses his halo in the mud and prefers to leave it rather than risk his life in the traffic. An acquaintance, eager to be helpful, suggests that he check with the police or advertise its loss.

God! no. I'm fine here. You're the only one who recognized me. Besides, I'm bored with dignity. And then, I'd like to think that some bad poet will pick it up and put it on his head. Make someone happy, what fun! and especially someone who will make me laugh. Think of X, or Z. Hah! That will be pretty amusing!

The poet is the man who renounces his illusions and bears ironic witness to the illusions of others.

But the irony does not stop there. The figure of the poet is unmistakably undercut by the cruel fatuity of his own language. Having forsworn his dignity, he becomes one of those absurd but rather vicious *farceur* like the dandy in "Un Plaisant," who imagines that he is fatally subverting social convention when he extends the season's greetings to a misused, old donkey. In "Perte d'Auréole," Baudelaire finds himself once more between superstition and the Cult of Reason, between the deluded dignity of the bad poet and the deluded demystifications of his hero. The subject of the poem is in fact the halo whose bizarre reality within the poem's prosaic world is never questioned. It somehow points to the truth hidden in the absurd pretensions of the poet who wears it and in the demystifying pretensions of the poet who renounces it — a truth which Baudelaire throughout his critical work is forever trying to discern behind the pose of the Parnassians and behind the anti-poetic rhetoric of the Realists. The halo in this poem points in a very ambiguous way to the realm of the *surnaturel,* to which Baudelaire constantly aspires, but which we hestitate even to name in view of the confusions and complexities which overlay this much abused word.

It would perhaps help to clarify this notion if we returned to the historical perspective from which we began. For Baudelaire, superstition, in its various forms, is considered somewhat ironically to be the reservoir of all truths. In another note he remarks the "Supremacy of the pure idea in the Christian as in the Communist." The pure idea which belongs both to Christians and Communists, which revolution takes over from superstition and preserves in the very negation of superstition, is often named by Baudelaire; it is *utopia.* The revolution negates the pure idea of Christianity in favor of the Cult of Reason, but the utopian vision of a world made rational is merely the inverted reflection of the terrestrial paradise. It is the purity, the ideality of utopias which make impossible their realization, but, paradoxically, it is their ideality which is their truth. The violence which Baudelaire directs against the utopians — "those entrepreneurs of public happiness" — is aimed not at those who merely create fictions but at those who in the name of fiction traffic in human manipulation. When he attacks utopians, Baudelaire is not without the knowledge that utopia is one of the most persistent themes of his own work.

Richard Klein

Both versions of "L'Invitation au Voyage" are extended evocations of that ideal country to which he longs to travel; he names his own utopian aspiration – the nostalgia for a country which one does not know. The utopia may belong to a hypothetical future or be lost in the past of man's beginning: "J'aime le souvenir des époques nues." Or it may be a dream of Greece, a mythological Holland, or, in "L'Essence du Rire," the projection of a time before man's fall: "In the terrestrial paradise, that is, in the milieu where all things created seemed good to man, joy was not found in laughter." A parenthetical comment on this terrestrial paradise insists on the purely imaginary, fictional character of the utopia: "In the terrestrial paradise (let it be supposed in the past or yet to come, memory or prophecy, like the theologians or the Communists)." When Baudelaire wants to say something nice about the Revolution of 1848, he singles out its utopian pretensions, that element which both contributed to its explosion and guaranteed its failure: "1848 was amusing only because people made utopias like castles in Spain." What amuses Baudelaire is the way revolution stirred the popular imagination to create an abundance of romance. In fact, he suggests that his own intoxication in 1848 was provoked by literary influences: "My intoxication in 1848. Literary intoxication; remembering books I had read. (Souvenirs litteraires)." For Baudelaire revolution is a temptation and a danger precisely because it prompts this kind of confusion between imagination and reality; it encourages the poet to mistake the truth of his utopian vision, to imagine that because he can conceive a better life, that life is within reach. At the end of *Mon Coeur Mis à Nu,* Baudelaire cries out: "Because I understand a glorious existence, I think myself capable of realizing it. O Jean-Jacques!" Throughout Baudelaire Rousseau is the figure of the sentimental poet. At the end of the "Poème du Haschisch," he is emblematic of the man intoxicated by the Ideal, who imagines that he has attained the elevation to which he aspires, who thinks he has become God: "Jean-Jacques had drugged himself without hashish."

Baudelaire's remark on the power of literature to influence a revolutionary situation confirms on an individual level one of the most astonishing insights of Marx. In "The 18th of Brumaire," Marx, writing from London, tears the veil of ideology from the Revolution of 1848.

> Just when men seem engaged in revolutionizing themselves and things, in creating something that has never yet existed, precisely in such periods of revolutionary crisis they anxiously conjure the spirits of the past to their service and borrow from them names, battle cries, and costumes, in order to present the new scene of world history in this time-honored disguise and this borrowed language.

Both Marx and Baudelaire seem to be denouncing the same mystification. The social revolution signifies its failure by the eagerness with which it borrows the rhetoric and costumes of an earlier age. Baudelaire finds it amusing; Marx calls it a farce. But whereas for Marx the comedy of utopianism is the inevitable spectacle of bourgeois revolution, Baudelaire denies that revolution can ever escape the illusions of its own poetry. Marx counters by insisting that the "social revolution of the nineteenth century cannot draw its poetry from the past, but only from the future. It cannot begin with itself until it has stripped itself of all superstition from the past." For Baudelaire, the cardinal superstition, the doctrine which is the very ground of Marx's optimism, is the progressive notion that the industrial system can be put to use to change the quality of human existence. Marx indicts the utopian socialists for failing to describe the means by which one can pass from the alienation of labor to its liberation. For him,

> The development of the industrial proletariat is, in general, conditioned by the development of the industrial bourgeoisie. Only under its rule does the proletariat gain that extensive national existence which can raise its revolution to a national one, and does itself create the modern means of production, which become just so many means of its revolutionary emancipation.

For Baudelaire those means of production, far from providing the possibility of revolutionary emancipation, are — whatever the quality of men's relation to production — the source of man's progressive dehumanization. While for Marx technology was neutral, merely a tool in the hands of a certain class, for Baudelaire it is the instrument of man's self-destruction. "Technology," he says,

> will have so americanized us, progress will have so atrophied our spirit, that nothing in the sanguinary, sacrilegious, or anti-natural dreams of the utopians will be comparable to these positive results.

It should be clear that Baudelaire, whose sympathy for the poor and estranged is one of his most impressive themes, was directing his anger against the reign of bourgeois society. One cannot doubt that if it came to revolution, he would have taken the most intense pleasure in destroying that society in the name of the "captives, the vanguished . . . many others besides." But he would not be duped by the promise of revolution:

> Theory of true civilization. It is not in gas, in steam, nor in talking tables. It is in the diminuation of the traces of original sin.

> There can only be progress (real, that is to say, moral progress) in the individual and by the individual.

The writer who seeks to put his imagination to work to reform society shares the absurd destiny of the poet in the famous prose poem, "Assomons les pauvres." Having read many bad utopian authors, he leaves his house fascinated by his own utopian scheme, "the germ of an idea superior to the wives' tales the lexicon of which I had recently scanned." He finds an old beggar, beats him up until the man in a rage "proves" his dignity by beating up the poet in turn. Bloody and black-eyed, the poet gives the man his purse and urges him to share the money with his companions by applying the same theory: "He swore to me that he had understood my theory and would follow my advice." The utopian poet is satisfied with the assurances, duped by his own superior idea into giving up his purse and taking a beating in the bargain. Baudelaire is not duped, however: "I have never been a dupe. I say *Vive la Révolution!* as I would say *Vive la Destruction! . . . Vive la Mort!*"

Nothing it seems is left of revolution or utopia. The words themselves have been exhausted, endlessly undercut by Baudelaire's ironies. The poet can view them only with bitter laughter. In one terrible phrase, Baudelaire sums up the Revolution of 1848: "1848 was charming only in the excess of its ridiculousness." The Revolution was a farce because neither the revolutionaries nor their opponents even began to diagnose the source of man's misery: "It is not particularly in political institutions that the universal ruin, or universal progress (the name little matters), will appear. It will be in the degradation of human hearts."

Yet at the very moment when the critic believes that Baudelaire has transcended all commerce with revolution and utopia, he recalls that the "degradation of human hearts" provoked Baudelaire to write a book entitled *Mon Coeur Mis à Nu* and that he borrowed the title from a passage in Poe:

> If any ambitious man have a fancy to revolutionize at one effort the universal world of human thought, human opinion, and human sentiment, the opportunity is his own — the road to immortal renown lies straight open and unencumbered before him. All that he has to do is write and publish a very little book. Its title should be simple — a few plain words — "My Heart Laid Bare." But this little book must be *true to its title*.
>
> . . . But to write it, there is the rub. No man *could* write it, even if he dared. The paper would shrivel and blaze at every touch of the fiery pen.

Baudelaire dared to write the book. He aimed to serve humanity not by trying to legislate its happiness but by sacrificing his own happiness, by laying bare his heart and revealing it to the world. Therein lies the real sacrifice which superstition consecrates under all its disguises. The book was not published by Baudelaire, as if to confirm Poe's prediction. Though it aims directly at revealing the poet's heart it succeeds only in accumulating the ironic masks with which he hides. The revolution has to find more oblique paths: "The destiny of poetry is a great one. Joyful or mournful, it always possesses a divine, utopian character. It ceaselessly contradicts facticity [*le fait*], on pain of ceasing to exist." Poetry does·not evoke the utopia as a promise to which action may aspire, but as a pure fictional projection through

Richard Klein

which the negativity, the finitude of the human condition may be revealed. The poet is not attempting to found the utopia but to become conscious of its irrevocable absence within the world. And when an exquisite poem brings tears to one's eyes, these tears are not the proof of an excess of pleasure, they are rather the witness of an irritable melancholy, of a solicitation of one's nerves, of a nature exiled in the imperfect who would like to seize immediately on this earth the revealed paradise. Not pleasure or consolation, poetry can only disclose man's estrangement. The poet is always the man in exile, Ovid's man, who lifts his eyes to the heavens but can never return. His highest function, his "revolutionary" role, is not to urge revolt or promise utopia − all that is illusion which poetry unmasks − but to bear witness in the presence of the barbarians to the imperfection inherent in man's being-in-the-world. When the poet speaks seriously of revolution he can only say, ironically, "Vive la Mort!"

Antonio Regalado García

The counterrevolutionary image of the world

Juan Donoso Cortés (1809-53) belonged to the first romantic generation in Spain. He became a prominent liberal conservative politician in the 1830s and 1840s and was ambassador to Paris and Berlin. Partially as a consequence of the 1848 revolutions, he abjured his liberalism in the Spanish parliament on January 4, 1849, in a famous speech which was widely distributed and elicited responses from many. Alexander Herzen made one such response in Proudhon's publication *Voix du Peuple,* and this answer caused the denunciation of the newspaper and its closing. Donoso's famous book, *Ensayo sobre el catolicismo, el liberalismo, y el socialismo,* was published in Spanish and French in 1851; it became a best seller and had as apocalyptic a success as Spengler's *Decline of the West* had later. His reputation was spread by Montalambert, and he influenced Schelling, Ranke, Metternich, Bismarck, and Friedrich William of Prussia.

Donoso was condemned by his enemies as a reactionary, but in the twentieth century he has been reevaluated in Spain, Germany, and France as an accurate observer whose prophecies came true in many cases, in particular his awareness of socialism and of the future political role of Russia. Karl Löwith says of Donoso that

he describes bourgeois society exactly in the same terms as Kierkegaard and Marx: as an undifferentiated class *discutidora,* without truth, passion, or heroism. It eliminates hereditary nobility, but does nothing to combat the aristocracy of wealth; it accepts the sovereignty neither of the king nor of the people. Hatred of the aristocracy drives it to the left, and fear of radical socialism to the right. The opposite of its wordy indecisiveness is the decisive atheistic socialism of Proudhon. In contrast to him Donoso Cortés represents the political theology of the counterrevolution, to which the French Revolution, which declared man

Antonio Regalado

and the people sovereign, appeared as a revolt against the created order.[1]

Donoso saw the choice facing Europe after the 1848 revolutions as either the dictatorship of government or the dictatorship of revolution. Donoso incorporates into his thought the dialectic of revolution and counterrevolution which from 1789 to 1848 offers several stages: the French Revolution and the counterrevolutionary reaction, the attempt at a liberal synthesis, and the rise of socialism as an extreme form of revolution. Donoso experienced the liberal attempt at synthesis and reacted against it and against upcoming socialism by returning to the response of the first counterrevolutionaries, especially that of Joseph De Maistre, which he applied to a new phenomenon, that of the third stage of the dialectic, the rise of socialism in the 1840s. The following passage of the *Essay* is characteristic and revealing of Donoso's thought. The passage shows closely the language of revolution and counterrevolution, a language that has an oratorical bent in a fully developed literary expression. The passage is addressed to the revolutionaries, particularly to Joseph Pierre Proudhon.

> Delinquent and fallen man was not made for truth, nor truth for delinquent and fallen man. Between the truth and human reason after the fall of man, God has placed an everlasting repugnance and an invincible repulsion. Truth carries within itself the titles [i.e. proofs] of its own sovereignty, and does not ask permission to impose its yoke, while man, since he revolted against his God, does not consent to any other sovereignty except his own, unless the others ask first of him his consent and his permission. That is why when the truth is placed before his eyes, then, at once, he begins by denying it and to deny it is to affirm himself as an independent sovereign. If he cannot deny it, he enters into a struggle against it and fighting against it he fights for his own sovereignty. If he triumphs, he crucifies it; if he is conquered, he flees; escaping he thinks he escapes from his servitude, and crucifying it, he believes he is crucifying his tyrant.
>
> On the contrary, between human reason and the absurd there is a strange affinity, a very close relation. Sin has united them through the bond of an indissoluble wedlock. The absurd triumphs totally over man, because he is bereft [lit. "naked"] of all rights prior to and superior to human reason. Man accepts reason absolutely, because he comes [into the world] naked, because having no rights he has no pretensions. His will accepts him because it is the son of his understanding, and the understanding takes pleasure in him because it is his own son, his own *logos*, because it is a living testimony of his creative power. In the act of his own creation man becomes like God and he calls himself God. And if

[1]Karl Löwith, *From Hegel to Nietzsche; The Revolution in Nineteenth-Century Thought*, trans. David S. Green (New York, 1964), pp. 251-52.

he is God in the manner of God, everything else is less. What does it matter if the other be the God of the truth, if he is the God of the absurd? At least he will be independent like God; he will be sovereign like God; worshipping his own work, he will worship himself; magnifying it he will magnify himself.

You who aspire to subjugate the peoples and dominate the nations and exercise an empire over human reason, do not proclaim yourselves holders of clear and evident truths; and above all do not declare your proofs if you have them, because the world will never recognize you as masters, but rather it will revolt against the brutal yoke of your evidence. Proclaim, on the contrary, that you possess an argument that destroys a mathematical truth; that you are going to demonstrate that two plus two are not four but five; that God does not exist, or that man is God; that the world has been until now the slave of shameful superstitions; that the wisdom of the centuries is nothing but sheer ignorance; that all revelation is an imposture; that all government is tyranny, and all obedience servitude; that the beautiful is ugly and the ugly is beautiful; that good is evil, and evil is good; that the devil is God and God is the devil; that outside this world there is neither hell nor paradise; that the world which we inhabit is a present hell and a future paradise; that liberty, equality, and fraternity are dogmas incompatible with Christian superstition; that theft is an imprescriptible right, and that property is theft; that there is no order but in anarchy and no anarchy without order; and be sure that with this single proclamation the world, amazed by your wisdom, and fascinated by your science, will pay close and reverent attention to your words.[2]

Donoso Cortés opposes delinquent and fallen man (*el hombre prevaricador y caido*) to the truth. Through his breach of trust (*prevaricación*), man has plunged into a world of sin and corruption, from which he can be redeemed through a reinstatement into truth (*verdad*), whence emanate revelation, grace, and divine providence. This truth is not that of rationalism, the *adequatio rei et intellectu* of the scholastics, reinterpreted in the eighteenth century as the internal coherence of thought, reason, independent of transcendence or any external factor alien to itself. In opposition to this rational truth (*la razón humana*) stands the truth in the sense of the *'emunah* of the Old Testament, meaning security, trust, being, God, the absolute truth, for God alone is absolutely faithful. Human reason does not correspond to the truth, for human reason is precisely the deviation from trust and the supreme mark of man's infidelity.

Donoso accepts the premises of the first catholic counterrevolutionaries, most notably Joseph De Maistre (1753-1821) and Franz von Baader (1765-1841). They react to the French Revolution, which is identified in their minds with the entire process of rational-

---

[2]Translated from Juan Donoso Cortés, *Ensayo sobre el catolicismo, el liberalismo, y el socialismo* (Madrid, 1851), pp. 65-68.

ism since the Renaissance, culminating in the Enlightenment, through a reassertion of a catholic world order. Baader, less well known than De Maistre, states clearly the grounds for the counterrevolutionary position. He sees the Christian state as the only one truly universal (catholic) and able to conciliate the inherent contradictions of man's nature. He sees the modern secular state as a product of human reason which, having disengaged itself from God, has alienated man from the truth, the only basis of order, and thrown him into anarchy and corruption. Baader denies modern man's claim to absolute autonomy and envisions authentic liberty in a necessary dependence upon God. His stupendous interpretation of the revolt of Lucifer illustrates the fundamental premise of catholic counterrevolutionary thought. Through his revolt, Lucifer attempted to reach the plenitude of being predicated only of God. God chastised Lucifer by depriving him of any participation in being and condemning him to nothingness, then out of mercy abrogated this first command. But Lucifer was already on the way to nothingness. This being on the way to nonbeing, braked by God's second command, is matter itself, the world and fallen man. Revelation, grace, and divine providence are the processes by which God extends his merciful hand to man to stay his plunge into the abyss of nonbeing and raise him toward a salvation, a return to being, which he could never achieve merely by his own efforts. Truth, which is God's plenitude of being, is beyond the reach of treacherous and fallen man, the betrayer of that trust, that truth. Man's reinstatement into being is only possible through redemption, not through the revolutionary principles of liberty, equality, and fraternity.

The French Revolution, in accordance with rational premises, attempts to change that accumulation of habits and institutions persisting in the present, which is the traditional world. Yet that present moment of the past, those patterns of behavior and institutions, resist change as dictated by reason. The latter has not taken into account the fundamental contingency and complexity of the world it seeks to change. Counterrevolutionary thought is based on a solid reality, the actual failure of the Revolution to change the world as prescribed in its abstract principles. From its theological perspective, counterrevolutionary thought sees the Revolution not as man's taking the reins of his own destiny through rational planning of the future, but rather as a working of God's ways among men. History is guided by divine providence, not by the rational idea of human progress. In this spirit De Maistre interpreted the revolutionary process in 1796: "On ne sauroit trop le répéter, ce ne sont point les hommes qui mènent la révolution, c'est la révolution qui emploie les hommes."[3] The Revolution had not attained its goals, but it had jolted the traditional structure of society so that it could never again be the same and therefore had elicited the counterrevolutionary response, which was forced to explain the Revolution in a manner satisfactory to its philosophical premises. The counterrevolutionary thinkers cleverly attack the Revolution in its Achilles' heel, in its dogmatic rationalism, in its blindness to the nature of history and the limitations of abstract thought. Yet this historical sensitivity of the counterrevolutionary is vitiated by the invocation of an all-purpose explanation, the deus ex machina of divine providence, to account for the undeniable reality of the Revolution.[4]

To understand the dialectical movement of revolution and counterrevolution, we must glance briefly at the first dialectical stage which roughly stretches from 1789 to the return of Napoleon from Elba in 1815, a stage which carries within it the second one. The failure of the French Revolution to actualize its rational plans not only nourished the counterrevolutionary spirit but provoked a reappraisal within the revolutionary movement, which led to an attempt to transcend rationalism, to learn to think historically, to integrate the past with the future. Counterrevolution becomes the pedagogue of revolution, and vice versa; thus the possibility of a synthesis, of a conciliatory

[3]Joseph De Maistre, *Considérations sur la France* (Lyon, 1822), p. 9.
[4]The entire mechanism of revolutionary rationalism is well expressed by Descartes when he says in his fourth Meditation that everything conceived by reason is thought as it ought to be, and it is thus impossible for the intellect to err. Yet, he asks, whence come my errors? They come, he says, from the will, which being more ample than understanding cannot be contained within the same limits but extends itself to phenomena which it does not understand and thus errs, confusing true and false, good and evil. This is why man errs and sins. Truth is guaranteed by Cartesian rationalism, if man uses properly his ability to reason. Thus is established the autonomy of reason from the world of contingency and accident, from the fallen condition of man, and from history. Such an attitude is fundamentally blind to the fathomless irrationality of history, to the world or domain of the will, where error and sin prevail. It is easy prey for the counterrevolutionary critic who denies the disengagement of pure reason from the will and rather sees both of them entangled in acts of error, sin, and rebellion.

position, is made possible. Hegel, the first philosopher in the essence of whose thought a historical consciousness is embodied, records sensitively the changes brought about by the Revolution. In the 1790s, illuminated by the fervor of youth and the fireworks of the French Revolution, Hegel indeed saw that the Revolution was not leading to liberty, but to a new despotism. Yet he explained this as a necessary evolution. The emancipation of the individual brings about the Terror and the destruction of liberty (a typical counter-revolutionary argument), but the real emancipation will ultimately be achieved by the development of the state. Hegel had to correct this early optimism. In the preface to the *Phenomenology of the Spirit* (1807), finished in Jena in 1806 as the guns of Napoleon were pounding nearby, he no longer sees the state as the instrument of emancipation. For the time being, liberty must retreat into the privacy of the mind without expecting that a political and social reality correspond to it. Hegel justifies this position by saying that the new is not the real, the revolutionary; it is as yet only the newborn, not a mature organism, just as the grown tree is not merely the roots nor the bud. History takes its time; it may not be accelerated mathematically by the absolute and immediate claims of reason.

The step backward represented by the Napoleonic dictatorship, following the initial step forward of the Revolution, implies not only the counterrevolution but also the necessity for reason to adapt itself to the two realities, the emerging one, which has not fully developed, and the old one, not completely dead but still possessing a vitality which in part is communicated to it by the very birth of the new world itself. Thus the possibility of doctrinaire liberalism as a conciliatory political philosophy arises. Such a liberalism came to flower in France during the Restoration (1815-30) and the July Monarchy (1830-48) and was elaborated into political theories, philosophies of history, charters, and constitutions. This synthesizing movement may already be seen in the compromise forced upon Napoleon during the Hundred Days. The least likely person to yield to constitutionalism and representative government, he nevertheless found the political climate alien to a dictatorship based on the myth of popular sovereignty.

Napoleon's giving in to constitutionalism already represents the second moment in the dialectics of revolution and counterrevolution. Donoso Cortés also experienced that second moment and championed liberalism until his conversion to a counterrevolutionary position after the 1848 Revolution. It was then that he came to see liberalism not as the synthesis, but as leading to a third movement, the emergence of socialism.

Returning to Donoso Cortés' text one reads "that truth carries within itself the titles of its own sovereignty and does not ask permission to impose its yoke, while man, since he revolted against his God, does not consent to any other sovereignty but his own, unless the others ask first of him his consent and his permission." Two concepts of history based on different interpretations of sovereignty are opposed to each other: that of God's sovereignty, through which divine providence is exercised, and that of man's claim to his own sovereignty, to the making of his own history. Donoso associates man's claim to sovereignty with the claims of reason to autonomy and the development of the secular idea of the state since the seventeenth century.[5]

Theological language such as that of Donoso is not the property of the counterrevolutionaries alone. Joseph Pierre Proudhon (1809-65), the libertarian socialist at whom Donoso's attack is chiefly aimed, used theological language himself in his attack on traditional society and counterrevolution. Proudhon saw that the beliefs of traditional society, although false from a revolutionary perspective, were pragmatically and therefore dialectically true, insofar as they motivated the behavior of traditional society and institutions. God does not exist, but the men who believe in Him and act accordingly do exist; therefore, God is a reality to be coped with. Proudhon, who was a biblical scholar of sorts and who sprinkled his works with biblical imagery, resolved to attack God as the great enemy of progress and liberty. Proudhon sees history moving toward the total

[5]Hobbes, for example, made the political sovereign the absolute source of the laws, and for him the divine and natural laws have legal significance only insofar as the sovereign interprets and accepts them. For Rousseau, authority is grounded rationally through the sovereignty of the "general will" which remains the sole arbiter of what benefits itself. The revolutionaries carried this claim to sovereignty even further by denying the "truth" which makes itself visible in history through "revelation, grace, and divine providence," and from which could be derived the only sovereignty Donoso could accept.

emancipation of man from God. This is achieved first by equality before God; a second stage brings equality before conscience or reason (as in seventeenth-century rationalism), and a third (the French Revolution), equality before the law. The future heralds the complete equality of man with man within a purely human order. To achieve this goal of liberty and progress man must fight God, whom Proudhon calls "anti-civilisateur, anti-libéral, antihumain." Thus the revolutionary is forced to use the language of his counterrevolutionary antagonist. Donoso turns this to his polemical advantage as he parodies Proudhon's style and thought.

Donoso finds a secret affinity between the absurd and human reason, which are linked by sin in an indissoluble marriage. By disengaging itself from truth, human reason achieves a false autonomy and falls into fundamental absurdity. This absurdity of reason was witnessed by Donoso not only on the existential plane but on the political one as well: the failure of abstract constitutions as applied to concrete historical situations. Reason runs inescapably into the absurd, for it cannot cope with contingency, evil, and suffering. Modern revolutionary man is thus an absurd creature, an imitator and displacer of God, who claims to supplant Him and calls himself by His name, "and who cares, says this man, if the other is the God of the truth, when he is the God of the absurd." Donoso sees man's claim for autonomy through reason as a sinful act of will. Thus an extreme subjectivism, projected over the canvas of rational planning, is the essential characteristic of revolution. Proudhon finds an appropriate image for revolutionary man when he calls him "the indefatigable Satan who reasons unceasingly." To this act of implacable will of the indefatigable Satan (the antagonist of counterrevolution) is related a factor of which Donoso was not consciously aware, but which conditioned his own thinking, and which he tried to understand as human reason, that is, the phenomenon of world-view, inseparable from extreme subjectivism and from the dialectic of revolution and counterrevolution.

To understand this key phenomenon one must glance back briefly at a world where revolution in the modern sense was impossible, that is, the medieval world, which the counterrevolutionaries attempted to resurrect as the antidote to revolution. In the medieval order there could be no world-view such as we, in our historical self-consciousness, can deduce. For medieval man (in the proper sense) the world is a static order with a hierarchy of existents, where God the creator is the absolute frame of reference, holding the world together through the analogy between Himself and man. A world-view in the modern sense implies an awareness of historical relativity, in whose light the perceived world order is seen as a contingent image manufactured by man through reason to change the world and sustained against the past and for the future. Grace, revelation, and divine providence dissolve before the channeling of man's will through reason and the forging of a world of man's own making. This revolutionary willing of the future implies a counter-willing against the past; that is, the future is willed insofar as the past is negated, willed to destruction. The counterrevolutionary participates in this drive of modern man, for he wills the past and counter-wills the future in a reversal of the dialectical movement. He must resurrect the traditional world order, but he can do this, although he does not fully realize it, only by making that absolute into its opposite, a world-view. The emergence of world-views and the disengagement of man from a created order posited as absolute release the utopian aspirations of human nature in a Faustian procreation of ever new futures.

The rise of the age of world-views constitutes a new reality which affects the very core of literature. Through it arises the possibility of becoming consciously committed, a revolutionary phenomenon unthinkable within the system of beliefs of medieval man. The latter is committed a priori and without question by the fall in corruption and sin, committed to the effort toward salvation through redemption and grace. In that system of belief, individual souls are indeed saved, yet the efforts are not merely individual, for man's freedom to will his salvation is futile without God's merciful cooperation. Commitment in the modern sense means commitment of the person, of the will, to an image of the world, posited as an aspiration to be achieved and consciously opposed to other antagonistic images of the world. This commitment, implying an ethical choice and a concept of the nature of man, is possible only when man has disengaged himself from God. Only when man is liberated from the concept of an absolute static order is he free to choose among alternative images of the world to be willed. This is Sartre's revolutionary idea of *engagement,* the atheist's ethical imperative of commitment to a cause. Here man is not committed a priori, but, burdened by absolute and total responsibility for his actions, he must himself choose absolutely to become committed.

These realities act as partly unconscious determinants behind Donoso's thinking. When he asserts that the absurd triumphs over man because man is bereft of all rights (*desnudo de todo derecho*) prior and superior to human reason, that man arrogates to himself through reason rights which are merely human creations in contradiction to truth, and that the contradicted truth has its own rights and does not ask permission to implement them, he is talking, from his counterrevolutionary perspective, about the problems of worldview, created order, and commitment. Commitment is only possible for man in his own creations: rights, constitutions, principles. These are the products of reason, for man is devoid of them prior to the use of reason. The revolutionary antagonist infiltrates to the very core the counterrevolutionary position. Hence the anguish of the counterrevolutionary, the splendid spectacle of Donoso's struggle against the inevitable, the passionate distortion, pride, and tragic heroism which fill his writings. By its very nature the counterrevolutionary spirit — as incarnated in a man like Donoso, whom his friend Veuillot called the "pilgrim of the absolute" — is opposed not only to socialism but to the liberal bourgeoisie, the greatest enemy of the heroic search for the absolute. This bourgeoisie sought to integrate the extremes of revolution and counterrevolution, an integration which Donoso himself attempted but discarded.

During the 1830s and 1840s Donoso formulated a political philosophy based on the thought of the French doctrinaire liberal school which, as we said before, he later came to see as the second moment in a revolutionary dialectic. Benjamin Constant, Royer-

Collard, and Guizot were his main sources. Guizot elaborated a philosophy of history for doctrinaire liberalism, seeing European history as the slow but sure rise of the middle class and the upsurge of representative government. The bourgeoisie is the axis of modern Europe, its unifying center, which according to Guizot does not exclude but rather assimilates other social classes. Although Guizot pays lip service to divine providence, a counterrevolutionary would see his philosophy of history as fundamentally atheistic. For the liberal Donoso, reason actualizes itself in the social world through the communion of intelligent beings. It transcends the individual; it is in man, but it is not man. The unique essence of man is his freedom, yet this freedom resists association or dependence. Reason is equal to reason, i.e. to itself: it attracts itself. One liberty, however, being purely individual, is not equal to another liberty: liberties repel each other. Politics is seen as the struggle to integrate reason and individual liberty. Thus government must fight against the invasions of extreme individualism upon the social order but only insofar as is necessary to maintain a balance. If government transgresses its limits, it becomes itself the invader of liberty. Social reason and individual freedom have to coexist, and human liberty must express only that amount of freedom which will preserve society and therefore itself. At this stage Donoso does not identify reason with an extreme individualism, but opposes reason to it. Years before 1848, however, his faith in liberalism began to cool. The continuous emancipation of human reason now appeared to him to lead to self-adoration. The French Revolution was a bloody commentary on the emancipation of reason and ought to have been its providential termination. While acknowledging his debt to liberalism, Donoso now criticizes it for being too conciliatory, fit only for an age of transition, not for the new age which is dawning and which demands a creative and dogmatic philosophy. This presumption corresponds both to his turn to a reactionary position and to the rise of socialism, specifically Marxism.

Donoso saw with great perspicacity that instability within liberalism which would lead to socialism. For him the philosophy of liberalism reverted fundamentally to the cry of the Abbé Sièyes on

Antonio Regalado

the eve of 1789: "Le Tiers embrasse tout ce qui appartient à la
Nation, et tout ce qui n'est pas le Tiers ne peut se regarder comme
étant de la Nation. Qu'est-ce que le Tiers? Le Tiers Etat c'est tout."
But the Third Estate was not everything for Donoso, who saw liberalism as indifferent to religious, economic, and social problems, indifferent to the masses, and impotent to cope with the new dogma of
socialism. Although liberalism reformed the feudal concept of property, making it accessible to individual initiative and enterprise, it also
created a class concept of property upon which its system of representative government was grounded. It was precisely from this angle
that Marx criticized the concept of the rights of man as envisioned
by the French Revolution. He did not see them as universally applicable but rather as privileges of the bourgeois class. The 1848
revolutions confirmed Donoso in the conviction that the revolutionary
drive was now in the hands of a socialism utterly hostile to the liberal
bourgeoisie's concepts of property and representative government,
and which attempted through a universal dogma to embrace all men.
Donoso calls this universal dogma of socialism, which throws open
the doors of the future to the proletariat, "a satanic theology," for
it sought to replace the universality of religion, the divine theology
of catholicism. He envisions the third moment of the dialectic as the
failure of the liberal synthesis, leading to a war to the death between
the dogmas of catholicism and socialism, between God and the proletariat. This dilemma was stated on the eve of the 1848 revolutions,
on the one hand, by Marx in the rallying cries of his *Communist
Manifesto* (1847) — "Workers of the world unite" — and, on the
other hand, by Kierkegaard in his *Literary Announcement* (1846),
where he asked whether it mattered if the generations of the future
were saved, if one lost one's own soul. This opposition echoes in the
thunderous prose of Donoso's *Essay*, in which is forecast the inevitable clash between the people, the socialist hordes, on one side of
the horizon and God on the other.

The last section of Donoso's text addresses itself to the revolutionaries and in particular to the Proudhonian socialists. Donoso
refers to them as those who seek to exercise empire over human rea-

son, warning them not to declare themselves possessors of "clear and evident truths," because the world will revolt against the "brutal yoke" of their "evidences." The Cartesian terminology used, "clear truths," "evidences," refers again to rationalism, but this counterrevolutionary "misology," this hate for reason, cannot cancel out the fact that Donoso himself is inescapably a child of the Revolution. Indeed he is Proudhon's "indefatigable Satan who reasons unceasingly" turned counterrevolutionary. Donoso suffers from what Bergson has called the *loi de double frénésie,* the contradictory tendencies which impel modern man into conflict and drama and which are externalized in conflicting possibilities of action. A century before Bergson, Hegel, observing the effects of the Revolution upon his contemporaries, had described this *loi de double frénésie* in the *Phenomenology of Mind* with his concept of the "unhappy consciousness," "the alienated soul, which is consciousness of self as a divided nature, a double and merely contradictory being." Donoso is involved in such a conflict, between the old world and the new, between tradition and progress, the regressive utopia of the past and the progressive utopia of the future, the kingdom of heaven and the classless society. Rejecting liberalism, the pragmatic conciliation of contradictions, he plunged anew into the *double frénésie,* out of which he wishes to escape into the catholic absolute, for him the only genuine conciliation of the extremes. From such a perspective he mocks the Proudhonian paradoxes, for they reveal too clearly to him his own contradictory nature and imperil his search for absolute certainty.

The paradox "God does not exist" predicates nonexistence of what is taken for granted to be the source of all being. It momentarily jolts the mind out of assuming that God equals plenitude of being. Donoso takes advantage of the psychological malaise evoked by the paradox to deny it on a merely logical basis as absurd, that is, as the equation of God (pure being) with nonbeing. However this device does not hide the fact that the paradox has an existential depth which is revealed in its very capacity to shock and which may not be erased by a facile appeal to the law of contradiction. Historically and psychologically the paradox is not absurd, for what the revolutionary is attempting to say through it is that God has been discovered by reason to be a fraud. This very fraud is passionately affirmed by the counterrevolutionary as a reality.

Revolution necessarily works in a negative relation to the material it wants to change; in Proudhonian terms it must fight it. The revolutionary paradox is thus a movement away from the past, from accepted opinion, by means of a destructive thrust at the past. The etymology of the word "paradox" is "doxa," common opinion, what is generally accepted, and "para," to set aside; thus a paradox is an opinion that contradicts or sets aside the commonly accepted one. The paradox "God does not exist" deviates from the common opinion which takes for granted God's existence. The "doxa" or common opinion is grafted in those traditional patterns of behavior which the revolutionary spirit wishes to destroy. Donoso's rhetoric appeals to that common opinion which everyone carries with him in order to discredit revolutionary reason as absurd, to make the reader see himself mirrored negatively in the paradox, menaced by it, to drive him to negate the paradox, and thus to escape from the shock which it induces into his prior state of acceptance. Kierkegaard, a great producer of counterrevolutionary paradoxes, was a master at turning around such assertions as "God does not exist" to prove that man chooses God by the very act of denying him and rebelling against him.

That "man is God" is an inversion of the Christian dogma that God became man in order to redeem man. To say that man is God, from the counterrevolutionary perspective, would mean the negation of God's divinity and the predication to God of man's corrupt nature. But for the revolutionary the opposite is true; the predicates of the divinity are truly man's property, for God is a mirage. Ludwig Feuerbach made this clear in his influential book *The Essence of Christianity* (1841), in which he said: "All metaphysical predicates of God are real predicates only when they are recognized as belonging to thought, to intelligence, to the understanding."[6] These paradoxes are inversions of values, not the creation of completely new values,

[6]Ludwig Feuerbach, *The Essence of Christianity* (New York, 1957), p. 37.

for the revolutionary affirmation that God does not exist or that man
is God simply demotes the predicates from a transcendental to an
immanent level. The revolutionary says that man is really God, for
the predicates he attributes to God are man's own creations. That is
why the affirmation of the paradox has to be a negation of the common opinion from which it deviates. The revolutionary paradox is a
parasite of counterrevolution, which it must forcibly negate in order
to affirm itself. The assertion that "the wisdom of the centuries is
nothing but pure ignorance" annihilates the very claim to validity of
the counterrevolutionary position, which implies that wisdom is the
accumulated process of historical experience. That "all government
is tyranny," from the revolutionary perspective, means that government as conceived by the ancien régime and by the liberalism that
tried by compromise to reconcile it with liberty is tyranny. This paradox is aimed at the doctrinaire liberal synthesis, according to which
only a properly devised government can protect liberty. "That all
obedience is servitude" is the logical consequence of the preceding
and enters an ethical as well as a political plane. The counterrevolutionary finds freedom only in dependence upon a transcendental
authority represented in the world by a catholic state, and the liberal
finds liberty in a kind of restraint of liberty itself for the sake of
social harmony and the protection of that very liberty. These paradoxes explode the common assumption that identifies order with
liberty, with government, and with obedience. Thus in the paradoxes
are contained the three moments of the dialectic: revolution, counterrevolution, and the attempt at synthesis.

"The ugly is beautiful" refers to the same inversion of values on
an aesthetic plane. One thinks of the conflict between romanticism
and classicism, and in particular that part of the romantic movement
associated with liberalism and the revaluation of such unclassical
models as Shakespeare and Calderón. Donoso had in all probability
authors like Victor Hugo in mind. "The devil is God and God is the
devil" refers to the inversion of values brought about by the angelic
rebellion and man's eventual political revolt. This inversion can be
seen in Byron's *Cain* (1821) and informs all of nineteenth-century

literature. It is best expressed poetically by Baudelaire (an admirer of Joseph De Maistre) in his "Litanies de Satan," where he associates Satan with fallen man, with progress and revolt, with Proudhon's "indefatigable Satan who reasons unceasingly":

Baton des exilés, lampe des inventeurs,
Confesseur des pendus et des conspirateurs

Père adoptif de ceux qu'en sa noire colère
Du paradis terrestre a chassés Dieu le Père.

"This world is a present hell and a future paradise" means the present state of society is to be changed by revolution into a future paradise. "Property is theft" refers specifically to the answer given by Proudhon to the question he asked himself in the book titled *Qu'est-ce que la propriété?* (1840), a slogan which, besides scandalizing the bourgeoisie, became the war cry for the entire socialist movement. This paradox inverts the value of property as the counterrevolutionaries saw it (for Burke in 1790 the Revolution would be acceptable if it maintained, among other things, "morality and religion," "the solidity of property," "peace and order") and as the doctrinaire liberals saw it as well. But it condemns property in terms of a moral judgment which common opinion associates with the radical opposite of property, with theft, from the point of view of the morality of property itself.

In the course of his attack upon Proudhon, Donoso calls him not a person but a personification, a consequence of all the "contradictory principles, of all the absurd premises, of three centuries of rationalism." Proudhon is condemned always to appear original without being so, for who can appear more original than he in whom is concentrated all the contradictions of three contradictory centuries? And who is in reality less original than he who is the consequence of three centuries of rationalism? Donoso mocks Proudhon's attempt to find an equation for all contradictions, a thesis for all the antinomies; Proudhon's synthesis is no more than the beginning of a whole series of contradictions. Caught between property (the thesis) and communism (the antithesis) he searches for synthesis in the concept of nonhereditary property, which is no property; consequently his synthesis does not resolve the contradiction but merely devises a new manner of negating the thesis and affirming the antithesis. When, continues Donoso, in order to formulate the synthesis which is to integrate authority (the thesis) and liberty (the antithesis) Proudhon denies government and proclaims "anarchy is order," this synthesis is nothing else (if he means by that no government at all) than the negation of authority and the affirmation of human liberty. If he means that the source of authority is not to be found in the state but in society, he denies the antithesis and affirms the thesis, denying liberty and affirming authority or "the omnipotence of communism." Where, asks Donoso, is the conciliation; where is the synthesis? Monsieur Proudhon shows strength only when he is content to remain the personification of modern rationalism, in nature absurd and contradictory, and he is weak whenever he shows himself and ceases to be a personification and becomes a mere person.[7]

Marx too was a severe critic of Proudhon, attacking in him a rationalism within which production, credit, money, and division of labor could be conceived of as "fixed inmutable categories." Thus, says Marx, "if we abstract from every subject all the alleged accidents, animate or inanimate, men or things, we are right in saying that the final abstraction, the only substance left is the logical categories." The real world "is drowned by rationalists." Such categories are not eternal; they are, like the relations they express, "historical and transitory products." For Proudhon, says Marx, dialectic is a dogmatic distinction between good and bad. Proudhon moves from thesis to antithesis to synthesis, and then to the realization that they all are "merely contradictory hypotheses." By taking the economic categories one by one and making one the antidote to the other, he manages to "make with this mixture of contradictions and antidotes to contradictions, two volumes of contradictions which he rightly entitles *The System of Economic Contradictions.*" "Proudhon," continues Marx, "wants to be the synthesis. He is a composite error,

---

[7]Donoso Cortés, *Ensayo,* pp. 324-26.

he is merely the petty bourgeois, continually tossed back and forth between capital and labor, political economy and communism."[8]

Despite the attacks of his opponents of the extreme right and extreme left, Proudhon appears in retrospect as a valid political thinker and social prophet. But what do these attacks have to tell about the impact of revolutionary and counterrevolutionary thought upon literature, world-view, and individualism? Both Donoso and Marx attempt an explanation of history which copes with its relativity, Donoso by producing from his bag of tricks a divine providence that explains all deviations, and Marx through the dialectic of historical materialism, which explains the contradictions as moments in the class struggle. Both attitudes are based on sharply accurate observation but carry within them the idea of utopia. The catholic and regressive utopia of Donoso involves the reinstatement of history into an absolute order, which cancels out the world-view represented by the Proudhonian paradoxes. Marx also sees history as a continuous transition from one stage to another, from one world-view to another, and as the conflict between the world-views and the social classes that uphold them. Conditioned by the evolving processes of material production, these world-views develop toward the synthesis, the communist utopia, in which the contradictions are resolved by the triumph of the proletariat. Thus the utopia of the classless society is reached, which ideally implies the end of world-views and the attainment of a "real world" of authentic human relations, psychologically analogous to the absolute of Donoso. Donoso's critique of socialism was aimed at Proudhon, for Marxism had barely begun to emerge, but this characterization of it as a "satanic theology" is an apt one. The Marxist utopia in its relentless optimism negates the possibility of tragedy, while the Donosian utopia is profoundly tragic, for it deals not with the hope of actualizing values in the future, but with the hopeless effort to maintain at all costs values which are absolute and irreplaceable, which it sees as being irremediably lost before the onslaught of socialism. For whatever reasons, very little great literature

[8]Karl Marx, *The Poverty of Philosophy. Answer to the "Philosophy of Poverty" by M. Proudhon* (1847) (Moscow, n.d.), pp. 99-168.

has been produced out of the Marxist position, while a great deal has arisen from positions analogous to those of Donoso or Proudhon.

The idea of world-view is intimately linked to an extreme subjectivism which both Donoso and Marx criticize and identify with bourgeois liberalism and rationalism and their offshoots in Proudhonian socialism. Donoso, however, foresaw very clearly the evolution of this extreme individualism into a rampant anarchism which would lead to communist statism. Such subjectivism is denied on the right because, as Donoso says, "man is only free when he is the slave of God," and on the left because the liberty of each is relative to the liberty of all and guaranteed only in the classless society. Max Stirner, execrated by Marx as the epitome of bourgeois egotism, shows this subjectivism carried to the extreme in his formulation:

My power is my property;

my power gives me property;

my power am I myself, and through it am I my property.[9]

Fichte, the romantic philosopher, incarnates in his thought the voluntarism so typical of the revolutionary epoch by saying that the I finds itself only insofar as it finds itself willing. Each I is the absolute point of departure for a philosophy and implies a faith and a liberty. The self arises out of a feeling of limitation, out of its opposition to the nonself. Fundamentally the I is pure activity, a subjective freedom that precedes any determination of the ego. Fichte gave his concept of will a transcendental dimension, channeling it in terms of moral action, while Max Stirner reduces will to a quality of pure egoism. This voluntarism, which attempts to equate thought with being, contemplation with action, animates all thought in the revolutionary epoch, and it is no coincidence that the most influential philosophical work of the century, published by Arthur Schopenhauer in 1818, carries the title *The World as Will and Representation*.

But the thinker who most profoundly reflected upon willing and freedom was Schelling in his *Philosophical Inquiries into the Nature of Human Freedom* (1809), where he said: "Will is primordial being,

---

[9]Max Stirner, *The Ego and His Own; The Case of the Individual Against Authority* (1844), trans. Steven T. Byington (New York, 1963). p. 185.

and all predicates apply to it alone — groundlessness, eternity, independence of time, self-affirmation. All philosophy strives only to find this highest expression." Schelling discusses will from a perspective that has many analogies with the counterrevolutionary position. He sees evil as the very exaltation of self-will, for will, when it deserts its supernatural status in order to make itself as general will and also particular and creature will, leads to disorganization within itself and outside itself. Man's will is a nexus of living forces; only insofar as it abides in its unity with the universal will the forces remain in the divine measure and balance.

But hardly does self-will move from the center which is its station, than the nexus of forces is also dissolved. In its place a mere particular will rules which can no longer unite the forces among themselves as before, but must therefore strive to form or compose a special and peculiar life out of the now separate forces, an insurgent host of desires and passions — since every individual force is also an obsession and a passion.[10]

Donoso Cortés stated clearly, but within a theological and counterrevolutionary framework, this dilemma of man's freedom to will in an age of ideology. The following passage from his *Essay,* which was so much liked by the aging Schelling, gives a lucid and terse picture of that *loi de double frénésie* which besieges the modern will in a continuous struggle between good and evil.

Free will of man is the masterpiece of creation and the most portentous, if it is permitted to speak thus, of all divine portents. All things are invariably ordered in relation to it in such a manner that creation would be inexplicable without man, and man would be inexplicable if he were not free. His liberty is at the same time his explanation and the explanation of all things. But who will explain that very high, inviolable, holy freedom, so holy, so high, so inviolable that the one who gave it to him cannot take it away from him, and with which freedom he can resist and conquer the one who gave it to him, with an invincible resistance and a tremendous victory. Who will explain in what way, with that victory of man over God, God is finally the victor, and man is finally conquered, man's victory being a real victory, and the conquering of God a real conquering. What kind of victory is that, which is followed necessarily by the death of the victor? And what conquest is that which ends in the glorification of the conquered one? What does paradise mean, the reward for my defeat and hell the punishment for my victory? If my reward is

[10]Friedrich Wilhelm Joseph Schelling, *Of Human Freedom,* trans. James Gutmann (Chicago, 1936), pp. 24, 41.

in my defeat, why do I naturally reject what saves me? If my condemnation is in my victory, why do I crave naturally the very thing that condemns me?[11]

The attempt to rechannel that will either through the ideology of socialism, liberalism, or the catholic state is the attempt to relate again those forces to a central nexus. The man of letters is caught in this dialectic, which he attempts to transcend through an even more reckless and individual exercise of the will. With romanticism the man of letters adopted the role of the priest, the prophet, the creator, God (Fichte and Carlyle in particular theorize regarding this), yet the need for certainty was not satisfied by such an autonomy. The past, memory, became the raw material of willing and representation, the road to freedom. The moment that man wills to remember more than can be contained in any given world-view he will automatically reshape that world-view; if he remembers too much his reshaping of the status quo will be radical, making him either a revolutionary or a counterrevolutionary. Willing the future and counter-willing it are the essential mechanisms of revolution and counterrevolution. This willing creates a struggle between world-views, producing on the secular plane the typical modern forms of relativism, pragmatism, and skepticism, which secretly search for absolute certitude. for a rest from the dynamism of willing and representation.

[11]Donoso Cortés, *Ensayo,* pp. 103-04.

Roman Jakobson

The generation that squandered its poets (excerpts)

Lost. Ours is a lost generation. Roughly, those of us who are now between 30 and 45 years old. Those who, already fully formed, entered into the years of the Revolution not as unmolded clay, yet still not rigidified, still capable of adapting to experience and change, still capable of a dynamic rather than static understanding of our situation . . . .

[Then came] the execution of Gumilyov (1886-1921), prolonged spiritual agony, unbearable physical torment, the demise of Blok (1880-1921), cruel privations, and the death of Khlebnikov (1885-1922) under circumstances of inhuman suffering, the premeditated suicides of Esenin (1895-1925) and Mayakovsky (1894-1930). Thus, during the third decade of this century those who inspired a generation perished between the ages of 30 and 40; and each one of them shared a sense of doom, so sustained and vivid, that it became insupportable . . . .

The poetry of Mayakovsky, from the first verses . . . to his last lines, is one and indivisible. The dialectical development of a single theme. An extraordinarily coherent symbolic system . . . .

A Mayakovskian mythology?

His first collection of poems is called *I*. Vladimir Mayakovsky is not only the hero of his first play, but the very title of this "tragedy" . . . .

The "I" of the poet is a battering ram, thudding into an impregnable future; it is a will "hurled over the last perimeter" toward a future personified, toward an absolute fullness of being: "one must rip joy from the days yet to come" . . . .

Opposed to this creative urge toward transforming the future is the stabilizing force of an immutable present, covered over, as this present is, by a stagnating slime, which stifles life in its dense, hardened mold. The Russian name for this element is *byt*[1] . . . .

Stasis still reigns. It is the primordial enemy of the poet, and to this problem Mayakovsky never ceases to address himself . . . . If we thought to translate the Mayakovskian mythology into the language of speculative philosophy, the exact equivalent for this enmity would be the antinomy between the "I" and the "not-I." A more adequate term for this enemy is not to be found . . . .

The basic fusion of Mayakovsky's poetry with the theme of revolution has been remarked on numerous occasions. But another indissoluble combination of motifs in Mayakovsky's work has gone unnoticed: revolution and the death of the poet . . . .

The poet catches the music of the future in an insatiable ear, but he is not fated to enter into the Promised Land. A vision of the future is inseparable from the most essential pages in Mayakovsky . . . . For Mayakovsky, the future is a dialectical synthesis. This removal of all contradictions finds its expression in the playful image of Christ at checkers with Cain, in the myth of a universe permeated by love, and in the proposition: "The commune is a place where bureaucrats will vanish and there will be poetry and song." The present disjunction, the contraries of workaday life and poetry, "the delicate business of the poet's place in the working class" is one of Mayakovsky's most acute problems. "Who needs it," he said, "that literature should occupy its own special preserve? Either it should appear in every newspaper, every day, on every page, or it's totally useless. The sort of literature that is dished out as dessert can go to hell."

Mayakovsky has an unshakable faith that there are heights yet to be scaled, that beyond each rising plateau of revolution is "the

[1] A virtually untranslatable Russian word whose wide semantic umbrella covers such concepts as Philistinism, vulgarity, the commonplace, the daily grind, and so on. (translator's note).

real heaven on earth," the only possible resolution of all contradictions. *Byt* is only a surrogate for the coming synthesis; it does not remove contradictions, but only conceals them . . . The "hero" of Mayakovsky's unsparing sarcasm is the *yes-man. (Mystery Buffe)* . . . Obstacles in the road to the future — this is the real significance of the actions of these "phonies." The engine of time will surely spit them out . . . .

Khlebnikov and Mayakovsky accurately forecast the Revolution (including even its dating) — a detail — but not an insignificant one. It would seem that never has the fate of the author been laid bare with such pitiless candor in his own words as it has in our own day. Impatient to know life, he came to recognize it in his own creations . . . .

The motif of suicide, so alien to the thematics of the Futurist and "Left Front" groups, continually recurs in the work of Mayakovsky, from his earliest things in which madmen hang themselves in an uneven struggle with *byt* (the Director, the Man with the Two Kisses), to the scenario, "How Are You?" in which a newspaper article about a girl's suicide reduces the poet to terror . . . .

To give a résumé of Mayakovsky's poetic autobiography (if you wish, his litho-montage): the unprecedented anguish of the present generation was nurtured in the poet's heart . . . .

The theme of suicide, as it further developed, became more and more pressing. Mayakovsky's most intense poems, *Man* (1916) and *About This* (1923), are devoted to it. Each of these works is an ominous song of the victory of *byt* over the poet; their leitmotif is "Love's boat has capsized against the daily grind" (a line from Mayakovsky's valedictory letter). The first is a detailed depiction of Mayakovsky's suicide. In the second, there is already a clear extra-literary sense of this theme. It is already the literature of fact. Once again — but even more disturbingly — the images of the first poem file past, the keenly observed stages of existence: the "half-death" in the vortex of the terrifying trivial, then, the "ultimate death" — "The lead's in my heart! I can't even shudder!" This theme of suicide had hit so close, it became impossible to depict it further ("it's no use enumerating our mutual pains, woes, and wrongs"). Exorcism was needed; propaganda indictments were necessary to slow down the impetus of the theme. *About This* already initiates this long cycle of exorcism . . . . The lines to Sergei Esenin are the apex of this cycle. Devised to neutralize the impact of Esenin's death poem — such, in the words of Mayakovsky, was the special aim of this verse. But when you read it now, it sounds even more sepulchral than Esenin's last lines. These lines place an equal sign between life and death, while Mayakovsky, speaking on the same day, adduces an argument for life — it's harder than death. This is the same sort of enigmatic propaganda for life as occurs in Mayakovsky's earlier lines to the effect that disbelief in the afterlife only ceases before the bullet strikes. Such, too, are his farewell words: "stay happy."[2]

After Esenin's death poem, Mayakovsky says, his death became a literary fact . . . . Approaching autobiography, Mayakovsky remarks that the facts of a poet's life are interesting "only if they are upheld by the word." But who would dare assert that Mayakovsky's suicide is not upheld by the word? "Don't gossip," adjured Mayakovsky before his death. Yet those who stubbornly draw boundaries between the "purely private" fate of the poet and his literary biography create an atmosphere of private and malicious gossip . . . .

Toward the end of Mayakovsky's life, his odes and satires totally overshadowed the renown of his elegies, which, parenthetically, he identified with the lyric in general. In the West, the existence of a basic core in Mayakovsky's poetry was not even suspected. The West only knew the "drummer of the October Revolution." Explanations for this success of his propaganda pieces could be given in various ways . . . . In 1923, Mayakovsky had come to the end of the road as far as the

[2]The last message in Mayakovsky's suicide note of 12 April 1930 (translator's note).

Roman Jakobson

elegaic mode was concerned. His journalistic verse served as poetic storage bins; they were experiments in manufacturing new materials and in working over untested genres. To my skeptical comments about these poems, Mayakovsky replied: later you'll understand even them. And when the plays, *The Bedbug* and *The Bathhouse,* followed, it really did become clear what a huge laboratory experiment in language and theme Mayakovsky's latter-day poems were, how this labor was masterfully exploited in his first efforts in the area of prose drama, and what inexhaustible potential for growth was secreted in them.

Finally, in connection with its social setting, the journalistic verse of Mayakovsky represented a shift from an unrestrained frontal attack toward an enervating trench warfare. As always, *byt* pounces back with a swarm of heartbreaking trivia . . . . Its onslaught cannot be held in check by grandiloquent pronouncements "in general and in toto," or by theses on Communism refracted through poetic devices . . . . The invention of strategies for describing "trifles, empowered to further the true step into the future" − this Mayakovsky deemed the proper civic duty of the poet.

Just as one mustn't reduce Mayakovsky the propagandist to a single dimension, so, too, one-sided interpretations of the death of the poet are shallow and opaque . . . .

How can one speak of a private episode, when, in the course of a few years, the whole bloom of Russian poetry was brushed aside?

At age 31, Ryleev was executed. At 36, Batiushkov went mad. At 22, Venevitinov died; at 32, Del'vig. At 34, Griboedov was killed; at 37, Pushkin, and at 26, Lermontov.[3] Their fate has more than once been characterized as a form of suicide. Mayakovsky himself compared his duel with vulgarity with the duels of Pushkin and Lermontov. There is much in common in the reactions of society in both

[3]The above were all prominent figures, unequally gifted, in nineteenth-century Russia's Golden Age of poetry (translator's note).

periods to these premature losses. Once again, a feeling of sudden and profound emptiness burst forth, an oppressive sense of an evil destiny lying heavily on the spiritual life of Russia . . . .

There are some countries where ladies' hands are kissed, and others where one merely says, "I kiss your hand." There are countries where Marxist theory is answered by Leninist practice, and countries where the madness of the bold, the bonfire of faith, and the Golgotha of the poet are not merely figurative expressions . . . .

The correspondences between the biographies of a generation and the march of history are intricate. Each age accumulates its own inventory of requisitions taken from the private sector. History takes and makes use of Beethoven's deafness, Cézanne's astigmatism. The life span of a generation and its term of service in history's conscription is both varied and symptomatic. History mobilizes the youthful ardor of one generation and the tempered maturity or aged wisdom of others. Their role is performed, and yesterday's rulers of men's minds and hearts depart from the proscenium to the backstage of history to live out their years in private as spiritual profiteers or paupers. But sometimes it happens otherwise. Our generation emerged at an extraordinarily young age: "We alone are the countenance of our time. The trumpet of time blows for us." . . . Meanwhile, its voice and enthusiasm were cut short, and its allotted quota of emotions — of joy and sadness, of sarcasm and rapture — was expended; and yet, the constant paroxysm of a generation turned out, after all, to be not a private fate, but, in fact, the countenance of our time, smothered by history.

We strained toward the future too impetuously and avidly to leave any past behind us. The links in the chain of time were broken. We lived too much in the future, thought about it, believed in it; the self-generating evils of the day did not exist for us. We lost a sense of the present. We were the witnesses and participants in the great socialist, scientific, and other such cataclysms. *Byt* remained. Like that splendid hyperbole of the young Mayakovsky, "the other foot was still running along a side street." We knew that the thoughts of our fathers were already in discord with their surroundings. We read harsh lines alleging that our fathers fought in the hire of the old, unventilated commonplaces. But our fathers still had remnants of faith in their convenience and social utility. To their children was left a single, naked hatred for the ever more threadbare, ever more alien cast-offs of the vulgar reality . . . .

Nor is the future ours. In several decades, we shall be cruelly invoked as the children of the last century. All we had were compelling songs of the future; and suddenly these songs were transformed by the dynamics of the day into a historico-literary fact. When singers are killed and their song is dragged into museums and pinned to the wall of the past, the generation they represent becomes even more bankrupt, orphaned, and displaced — disinherited in the most authentic sense of that term.

(1930)

Translated by Dale E. Peterson

Michael Holquist

The Mayakovsky problem

The Russian experience of 1917 is of unique importance in the study
of literature and revolution for a number of reasons: our closeness
(not only in time) to the events; the fact that the C.P.S.U. concerned
itself so insistently with literary problems; the complex responses of
the artists involved; and the thoroughness with which they documented those responses. But what is perhaps the most compelling
reason for the importance of the Russian upheaval in such a study
has emerged only in the last few years. It was immediately clear that
the first decades of this century had given birth to a great Russian revolution, but it is now becoming increasingly apparent that the same
years witnessed the rise of a great new Russian literature. The age
of Pushkin has traditionally been known as the Golden Age of Russian
poetry, but the conviction is rapidly growing that the years from
(roughly) 1890 to 1920 constitute at least a second Golden Age and,
possibly, a period of even richer significance than the twenties and
thirties of the nineteenth century. Taxonomy is to literary history
what alchemy is to physics, so the point will not be labored here.
Suffice it to say that among the poets caught up in the events of 1917
and their aftermath were Ivanov, Blok, Pasternak, Esenin, Akhmatova, and Mandelshtam (to name only the more prominent).

To make meaningful the interaction of political events and any
one of these figures would require at least a book. In some cases such
books have been written by Soviet scholars, but their zeal has all too
often not been sufficient preparation for the complexities involved.
The one poet of the period who more than any other has been the
subject of such studies is Vladimir Mayakovsky — and his case, paradoxically, remains the most confusing of all. It may well be that a
definitive statement of Mayakovsky's relationship to the Revolution is

Michael Holquist

not possible. Certainly the present article will not attempt anything so grand. Rather, the intention here is to present only a *Problemstellung*, a series of quotations from widely varying sources which will, hopefully, provide some minimal data for coming to grips with the problem of a great poet in time of revolution.

There have been those who maintained that Mayakovsky was merely a talented adventurer, that he had nothing to do with the real Revolution, despite all his attempts at involvement. On the other hand there are those who hold that Mayakovsky's life and work are at the core of the Revolution's meaning. In the material which follows, an attempt has been made to present a spectrum of views, circumscribed by these poles of opinion. Thus the arrangement is more polemical than chronological.[1]

Lenin[2]

Lenin's politics were revolutionary, but his literary taste was distinctly retrograde. Pushkin and Turgenev were favorites. As he once admitted, for one raised on Nekrasov[3] contemporary literature was difficult to understand, much less appreciate. He particularly objected to Russian Futurism.[4] In 1921, in a letter to M. N. Pokrovsky (leader of the State Publishing House) he appeals for Pokrovsky's aid in combating the influence of the Futurists. There is something almost pathetic in the note's final words: "Can't we find some reliable *anti*-Futurists?" In the same year Lenin was highly incensed that Mayakovsky's poem *150,000,000*[5] was printed in an edition of 5,000 copies: "Rubbish! Stupid, double-dyed stupidity and pretentiousness! In my opinion only one out of ten such things should be published, and then in *no more* than 1500 copies for libraries and eccentrics."

[1]Although it will be obvious that, for the Soviets at least, a progression from doubt about Mayakovsky's role in the Revolution to the conviction that he is *the* poet of the Revolution is a function of chronology.
[2]Citations from *Novoe o Mayakovskom* (*Literaturnoe Nasledstov 65*) (Moscow, 1958). Hereafter referred to *Lit. Nas.*
[3]A nineteenth-century poet famous for his civic verse, which at its weakest is extremely sentimental.
[4]In which Mayakovsky was the most prominent, or notorious, figure. This group should not be confused with the posturings of Marinetti and his followers, who have only the name Futurism in common with the Russians.
[5]A jingoistic comic epic in which Ivan defeats a giant Woodrow Wilson in hand-to-hand combat.

When he had read the copy of *150,000,000* which Mayakovsky personally sent to him, Lenin's comment was, "You know, this is very interesting literature. It is a special type of communism. It's hooligan-communism!"[6]

Bunin[7]

Lenin was not alone in objecting to Mayakovsky as a hooligan. An index to the complexity of Mayakovsky's position is provided by

[6]Lenin was not above using Mayakovsky's poetry when it suited his purpose of the moment, however. In the following year, 1922, Mayakovsky wrote a poem ridiculing Soviet bureaucrats. Lenin, while reserving judgment on the work as poetry, thought its "political" content sound enough to use in his campaign against governmental red tape.
[7]Citations from Ivan Bunin, *Vospominanija* (Paris, 1950).

the fact that one of the most violent anti-Bolsheviks among émigré authors, Ivan Bunin (who called Lenin a syphilitic), objected to Mayakovsky on much the same grounds:

> Having seemingly become a flaming Communist, [Mayakovsky] only strengthened and developed to the most extreme degree everything which added to his own glory — being a Futurist, stunning the public with his coarseness and his predilection for everything vile . . . he wrote about America [for instance]:
>
> Mama
> Gave the Child
> Her breast.
> The child
> *With drops on his nose*
> Sucks
> As if
> It were not a breast, but a dollar —
> Occupied with serious business.

Lenin preferred Pushkin and so, of course, did Bunin, who was particularly upset by Mayakovsky's demand that all past literature should be thrown out:

> And thus Mayakovsky becomes the unfailing servant of the party, begins to raise an uproar, the same sort he had made while still a Futurist: to yell "enough of living according to the laws of Adam and Eve," that it is time, "to jettison Pushkin from the ship of today . . ." and then me . . . "art is not a toy for the proletariat, but a weapon. Down with Buninism, all hail to the advanced circles of laborers!"

But Bunin's reaction to Mayakovsky was occasioned by more than personal pique. As an émigré,[8] a victim of the Revolution, he was particularly sensitive to its excesses, its cost in blood and tears. He despised Mayakovsky most of all for having been the rhapsodist of Bolshevik cruelties: "I think that Mayakovsky will remain in the literary history of the Bolshevik years as the lowest, most cynical, and

---

[8]Khodasevich (another émigré), whom Nabokov has called the greatest Russian poet of the twentieth century, also attacked Mayakovsky.

harmful servant of Soviet cannibalism in the area of literary en-
comiums and their resultant influence on the Soviet rabble."

What Lenin and Bunin (and many other smaller men, such as
the notorious party hack, V. V. Ermilov) objected to in Mayakovsky
was his Futurism or "hooliganism." By this they meant Mayakovsky's
penchant for poetic and lived hyperbole. To Lenin, Mayakovsky's
bohemian life and experimental poetry were not consonant with the
high ideals and noble sacrifices of the Revolution. To Bunin, the same
qualities in Mayakovsky were seen as harmful not to the Revolution,
but to its victims, in that Mayakovsky's extremism had its sinister
impact on future cadres of Dzerzhinsky's.[9]

Andrey Sinyavsky[10]
Soon to become a victim of the system he so brilliantly dissected
(as Abram Tertz) in his essay "On Socialist Realism," Sinyavsky
wrote: "Mayakovsky soon found out what he could and what he
could not laugh about. He could not permit himself to laugh at Lenin,

[9]F. E. Dzerzhinsky, chief of the secret police, whose words were held up as ideal for Soviet
youth in a Mayakovsky poem.
[10]*The Trial Begins* and *On Socialist Realism* (New York, 1958).

Michael Holquist

whom he praised to the skies, any more than Derzhavin[11] would laugh at his empress."

Pasternak[12]

While Sinyavsky is concerned with large-scale comparisons between Soviet and Czarist imperialism, a system in which Mayakovsky is reduced to the role of courtier, Pasternak sees Mayakovsky's involvement with the Revolution as a personal tragedy. *150,000,000*, the poem which Lenin attacked as evidence of Mayakovsky's unreconstructed Futurism, is for Pasternak a symbol of Mayakovsky's abandonment of Futurist principles.

> [Mayakovsky] read *150,000,000* to his own intimate circle. And for the first time I had nothing to say to him. We met in Russia and abroad, we tried to continue our intimacy, we tried to work together and I found myself understanding him less and less . . . . While he existed creatively, I spent four years getting used to him and did not succeed. Then I got used to him in 2 hours and a quarter, which was the time it took to read and examine the uncreative *150,000,000*. Then I languished for more than ten years with the acclimatization. Then lost it in tears all at once when *At the top of his voice*[13] he reminded one of himself, as he used to do, but now already from the grave.
>
> It was not impossible to get used to him but to the world he controlled and either set in motion or stopped at his caprice. I shall never understand what benefit he derived from the demagnetizing of the magnet, when, retaining its whole appearance, the horseshoe which before had reared up every idea and attracted every weight with its twin poles, could no longer move a single grain. There will hardly be found another example in history when a man who was so far advanced in a new proficiency should renounce it so fully, in the hour foretold by himself when that proficiency even at the price of inconveniences would have fulfilled such a vital need.

[11]Greatest Russian poet of the eighteenth century and court functionary under Catherine II.
[12]*Safe Conduct, an Autobiography, and Other Writings* (New York, 1958).
[13]Refers to Mayakovsky's last poem, associated with his suicide.

Max Eastman[14]

Eastman, who was in the Soviet Union just after Mayakovsky's suicide, makes a different point. For Lenin Mayakovsky *may* have been a great poet, but he was politically suspect. Pasternak feels politics destroyed the poet. Eastman's idea is that Mayakovsky failed politically — *precisely because he remained a great poet.*

> [Mayakovsky] came straight over to the Bolshevik revolution, bringing all his futuristic apparatus with him — the verbal circus work, the rhythmic and grammatic flying bars and colored paper hoops, and his intemperate imagination somersaulting through them — sometimes very flimsy, sometimes hardy and sublime . . . . The obvious fact that Mayakovsky failed as a leader of the proletarian culture because he was a momentous poet, and momentous poets are not institutions for cherishing other people's poetry, is another simple element of reality that can hardly sift through the conception of it which occupies the points of ingress to the brain of the dialectical materialist.

The party was aware of the apparent contradiction between Mayakovsky's strident, lyric self-dramatization and the role he was playing in the mass movement of the Revolution. After his death, *Literary Gazette,* often the party's voice on literary matters, said this of him: "The death of Mayakovsky showed how great was still his inner contradiction, how strong in him were still the petty bourgeois individualistic forces which he had wished to strangle by attacking the throat of his own song."

Trotsky[15]

In the case of Mayakovsky, as in so many other cases, Trotsky proved indeed to be a prophet. As early as 1923 he recognized that Futurism stood apart from the Revolution, but that it could be integrated.

> Mayakovsky's acceptance of the Revolution was more natural than any other Russian poet's, because it grew out of his

[14]*Literatura i Revoljucija* (Moscow, 1923).
[15]*Artists in Uniform* (New York, 1934).

Michael Holquist

whole development . . . . Mayakovsky came [to the Revolution] by the shortest route, that of rebellious, persecuted Bohemia. For Mayakovsky the Revolution was a deep, a true experience, because it fell with thunder and lightning on the very things Mayakovsky in his own way despised . . . [his] revolutionary individualism triumphantly poured itself into the proletarian Revolution, but it did not blend with it. . . . The dynamism of the Revolution and its stern courage were closer to Mayakovsky than the mass character of its heroism, deeds, and experiences. Just as the ancient Greek was an anthropomorphist and naïvely thought of nature's forces as resembling himself, so our poet is a Mayakomorphist and fills the squares, streets and fields of the Revolution with his own personality . . . the poet is too much in evidence . . . . When he wants to elevate man, he makes him into a Mayakovsky . . . . When the time . . . comes, when the cultural and aesthetic education of the toiling masses will destroy the wide gap between the creative intelligentsia and the people, art will look quite different from the art of today. In the development of that art, Futurism will show itself to have been one of the necessary links. And is this so very little?

Trotsky represents a median point between early uncertainty about Mayakovsky's role in the Revolution and the position Mayakovsky now holds in the Soviet Union as the voice and embodiment of the Revolution. Some evidences of this later development follow.

Stalin

"Mayakovsky is the best and most talented poet of our soviet epoch!"[16]

In 1930 Mayakovsky's books were removed from certain libraries for children because they were "not suitable," but in 1960[17] there appeared a book about Mayakovsky aimed specifically at children and called *Our Mayakovsky*. The cover speaks for itself. The

[16]Headline in *Literaturnaja gazeta* (December 1935).
[17]B. A. Leonidovna, ed., *Nas Majakovsky* (Moscow, 1960).

book contains articles on "Uncle Volodya," and its statement that "there isn't an educated person in the world who has not read or heard at least one work of the great poet of our Soviet nation" shows the degree to which Mayakovsky has been transformed into a national poet. The book appeared in an edition of 50,000 copies.

In the Soviet Union ten steamboats, three tanks, a bomber, a submarine, a subway station, a museum, a region in Georgia, a village in Armenia, a mountain in the Pamirs, various parks, theaters, and streets, as well as a major square in Moscow, are named after Mayakovsky.[18]

[18]Cited by Bunin, op. cit.

Michael Holquist

Mayakovsky has become an institutionalized subject of study. The Soviet Ministry of Education has published a volume of materials on him (2 editions: 1955, 25,000 copies; 1963, 14,000 copies) which includes the following suggested topics for research:

Mayakovsky in the struggle with bourgeois-decadent poetry.
The theme of building socialism in Mayakovsky's work.
The idea of Soviet patriotism in Mayakovsky's work.
The unmasking of bourgeois Europe and America in Mayakovsky's work.
Mayakovsky in the struggle against religion.
Principles of socialist realism in Mayakovsky.
Mayakovsky in the struggle for purity and richness in language of Soviet poetry.
The meaning of Mayakovsky's poetry during World War II.
Mayakovsky — great national poet.[19]

A popular biography of Mayakovsky (edition of 120,000 copies) appeared in 1965.[20] In this book Mayakovsky's association with Futurism, which so troubled earlier critics, is no longer a problem: "It is no accident that the start of Mayakovsky's poetic work belongs not to 1912 — the period when his poems appeared in Futurist anthologies — but to 1909, when, while in solitary confinement he created lines charged with revolutionary enthusiasm."

For better or worse, then, Mayakovsky has become the Soviet national poet. If the nuances in his work have frequently been lost under waves of party rhetoric, if his nose has been straightened for posterity on innumerable marble busts, such has been the fate of national poets at all times and in all places. The Soviets find in Mayakovsky the best of their Revolution — its sense of wonder, of power, its fun and its hurt. And his value as a symbol is not limited to heroic statuary, as can be seen in these lines from Evtushenko's long poem on the Bratsk hydroelectric station:[21]

[19]E. I. Naumov, *Seminarii po Majakovskomu* (Moscow, 1955, 1963).
[20]S. V. Vladimirov and D. M. Moldavskij, *Vladimir Vladimirovic Majakovskij* (Moscow, Leningrad, 1965).
[21]*Bratskij GES* (1965).

> . . . experiencing pain and grief,
> I can imagine everything —
>   but Mayakovsky
> In 1937[22] I cannot imagine.
> What would have happened to him
>   if that revolver
>   had missed?

Following are various images of Mayakovsky which dramatize in their own way the problem of his relation to the Revolution.

Mayakovsky, who had once been an art student, was in the habit of signing his letters to Lily Brik with little sketches of dogs and bears representing himself: I, *Lit. Nas.,* p. 131 (1923); II, *Lit. Nas.,* p. 135 (1924); III, *Lit. Nas.,* p. 141 (1924); IV, *Lit. Nas.,* p. 157 (1926); V, *Lit. Nas.,* p. 160 (1926).

A self-caricature from 1915: VI, *Lit. Nas.,* p. 110.

Photos of Mayakovsky: VII, *Lit. Nas.,* p. 51 (reading his poetry, 1929); VIII, *Lit Nas.,* p. 311 (reading for radio, 1927); IX (1930) from V. Katanjan, *Majakovsky* (Moscow,1956), p. 401.

Mayakovsky in official Soviet art: X, *Lit. Nas.,* p. 435 (statue by G. A. Kolpakova, 1954); XI, *Lit. Nas.,* p. 177 (statue by St. Konenkov, 1947); XII, *Lit. Nas.,* p. 340 (drawing by N. M. Avvakumov, 1938).

[22]Period of Stalinist repressions.

лотоооица, с плечом работающего в любом заводе, в любо[...]
(стр. 28). А в другом [...] [...] [...]ждает, что сама
разыгранная пролетку [...] а заводе, вы[...]
поставленная в професс[...]

Блестящую критику [...] [...]сства» дал Луна[...]
ном слове на этом же [...] [...]и Маяковского
Луначарский определяе[...] [...] [...]оветской литер[...]
реализм», как «широкую [...] [...]ескую литер[...]
этом на творческий [...] [...]исателей (в ча[...]
нова, Сейфуллиной [...] [...]же, что лучши[...]
ского, Асеева ника[...] [...]устово ложе ле[...]
о поэзии. Анализи[...] [...]ибок, он хара[...]
мальное понимание [...] говорит, что и[...]
жи[...] [...]и пропаганды
ле[...] [...]ности примити[...]
фо[...] [...] — Мы с тобою
ид[...] [...]ци. Заказывай [...]
пл[...] [...]естно будем делать.— В этом-то [...]
кл[...] [...]авление о художника[...] говорил Л[...]
ча[...] [...]уржуазно-декадентских течений в
кусстве: [...]ень мно[...] [...] так и остались [...] бурж[...]
ном лагере, а он са[...] [...]ривычку к та[...] [...]й по[...]
новке вопроса он п[...] [...]е: «Маяковский [...]ье на[...]
во время буржуазно[...] [...]ье выйти из [...] [...]ат[...]
выручил. Он станов[...] [...]а твердую поч[...] [...]но
всем забросить то, [...] [...]й декаданс» ([...]

ле[...] [...] [...]адачах неразр[...] много[...]
де[...] [...] [...]и содержании [...] про[...]
св[...] [...]орме произведения, маяковский вс[...]
ле[...] [...]ия. Содержание [...]ебует своей оп[...]
це[...] [...]кажают содержание. О сложном [...]

в своей [...] ссическе[...]
блеф?» на примере стихов В. Наседкина Маяков[...]
дойти поэт, воспевая Париж[...]ю Коммуну в ст[...]
тический принцип появился и в опенке Маяко[...]
войны в выступлени[...] РОСТА.
лефовцев утвержда[...] [...] содерж[...]
для нас является в[...] [...]литерату[...]
19[...] и[...] [...]ну этого
фо[...] ут[...] [...]ржание [...]
ни[...] по[...] [...]х роман[...]
ци[...] ж[...] [...]лее в го[...]
ше[...] то[...] [...]и попере[...]
и [...] л[...] [...]ы развяз[...]

самый ин[...]ресный [...] [...] вот в че[...]
Вот в чем наша пом[...] [...]тр. 34—
ского сказалось и влияние ошиоочных лефовск[...]
дожником непосредственно [...]жизни, представл[...]
содержание искусства. Задача художника — обл[...]

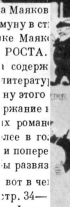

Victor Serge

Is a proletarian literature possible?*

In 1921, with the introduction of *Nep,* the Russian civil war ended. A move by Lenin scuttled the chaotic peasant revolt which followed the Kronstadt, Tambov, and Volga uprisings. That same year was the year of the great famine. Wrangel was still holding out in the Crimea but, by the end of the year, peace was in the air and the beginnings of a literary renaissance as well.

"Never have we had so many and such promising young writers," Maxim Gorky said later. I have already described this new generation of Russian writers in various articles for *Clarté. The Serapion Brothers,* a literary group speaking for peasant Russia (Boris Pilniak, Vsevolod Ivanov, A. Yakovlev, N. Nikitin, N. Tikhonov), was beginning to make itself heard at the same time as the young proletarian writers. In June 1923, the appearance of the review *On Guard (Na Postu)* in Moscow initiated a surprisingly vigorous struggle for a proletarian literature.

This was only a renewal of the attack however. During the heroic years 1918-21, at the height of the civil war and intervention, the *proletcults* had battled for a proletarian culture, founding circles in the smallest towns, covering city walls with posters, producing poets, putting on plays, elaborating theories, setting up courses, and even founding an international committee which lived out its allotted day.

This grandiose program was premature, and it was recognized as a failure. After all, what cultural work could be expected when every committed party member lived on 200 grams of black bread a day, plus three dried herring a week? Nevertheless the *proletcults* had formed the young poets Alexandrovsky, Kirilov, Vassily Kazin, and

*Translated from *Clarté, 12* (March 1, 1925).

Obradovitch, and their efforts were highly useful. It is a great thing when social war activists can give some thought to culture.

Such is the creative capacity of the Russian people that, after one year of peace, an entirely new literature emerged. It was a revolutionary literature, of course, but full of ambiguities and quick to change direction. Oriented sometimes toward mysticism, toward a kind of neo-nationalism, or even more often toward bourgeois thought, it was neither proletarian nor Communist. This was a surprise. Communist writers, still under the influence of other recent battles, immediately attacked the tendencies in this new work. The review *On Guard* was their organ.[1]

This was one of the best and most characteristic of the Russian reviews, irreproachable in presentation, easy to read, and rigorously consistent in ideological stance. Its claim was, in a word, to "bolshevize" the new literature. Volumes 2 and 3 carried the following lines on the flyleaf: "In literature we declare war without quarter on calumnious petit-bourgeois deformations of the revolution; we will denounce untiringly any petit-bourgeois literary deviations in our midst; we will found and defend a proletarian literature, for this is the only way to continue our party's glorious tradition." Another declaration specified further that the review "aimed at a Marxist-revolutionary criticism of contemporary literature" and "a merciless struggle against literary tendencies which, either openly or under a revolutionary guise, were inspired by reactionary ideas."

This was stating the problem with useful clarity and brutality. The time had come to shatter entrenched ideas, especially those of inveterate bourgeois hypocrisy, such as the ancient lie of art for art's sake when true intellectual culture is restricted to the propertied classes; the old ideology which separates thought and literature from politics when no one can escape his social class and our entire baggage of ideas and words belongs to a society in which labor and production are the dominant laws; and the idea prevalent in the democracies of

---

[1]Published under the direction of Boris Volin, G. Lelevitch, Semyon Rodov, with the collaboration of L. Auerbach, L. Sosnovsky, I. Vardin, Yu. Lebedinsky, A. Tarasov-Rodionov, and others.

the intellectual hovering above the class struggle on wings of printed paper. These deceptions may last for a long time in decadent Europe; on soil reclaimed by the Revolution they should be totally unmasked. A characteristic of these post-revolutionary Russian writers, however, was to avoid committing themselves. "If Russia evolves toward bourgeois democracy," I wrote two years ago in *Clarté*, "in ten years they will become perfect *gens de lettres*. If Russia approaches socialism, they will become Communist writers. They will drift with the tide." And the Communist Zorin told me, "You're right. Only, in the first case, it wouldn't take ten years; ten weeks would do it." When Communist writers attacked the equivocal ideology of Pilniak, the most representative of them, there erupted the literary counterpart of the current class struggle in Russia.

On Guard was a review of demolition and savage attack, as well as of criticism. No one was spared. Here Sosnosky defined Gorky as "the ex-falcon turned hedgehog" for his continual bitterness and obstinate defense of the old intellectuals. With complete justification the review condemned "the poetic counterrevolution" of the poet Maximilian Voloshin. Pilniak, Ehrenburg, and Nikitin were called calumniators of the Revolution. Mayakovsky came under heavy fire for his claims of a proletarian Futurism, Alexandra Kollantai for her novels on free love, Lunatcharsky for his theater, and the directors of the State Library for their clumsy editing. It published a kind of small anthology of "mutual attacks by Bolsheviks" which is a joy to read.

There are some critical studies in this review which seem to me hardly models of the style, among them, G. Lélévitch's Marxist analysis of Anna Akhmatova's love poetry from a class point of view. I note also Lebedinsky's vigorous study on "The Writer's Personality."

While this movement had strong points, it showed the reverse side of the coin as well. Sound and legitimate claims were carried to flagrant extremes. Criticism by lampoon became niggling at times, and the debate shrank in on itself. Dishearteningly oversimplified articles were published (Yu. Lebedinsky's "Subjects Awaiting Authors," for instance). The polemic against A. Voronsky, director of *Krasnaya Nov* and an old Communist writer who had contributed a great deal to the 1922 literary renaissance, grew as acrimonious as a strictly political one.

At last the Moscow Association of Proletarian Writers joined with *On Guard* to insist that the party intervene and set up a kind of "literary protectionism." It proposed with great pride "an artistic program, ideological in form and content, on which the future development of proletarian literature would be based."[2] *On Guard* demanded that the party undertake "the rational and tactical leadership in art," while the Association defined proletarian literature by its "Marxist-revolutionary world-view" which placed it "at the antipodes of bourgeois literature."

Here we come to the heart of the debate. The answers to this tendency which make the most sense seem to have come from N. Bukharin, whom no one could suspect of approving, even in literature, the laissez-faire attitude of old-style liberalism. "We should have a peasant literature," he said, as well he might, since peasants constitute ninety-five percent of the country's population, Also, "Don't forget that the cultural problem differs from the military problem in that it cannot be resolved by mechanical violence." Proletarian literature should assert itself by criticism and competition, not by restrictive measures against its rivals. "We must recognize that our proletarian writers should write works instead of theses." One work of art is more convincing than twenty platforms. And again, "Abandoning free competition is the best way to kill the young proletarian literature."

The Pilniaks and the Vsevolod Ivanovs, interpreting rural Russia's hesitations and confused thinking, should not be "beaten over the head" — at least not exclusively. It is better to influence them, to win them over if possible. Finally, Bukharin pointed out the danger of modeling writers' organizations on the party and the army. A multiplicity of groups and tendencies is necessary to liberty in the field of artistic creation, he felt, and the party should give Communists only directives of the widest latitude.

In the propositions submitted to the R.C.P. Central Committee

[2]Platform of the first conference of the Moscow Association of Proletarian Writers, 1923.

in the spring of 1924, A. Voronsky drew attention to a crisis in Russian literature due mainly to the *Nep*. He reproached the proletarian literature in the reviews *October* and *The Young Guard* for wallowing in "holy imagery," "official optimism," and "bureaucratic clichés." The romantic view of the Revolution, still ardent two years before, had declined. Bohemia returned with commerce. "We have lost one of our most talented poets," wrote Voronsky of Serge Esenin, "corrupted under our very eyes by Bohemian life." Young writers have a hard life: young proletarian writers were suffering from the contrast between what they hoped for and what the *Nep* offered. They were working in great physical misery. The suicide of one of them, N. Kuznetzov, drove home the meaning of many of the poems. B., for instance, noted simply:

> Over there ballerinas dance
> And hearts are filled with violets!
> While I freeze in front of the window,
> Clenching my fists, clenching my fists.

Volumes 1 and 2 (May and August 1924) of *October,* the review of the Moscow Association of Proletarian Writers, have appeared. Where the criticism produced by proletarian writers in *On Guard* seemed well-realized, here their work appears weak. On the other hand the poems are good (Ivan Doronin's "At War," Bezymensky's "The War of the Stages," A. Gvozdev's "Fragments on the War"). The romantic view of the war which poets still hold is obvious in the topics themselves. They cannot restrict or pare down their work, so the poems are long-winded, diffuse, and uneven, but they are lively and striking as well, with frequent flights of lyricism.

During the Revolution, as I noted earlier, poetry was much richer than prose. Here also the prose works are weak, too weak. A. Filipov's *At the Workbenches* rolls out an interminable story of factory life. With exasperating patience he has recorded several workers' remarks and gestures for a week, carefully eliminating, however, any swearing, rough language, crude jokes, or any of the recriminations which would certainly be heard in a country as ravaged as the Soviet

Union — in fact, almost everything that does not fit his preconception of workbench conversation. The story, in short, is as boring as an *image d'Epinal*. We mention it only because it is typical.

These really gifted writers are so hamstrung by their preconceptions and so theory-obsessed that, in the end, they can produce only flops. This work is not good proletarian literature because it is not good literature at all, in spite of a few successful pages. For instance, A. Tarasov-Rodionov, the author of *Chocolate,* a dramatic short story, attempted a great work (*Linev*) on the heroic year 1918 which was a total failure. The same thing is true for Yu. Lebedinsky who recently wrote *The Week,* one of the best works, if not the best, of the new Russian literature. *Tomorrow,* his novel on the revolution in Germany published in *The Young Guard,* was obviously so poor that even the author, with the greatest simplicity, agreed. The characters in these two novels are hopelessly stilted, made to order in a discussion on agitation and propaganda. In *Linev* there is a counterrevolutionary French officer imbued with the politico-economic principles of . . . . Frédéric Bastiat. Now there certainly is no lack of counterrevolutionaries in France or anywhere, but I cannot imagine that Frédéric Bastiat is still exercising a decisive influence on them. Here we catch the writer in the act of creating literature from abstractions. He follows this simplistic line of reasoning: French, radical, middle class, liberal economy, Bastiat. The character is a labeled store dummy.

The Association of Proletarian Writers has issued a number of statements of justifiable condemnation. One attacks the exclusive cult of form promulgated by the "formalist" school, founded in Leningrad by V. Shklovski, Professor Eichenbaum, and others. Another censures the Futurists' verbal acrobatics and the grandiloquence of *The Forge* (*Kuznitza*), a proletarian group which has dreamed of a cosmic revolution, no less. But then the Association asks writers "not to imitate bourgeois art forms, but to surpass them to create new forms" and, in addition, to write only "monumental" works on proletarian life. These pronouncements make good points, but the best theories must be adapted to concrete reality with a certain amount of insight. In the

Victor Serge

immensity of rural Russia, where cities are islands of advanced civilization, would a young writer *from a workshop* be able to *surpass* the expertise of bourgeois art methods? Perhaps, in isolated cases, after fifteen years of struggle and with good luck. But does literary apprenticeship ever start with monumental work? It appears highly dangerous, in short, to subject a young man's first creative efforts to this kind of unadulterated theory.

On the other hand, there are certain great accomplishments recorded in *October.* You must know where to find them and how to read them. Hidden in the back pages under the modest heading of news, we discover, for instance, that the *October* group will soon publish a dozen booklets of verse. Just like that! And that the fifty workers in the Workers' Springtime group have been turning out "intensive work in the last period, having tackled 15 plays, 76 short stories, 261 poems and 20 lectures, in 96 evening meetings attended by 450 writers." Don't laugh at these laconic statistics. Remember that two-thirds of these workers walk in the winter snows of Russia with holes in their boots. They don't go to the café. They work and write with the lovely candor of children determined to grow up.

The Vagranka group in the Rogoysko-Simonovsky suburb of Moscow is made up of sixteen workers who write for the press. Perkati-Polé, an old Bolshevik writer, a forgotten man, blind and dirt poor, gathers them in his comfortless lodgings and teaches them how to get rhythm into their verse and prose. There are not enough chairs; they crouch in a circle on the floor. They arrive smelling of tar, machine oil, and metallic dust. Naturally the works of this little literary group are still very imperfect, but you must agree that even the appearance of this group is of cardinal importance and promises more for human culture than any exquisite literary salon in Paris. In Tsarytsin an association of unpublished proletarian writers includes a locksmith, a turner, a cook, and some laborers; neither Pierre Hamp nor Gorky would make fun of that. We know that the Soviet press for years has been encouraging initiative among its correspondents — workers, peasants, soldiers, and sailors. There are thousands of them. In the backward countryside, obscurantism tracks them down and kills them. But we should be equally aware of a whole Russian Communist Youth literature, which includes remarkable poets like Bezymensky, Doronin, and A. Yarov, interesting prose writers like Seyfoulina and Artyom Vesioly, as well as critics and militants of un-questioned worth like Auerbach.

In a recent issue of *Literary News* M. Frédéric Lefebvre asked in an interview with the English novelist Swinnerton if it were possible for a poor man to get published in London. "It's practically impos-sible," the novelist answered, "for a man who is both poor and a pro-vincial." In Moscow, Tsarytsin, Tver, or Tashkent, a poor man *can* get published. A carpenter or a ferryman can write for the daily newspaper of his province or the capital, certain of receiving en-couragement if his work merits it.

This production of worker-correspondents, of little groups, of Communist Youth, this awakening of an entire people — imagine what fruit it will bear after fifteen years. Obviously Russian proletarians have already advanced beyond their brothers in the old cultivated Western countries. When a whole generation has matured in this at-mosphere of work, conscious of the duty to conquer culture and capable of doing so in actual practice since it has won the class war, we will have in proletarian literature something powerfully new, built on foundations laid by Lenin's generation.

Under the category of literary accomplishments several names spring to mind. Demian Biedny is an inexhaustible creator of truculent popular poetry. The social criticism of masters of proletarian journal-ism like Sosnovsky and M. Koltsov pictures the living face of Russia today, not those factory stories written to fit an official ideal.

Do these beginnings and these prospects justify a delay in the arrival of a true proletarian culture? In *Literature and Revolution* L. D. Trotsky gives an answer to this much debated question which seems virtually definitive. Culture is the product of centuries. The dictator-ship of the proletariat can only be a transitory period filled with struggle and hard work. Can it at the same time build a culture of its own? "There is some doubt of it since, during a revolution, destruction overbalances creation."

But after victory? "The more stable the new regime, the greater the possibility of creative cultural work and the more the proletariat will dissolve into socialist society, shedding its class attributes, that is, ceasing to be the proletariat." "The proletariat takes power with the precise intention of ending class culture forever and opening the way for human culture."

This is exactly our assessment. The development of any intellectual culture presupposes normal production, fairly high technology, well-being, leisure, and time. The time factor will diminish in importance since the masses by collective effort will produce works of culture at a rate beyond all hopes. But the revolutionary period, the period of transition from capitalism, will last decades, perhaps half a century. Until then, the workers' Republics will remain isolated strongholds in which the arts will take only the secondary place they now hold in capitalist society.

For Trotsky even the term "proletarian literature" is dangerous, since it "anticipates a fictitious future culture within the strict compass of the present." We feel, however, that it corresponds to the transitional period's hunger for new values. Many generations of workers may very possibly never know other times. More than anything they will have to fight; they will have to destroy and suffer enormously to remake the world. But like the armies of antiquity, they will have their bards, their story tellers, their musicians, and their philosophers. In order to conquer, the proletariat must be led by real thinkers and strategists who, like Marx and Lenin, have assimilated the essentials of modern culture. In short, the proletariat must have *its own* great intellectuals. It needs lesser ones as well, for the smaller but equally vital tasks. What is imperative is that both these groups serve it alone. Then the revolutionary work it accomplishes will have an intrinsic cultural value. In this historically limited sense, there will be, in fact there already is, a militant proletarian culture.

Translated by Anna Aschenbach

Richard Greeman

"The laws are burning" — literary and revolutionary realism in Victor
Serge

In the final chapter of Victor Serge's novel, *Birth of Our Power*,[1] the
narrator, a stateless revolutionary agitator of Russian extraction, has
just arrived in Red Petrograd, repatriated, as it were, to the land of
revolution. Behind him lie years of prison, a defeated revolution in
Barcelona, and, most recently, nearly two years of detention in a
French concentration camp as a "Bolshevik suspect." Before him lies
the capital of victorious revolution. The time is the terrible winter of
1918-19 — famine, civil war, the imminent seige of Petrograd. The
immediate problem for the narrator is to find lodgings for himself
and the families of the other returning "Captives of Imperialism"
whom he has left at the Finland Station. As the upper classes have
fled, there are plenty of empty houses in the half-deserted city, but,
paradoxically, they are unusable because there is not enough coal or
wood in Revolutionary Russia to heat them. After a series of comico-
tragic encounters with a "Soviet" bureaucracy newly born of revolution and already tinged with corruption, the narrator finally locates
suitable lodgings: the abandoned apartment of a former Counselor
of the Empire. Serge's description deserves to be quoted at length, not
only because it is, in a sense, the climax of the chapter and of the
novel, but because of the way in which the author's profoundly political and historical imagination turns essentially anecdotal materials
into a concretely significant structure.

> The Levines moved in there two hours later. It was on the second
> floor of a tall grey house, a series of twelve rooms abandoned to the cold,
> to the darkness, to the strange desolation of places where life has suddenly
> come to a halt. The grand salon seemed to have been turned topsy-turvy
> in a brawl. The grand piano, covered with a layer of dust, had been

[1]Translated from the French *Naissance de notre force* (1931) by Richard Greeman (New
York, Doubleday, 1967), 288 pp. Introduction by Harvey Swados, historical and biographical
notes by the translator.

pushed out into the middle of the floor. The naiad coming out of her bath, attributed to Brullov, which had smiled for twenty years over several generations of ladies, was hanging askew . . . . A cooking-pot full of mould was standing on the marble window-sill. In the open drawers of a little mahogany secretary you could see a jumble of photographs of children and schoolboys, shells from the Lido, cards post-marked Wiesbaden, a whole pile of those dusty nothings to which our memories cling: favors, ribbons, sachets, trinkets, calendars, old-fashioned jewelry. And fragments of letters: " . . . met Mama on the *Promenade des Anglais* . . . ." In Counselor of the Empire Benedict Illarionovitch Stavski's study, behind the master's straight-backed armchair bearing a carved monogram, the back wall was entirely covered by a glassed-in bookcase in which the massive volumes of the *Collection of the Laws of the Empire,* boxed in green cardboard, were lined up. One could easily imagine the late master, standing behind that table, as he appeared on a photograph which had been used to pick up sweepings in the next room: narrow forehead, stern monocled eye; an intelligent, egotistical industrialist, resembling a Roman senator; and a little girl bursting into that austere study clapping her hands: "Papa, little Papa, it's the revolution! If you knew how happy everyone is in the streets. I saw some soldiers with red ribbons, how pretty it is!"

I arrived there in the middle of the night . . . . The Levines had gathered in the smallest of the rooms, probably a nursery, furnished with two iron bedsteads with gilded balls on which only the mattresses remained — (one of them appeared to be stained with blood). This candle-lit room was like a corner in steerage on an immigrant ship. The children had fallen asleep on the baggage, rolled up in blankets. The mother was resting in a low armchair. The young woman, like a solemn child, with large limpid eyes which seemed by turns distended by fear and then victorious over the fleeting shadows, was dreaming before the open stove, the reddish glow of which illuminated from below her graceful hands, her thin neck, and her fine features. Old Levine's footsteps echoed on the floor of the grand salon, plunged in darkness. He entered, his arms loaded with heavy green-covered books which he dropped softly next to the stove. Silent laughter illuminated his ruddy face.

"The laws are burning!" he said.

The friendly warmth in front of which the young woman was stretching out her hands was coming from the flames which were devouring Tome XXVII of the *Collection of the Laws of the Empire.* For fun, I pulled out a half-burned page, edged with incandescent lace. The flames revealed these words forming a chapter-heading: *Concerning Landed Property* . . . and, farther down: *". . . the rights of collateral heirs."* (pp. 270-72)

Instinctively one understands that, given the conditions of the Russian Revolution and Civil War, somewhere, somehow, such an incident must have taken place once, if not many times, and that someone must have been on the scene to ironize about it. In any case, it is clearly a *trouvaille;* and, just as clearly, one can instinctively recognize that only someone intimately involved in the Russian Revolution could have found it and put it to use.

On the level of literary realism, the incident of "The laws are burning" is an example of the *petit fait vrai* which Stendhal prized so

highly for its undeniable authenticity and consequent ability to authenticate a whole idea, description, or emotional effect. "Realism" in this
context is merely a question of literary technique, of conditioning the
reader's response in such a manner that within a verbal context a
certain element will produce the reaction "this is true!" and so con-
taminate the rest of the passage. Yet this "true" or authenticating
element depends in turn on an elaborate web of relationships within
the context in which it must emerge as somehow inevitable. In creating these relationships Serge has produced a concrete social vision in
the passage which can be understood only in terms of referents *outside
of the text*: the transfer of power from one class to another in 1917.
The end result (provided the passage "works" on the level of literary
realism) is that the reader's comprehension of that historical abstraction ("the transfer of power") has been concretized, irreversibly
altered, and that the historical and political event has become part
of his vicarious "experience."[2]

How does Serge achieve this effect? The passage is divided into
two parts, the first a description of the empty, desolate, "public"
rooms of the apartment, culminating in an imaginary scene between
the former owner and his daughter, the second a description of the
warm, cosy, yet somehow mysterious nursery where the new occupants have gathered. The second section is parallel to the first in that
it too moves from description to a scene including a father and a
daughter, though this time it is "actual," not "imaginary" in the context. The passage is thus structured around a contrast between the two
families, the former occupants and the new ones, with a unity supplied
both by the "unity of place" and the rhetorical parallelism.

The tone of the first section is one of emptiness, desolation,
irreality, and a strange nostalgia — that of "places where life has suddenly come to a halt." This atmosphere is created through a description of the decor. The descriptive details are of two kinds: those

---

[2]It is in this sense that I concluded elsewhere: "That ineffable quality, 'what things were
really like'—the aspects, tone of voice, emotional context of a human event, personal or
historical—this is what the novelist's ear and eye can catch and what makes of his social
or historical fiction a truer record of living reality than the historian's data or the theoreti-
cian's rational frames" ("Biographical Note" to the Doubleday edition of *Birth of Our
Power* [p. 284], and, in a somewhat different context, in "Victor Serge and the Tradition of
Revolutionary Literature," *Tri-Quarterly*, No. VIII [Winter 1967], p. 50).

Richard Greeman

characterizing the social class and life-style of the former owners, and those which undercut this impression of the "normal" life of members of a stable, secure society by emphasizing the suddenness of their disappearance. The "salon," the "grand piano," the silly neoclassical painting of a "naiad" (with its satirical suggestion of inauthenticity in the words "attributed to Brullov"), the "marble" windowsill and "mahogany" secretary, the allusions to voyages to fashionable resorts like Venice, Wiesbaden, and Nice, the drawer full of trinkets and souvenirs suggestive of a shallow, romantic sentimentality, and finally the austere formality of the master's study leading up to the glassed-in, pretentiously boxed "Laws of the Empire" (the emblem of and political basis for all this upper-class comfort and stability), whose title precisely echoes the master's full title (Counselor *of the Empire* Benedict Illarionovitch Stavski") — all these elements of decor create the impression of a well-defined social milieu, the life of whose members the reader feels could be reconstructed on the basis of these artifacts. So far, the technique is that of traditional social realism.[3]

But there is a second series of details cutting across this impression and dislocating its elements: the piano has inexplicably been pushed out into the middle of the floor and is covered with dust; the painting hangs askew; the remains of an interrupted meal in a kitchen utensil are out of place in the salon (suggesting, perhaps, the flight of servants, the "lady" of the household turning an inept hand to cooking); the drawers have been left open; and, ignominiously, the master's photograph has been abandoned, later to be used as a dustpan. The effect is that of a visit to the ruins of Pompeii: the impression that a whole solid society has suddenly and mysteriously vanished off the face of the earth in the midst of preparations for hasty flight. The cause of this catastrophe is deliberately left unexplained until the word "revolution" in the daughter's imaginary speech at the end of the section, and an atmosphere of mystery is created where the reader is drawn into the text and obliged to imagine for himself the scene of

---

[3]Cf. Balzac's famous description of the Pension Vauquer in *Le Père Goriot* where the character of Mme. Vauquer is somehow "consubstantial" with that of her salon and where we feel we know her even before she is introduced.

departure which left these elements of decor in their present state of dislocation. Because of this "mystery," an impression is created not only of the suddenness, but also of the *permanence* of the family's disappearance. Indeed the reader understands that there is something irreversible about this disappearance not just of a family, but of a whole class and way of life whose foundation of existence has collapsed. They have all vanished into some irretrievable pluperfect; hence the sense of desolation and nostalgia for a society which, however decadent, is seen as forever gone.

Significantly, Serge has confined his description in this first section of the passage to the formal or "public" rooms of the twelve-room apartment (in opposition to the second section, which is set in the nursery), that is to say, rooms where the life, when it still existed, was already somewhat artificial and removed from reality. But reality does burst into these rooms with the naïve vigor and spontaneity of a little girl bursting in on her austere father — the news of the Revolution coming, characteristically, from the nursery and delivered, ironically enough, by a little girl who is too young to understand that the news means the end of her class' way of life and who can only see that the Revolution is, at this stage, as gay and spontaneous as herself.

Serge delivers this section of the passage from the point of view of an "author-omniscient," in subtle contrast to the second section, which is delivered, with more immediacy, through the persona of the narrator.[4] Moreover, by the end of this first section Serge has moved from the historical mode of author-omniscient, through a further remove from reality (the "reality" of the late master as he must have appeared at the time the photograph was taken), to a purely hypothetical mode: the little scene "one could easily imagine" taking place in the study.[5] Thus, where on one level there is a traditionally "realistic" movement in the text from pure description of physical objects, to description of people, to an actual scene, on the level of technique the text presents a contrary movement, from the concrete, through the

[4]Compare the initial sentences of the two sections: "The Levines moved in there two hours later" *vs.* "I arrived there in the middle of the night."
[5]The technique is reminiscent of the now-familiar cinematic flashback technique (whose ambiguities have recently been so overexploited by some of the "nouvelle vague" filmmakers) where the camera pans around a room, zooms in on an old photograph displayed on a bureau, and then dissolves into the scene in the "still" which suddenly comes to life.

problematical, to the hypothetical. In keeping with the theme of this first section — the disappearance of a certain social reality — the author places more and more layers of "literature" between the reader and the ever-receding "reality." This effect is striking in contrast with the second section of the text (to which the first is structurally parallel) where the theme is that of a new social reality literally and figuratively "moving in" to the physical context, and where the narrator, who is actually present, describes the scene.

Whereas the first section was characterized by the coldness and desolation of sudden and definitive absence, the emotional atmosphere of the second is one of intimacy, warmth, and humanity, combined with a certain feeling of insecurity. The reader is first struck by the physical restriction of the scene. We have moved from the emptiness of "twelve rooms abandoned to the cold" to the intimacy of a family "gathered in the smallest of the rooms" around the warmth of a stove. The darkness of the "candle-lit" room with the "reddish glow" of the "open stove," the sleeping children in their rolled-up blankets, the tired mother watching over her brood, the supposition that the room is a nursery — all these elements create a womb-like atmosphere. Serge has already noted the "good animal warmth" that emanates from this poor Jewish family (p. 251) and evoked the father's life-long struggles to provide warmth and food for his family while performing his revolutionary class duty. The simile with a "corner of steerage on an immigrant ship" has likewise already been applied to this family (p. 251), and it effectively characterizes the insecure existence of wandering Jewish proletarians forever seeking justice and a home. This theme of insecurity is reinforced by the impermanent way in which the family is "camping out" in this foreign milieu rather than taking possession of it and by elements like the young girl's fear of the "fleeting shadows" and the apparent trace of blood on the mattress — a mysterious and grim reminder that the "transfer of power" from one class to another which has given them this apartment was conquered by force and can be maintained only by force.

The passage evokes a whole complex of interconnected social, political, and historical relationships of individuals and classes which can be understood only in terms of an actual historical event *outside of* the text (the transfer of power of 1917) — an event which is in turn illuminated and made comprehensible for the reader with greater force and with more complexity through this purely "literary" text than it could be through any amount of abstract historical analysis.

It is within this context that the passage's climax (beginning with the exclamation "The laws are burning!") acquires a richness and symbolism that goes far beyond its purely "realistic" function as a *petit fait vrai*. On the lowest level, of course, Old Levine's exclamation is merely the punch line of an elaborately prepared pun, albeit a pun which depends on a precise historical situation for its effectiveness. Like any pun, this one is based on a simple verbal ambiguity.[6] Yet on another level, unresolved verbal ambiguity is the basis of much of the power of poetry. Since "laws" cannot "burn" in any material sense, the effect created by "The laws are burning!" as a verbally isolated expostulation is that of a Surrealist poem or an anarchist slogan; in either case it is a powerful image of the violence and destructive energy of revolution. Yet, as the text unfolds, the same destructive energy of the flames which "devour" Tome XXVII of the *Laws* is revealed as the "friendly warmth" toward which the young girl stretches out her hands, while the final image, that of *"Landed Property"* and *"the rights of collateral heirs"* framed in the "incandescent lace" of the flames suggests yet another possibility: that the social class represented by the Levine family, merely in order to survive, to keep warm, has been obliged to obliterate the society based on property and all its heirs (the class represented by the Stavski family) in the course of its struggle for existence. The image recapitulates Serge's portrayal of revolution throughout *Birth of Our Power*, where the masses are presented as moving toward revolution less on the basis of ideology than as an instinctive response to the pressure of the present, and where the progressive radicalization of the Russian Revolution specifically is seen in terms of the need to

[6]I.e. the word "laws" can signify a series of statements printed on paper or the material arrangements described or prescribed by these statements. A revolution having destroyed the arrangements of the latter, the former are deprived of their descriptive and prescriptive value and are hence reduced to their value as paper, a combustible substance. The old society has been destroyed. But the irony of the situation is that the new society's material existence is so precarious that its members are obliged to burn books to keep from freezing.

survive where there is no turning back.[7] Nor are the possibilities of the image by any means exhausted in these suggestions.

Serge thus brings his final chapter to a climax on a note of lyricism, but it is not the traditionally triumphal lyricism of Red Armies marching into the sunset. The vision is rather one of a necessary but ambiguous victory, of a new class placed precariously and uneasily in the seat of power, beset by internal and external threats and ironically conscious that the power which has been sought for so long and at such great cost will present greater problems in the future than any the powerless have ever dreamed of. Building up his effects slowly, on the basis of the most commonplace materials, and employing the traditional techniques of social realism to establish his context, Serge successfully gives his text the stamp of authenticity and then moves beyond the mimesis of reality to a realm of vision which includes history and poetry as its poles and where the text can be said to "authenticate" history as much as history "authenticates" the text.

The originality of Serge's vision may be seen as depending less on his undeniable talent as a creator than on the originality of our age of revolutions, the era which was ushered in by 1917 and has not yet closed. To me the basic difference between Serge's revolutionary realism and the no less visionary realism of a Balzac is historical. While Balzac was able to recreate the dialectic between the individual and society, establishing organic unity between the character and his milieu and thus arriving at a rival "reality" where the individual's destiny is seen as "problematic,"[8] it was not until the twentieth century that society itself — specifically bourgeois society — could be presented as problematic. This, I believe, is the originality of Serge's vision in *Birth of Our Power* — the ability to see bourgeois society in all of its forms not as *reality* (the limit on human activity) but as a historically limited arrangement destined to pass on to something else, and the ability to see the masses as a self-acting force capable of reshaping society. These two insights are ABC's to any student of Marx's *Manifesto,* but it is not a question of "applying" Marxism to

[7]Cf. Trotsky's concept of "permanent revolution."
[8]I am borrowing my terminology, though not necessarily my conclusions, here from Erich Auerbach.

the writing of fiction (although many have tried to do this and inevitably failed). Rather it is a question of the maturity of a revolutionary age which enables the sensitive artist to feel the earth trembling beneath his feet and a new society struggling to be born, or, in the case of a period (e.g. 1917) where an actual revolution has been made, to stand, as it were, on the shoulders of the masses shaping history and take on a new dimension as a historical individual and an artist. Be this as it may, it is clear that Serge was one of the few artists who absorbed the impact of 1917 on world consciousness and lived to tell the tale.[9] As his talent as a writer is indisputable, it follows that his place in modern literature is one of considerable originality and interest.[10]

Who was Victor Serge? Why does he appear as a stranger even in that part of our cultural tradition devoted to left-wing "political" literature, the first major translations and French reprints of his major works appearing only now, twenty years after their author's death and fifty years after the events that inspired them?[11]

Serge was a born revolutionary whose activity spanned three revolutionary generations (pre-World War I European anarchism, Bolshevism, and the Anti-Stalinist Left of the thirties and forties) and incorporated the revolutionary traditions of both Russia and the West. Yet, like all writers, he was always something of a maverick, and although he never hesitated to commit himself in action (his various imprisonments testify to that!), he was never a good "party man" and obstinately resists any effort to label him.

[9]The miracle of Serge's survival was attributable in part to his dual status as a Soviet citizen and a French writer with deep roots and many friends in Europe. Of the generation of Soviet writers to which Serge belongs, little needs to be said here except that the Stalinist counterrevolution, which crushed their talent, drove them to suicide, and eventually exterminated them, will have to do a lot more "de-Stalinizing" before it can rightfully collect the interest on the moral capital they created for the Revolution. The international solidarity that saved Serge in 1935 could not save them, and this fact accounts in part for Serge's unique position in the tradition of revolutionary literature.
[10]For a more detailed discussion of Serge's "place" and a further development of the historical ideas sketched here see my "Victor Serge and the Tradition of Revolutionary Literature."
[11]It is satisfying to note that this anniversary year of the Russian Revolution will be marked by a new paperback edition of Peter Sedgwick's excellent translation of Serge's *Mémoires d'un révolutionnaire* (Oxford), a new French reprint of the same work and of the monumental *L'An I de la Révolution russe* (Seuil), new editions of three early Serge novels—*Les Hommes dans la prison, Naissance de notre force,* and *Ville Conquise*—by Grasset, and my own translation of *Birth of Our Power,* the first in a series of three I have undertaken for Doubleday. I have also received reports of editions in Polish, Chinese, German, and Spanish, as well as a book club edition of *Ville Conquise* in Switzerland (Rencontres).

Richard Greeman

Born into a family of Russian "Narodnik" terrorists exiled in Belgium (1890), socialist "Jeune Garde" as an adolescent in Brussels, member of an anarchist utopian "colony" in the Ardennes (1908), anarchist-individualist editor of the Stirnerite *Anarchie* in Paris (1911), star of the infamous Bonnot trial of anarchist bandits (1913), convict in a French *maison centrale* for five years, syndicalist agitator in Barcelona (1917), detained for over a year in a French concentration camp as a "Bolshevik suspect" (1918) — these were Serge's credentials when he came to the Russian Revolution.

In Petrograd in 1919, though not yet a party member and still harboring anarcho-syndicalist sympathies, he was set to work organizing the administration of the Communist International under Zinoviev. He participated in Commintern Congresses, edited various international journals, exposed the Tzarist secret police archives, and fought in the defense of the city (1920-21). At the same time, he was constantly at loggerheads with the Bolsheviks over the treatment of libertarian and other "deviationists" by the *Cheka,* and he deliberately cultivated friendships among anarchists, left Social Revolutionaries, and Communist oppositionists, as his name had acquired protective value. Gorky, Pilniak, Yessenin, Blok, and Biely were among his literary acquaintances, and he sent a regular chronicle of Russian culture to Barbusse's *Clarté.* He served the Commintern from 1923-26 as a secret agent and editor of *Imprekor* in Berlin and Vienna, returning to Russia to take part in the last stand of the left opposition. (Some of Trotsky's last secret meetings with workers in Russia were held in Serge's kitchen.) The immediate cause of Serge's expulsion from the party (1928) was a brilliant series of prophetic articles on the Chinese Revolution, stigmatizing Stalin's blindly chauvinistic policies.

Serge took up writing seriously in 1928, as a substitute for political action. His early works (1929-35) were produced between spells of prison and in exile in Central Asia. His books were unprintable in Russia; several of the best were seized en route to publication in France. In 1935 some oppositionists raised the "affaire Victor-Serge" at the Communist-sponsored Congress for Defense of Culture in

Paris, and Stalin seems to have been embarrassed into releasing him, shortly before the Great Purges that would certainly have spelled his doom. Back in Europe, he was elected to the Central Committee of the Spanish POUM, campaigned against the Moscow Trials, translated Trotsky's works into French, and wrote voluminously — all under the constant harassment and slander of the Stalinists and their liberal allies. Even the Trotskyists cold-shouldered him for his independence. After the fall of France, he found a precarious exile in Mexico (where he died in 1947), the Anglo-American allies having closed their doors to him under Russian pressure. In the isolation and total poverty of his Mexican exile he wrote two of his finest works (*L'Affaire Toulaèv* and the *Mémoires*), but in spite of the friendship of Dwight Macdonald and George Orwell, it was impossible for him to publish. "It is hard to write for the desk drawer when you are past fifty," he said, "but every publishing house has at least one Communist and two conservatives . . . perhaps my name has become an obstacle to any work." He now lies buried as a "Spanish Republican" in the French section of the Mexico City cemetery — the funeral officials having refused the right to six feet of earth to a stateless person.

It is easy to understand why it took the beginnings of de-Stalinization in Russia and the birth of a New Left in the West to bring Serge's name back into circulation. His exemplary revolutionary career and lucid intellect have been an embarrassment to the establishments on *both* sides of the so-called Iron Curtain. However, what concerns us more directly is to try to discover the "exemplary" element in Serge's career as a *writer:* what light does Serge's life and work shed on the problem of literature and revolution?

Without attempting anything like a solution to this question, it is nonetheless possible to clarify a certain number of points on the basis of a study of Victor Serge. The first is that the genuine revolutionary has a distinct advantage over all others when it comes to creating a style and structure capable of expressing the spirit of his age. This is not to say that a great revolutionary is necessarily a great writer (although reading Trotsky's *History of the Russian Revolution* might suggest this). Nor is it merely a question of his drawing on the personal experience of revolution for "material" for a traditionally "realistic" portrayal.[12] Personal experience can be of great value to a writer (both Serge and Malraux are illustrations of that), but what I am driving at here is rather a matter of *internal* experience, of whether the individual has been able to match, on the level of understanding and feeling, the stage at which the masses have arrived in activity.[13]

In this respect Serge at his best is superior to Malraux. In Malraux, revolutionary experience and understanding are separate: one is never sure *why* his heroes commit themselves to action as heroically as they do. The revolutionary activity is all on the surface; the background is always that of the dilemma of the isolated individual facing an absurd universe. With Serge the relation is the exact opposite: revolution has been so internalized that it rarely appears on the surface but is always present in the background where it serves as the primary element of structure in the novel.[14] It is the unexpressed link between the two sections of the passage from *Birth of Our Power* analyzed above, and in the novel as a whole it structures and unifies an otherwise fragmented and kaleidoscopic series of episodes.

In fact it is precisely because the substructure is so deeply rooted in the soil of politics that Serge is able to create the impression of the free play of human feeling and experience (which is, after all, what one looks for in literature) on the surface. Serge's novels are thus entirely satisfying as "literature," as "fictions," having nothing forced or didactic about them — yet they are not merely impressionistic either. For Serge's class view of reality, his "ideology" so to speak, was so much a part of his way of looking at things, so deeply embedded in the structure of his imagination, that everything that flowed

[12]Literary realism is, after all, largely a matter of technique and is in no sense "revolutionary" as such. It is merely one of the many literary traditions on which a revolutionary artist can draw and, in spite of all the foolish dogmatism about "socialist realism," no thinking person would deny that a Mayakovsky was a revolutionary artist, and certainly not a realist.
[13]Where no such internal "revolution" has taken place, the artist or intellectual may ride on the crest of mass activity for a moment—participating in or even leading a revolution—but when the "moment" is over he will always slide back into bourgeois habits of thought, the basic dogma of which is the "backwardness" of the masses and the need to substitute something—state power, the party, ideology, or the heroic individual—for the actual dialectic of proletarian self-activity. Nor does this "backsliding" necessarily mean a return to the ivory tower or the bourgeoisie; it is of such "haughty vassals" that "revolutionary" bureaucrats are made. For a brilliant characterization of Bukharin as a tragic example of such well-meaning intellectuals, see Raya Dunayevskaya's *State Capitalism and Marxist Humanism* ("News & Letters," 415 Brainard, Detroit, Mich., 1967).
[14]In *Men in Prison* the word "revolution" appears only once, yet the novel is incomprehensible without the idea in the background.

from his pen was naturally and inevitably structured by it. It is from this structure, which underlies everything from the minutiae of description and surface technique to the overall architecture of the novel, that the work ultimately derives its significance.[15]

If the above is true, then the whole question of literature and revolution is placed in a new light. Much of the difficulty surrounding the question of "political" literature has come from asking the wrong questions. Too often it has been assumed that politics was necessarily some kind of vaguely dirty foreign matter grafted onto the pristine flesh of "pure" literature; too long has the true dialectic of literature and revolution been obscured by being presented as an either/or proposition; too often have the literati and the politicos been lined up in hostile camps — the former either disdainful of politics or afraid of losing their "souls" to it, the latter scornful of the essential "frivolity" of art yet ready to "use" it for alien purposes. Curiously, both sides — the dogmatists of "socialist realism" and the dogmatists of "art for art's sake" — share the same Manichaean view of the relationship between "ideology" and art. Rarely in these debates is it understood that there is such a thing as a political and historical imagination which can — as in the case of Victor Serge — produce works combining free creativity and political significance: works where political vision is the basis of literary structure. In fact it is just this concept — politics as vision — that is indispensable to an understanding of Victor Serge and, perhaps, of the whole question at issue.

Doubtless the acrimony with which this debate is usually carried on has genuine historical causes. Too many promising talents have been turned into "Agitprop" hacks or simply crushed for it to be otherwise.[16] The confusion arises out of a failure to distinguish between the case where "ideology" is *imposed* on an artist, either by a regime, a party, or his own personal compulsions, and the case of

---

[15]In *Birth of Our Power* this architectural effect is extraordinarily striking. The novel is constructed on an opposition between two cities, Barcelona and Petrograd, representing two faces of the Revolution. The novel's lyrical and ironic themes of "victory-in-defeat" and "defeat-in-victory" flow so naturally out of this opposition that the geography of the work generates its meaning.

[16]There is nonetheless something curious in the fact that revolutionary politics alone, of all world-views, is seen as so "alien" to literature. No one would dream of questioning the legitimacy of Dante's Christianity as an expression of *his* age. Catholic "ideology" is universally recognized as the structuring element in the *Comedy*. Why not apply the same standard to Serge and the writers of *our* age?

Richard Greeman

artists working under the spontaneous impact of revolutionary events on the free imagination. Perhaps it is because there have been too few of the latter (or rather that too few of the latter have been allowed to survive). In any case, it is unthinkable that something so momentous as the forces set in motion by 1917 should not find their proper expression in literature. Let us hope that the younger generation of writers in the Soviet Union or their counterparts in South America or on the New Left in the West will find the means to express the revolutionary impulse of our age and solve, in practice, the problem of literature and revolution. In the meantime, we have the exemplary career of Victor Serge, a genuine revolutionary and a genuine artist, to reorient our discussions. For, as Antonio Gramsci once wrote: "if the cultural world for which one struggles is a living and necessary fact . . . it will find its artists."[17]

[17]*Letteratura e vita nazionale* (Turin, 1950), p. 12.

Jean Pierre Morel

A "revolutionary" poetics?

First expounded in 1932, socialist realism is today the principal method of literary production and criticism in the U.S.S.R. and in several people's democracies. The very name "socialist realism" raises problems: certain Western critics consider it a mere propaganda slogan, but Marxist theorists, such as Lukács or Della Volpe, while disagreeing on the value of the term, treat it as a methodological concept. The importance of this expression is evident. For the first time, a literary doctrine proposes to define and to direct in a rational manner the entire revolutionary, marxist-oriented literary output. Moreover, from its very inception, this doctrine is linked with the more traditional aesthetics of "realism." Neither enterprise can be glossed over. Using general texts published especially in France at the time when the promulgation of socialist realism on an international scale was in its height, we would like to examine the rules which the theory sought to combine. It is not a question of judging the value of works produced according to the norms, but of evaluating the norms themselves, that is to say, testing their coherence within the framework defined by their formulation. Thus we shall be able to offer a provisional answer to the question, what gives reality to the "revolutionary" work? After all we cannot be sure that this reality is there, in the sense usually given to the term.

It stands to reason that we first consider this literary doctrine as containing the key of its own cohesiveness. We refrain from simply seeing in it, as did Trotsky, the fruit of the Stalinist regime.[1] The literary and political history of the U.S.S.R. must show the role played by the party in the elaboration of this doctrine at the time of the first five-year plans and certainly in conjunction with them.

[1]"Realism consists in imitating the provincial clichés of the third quarter of the last century; the 'socialist' aspect is visibly expressed, in that events which never took place are reproduced with the help of touched-up photographs" (Trotsky, "Lettre à *Partisan Review*," 1938).

Jean-Pierre Morel

The debates which brought it into being reach farther into the past, and it has outlived Stalin. A series of contemporary facts, of which we can make only a brief enumeration here (Lukács' recent works, international writers' conferences such as that of 1963 at Leningrad, the Nobel Prize awarded to Sholokhov, condemnations of Russian writers for the liberty they took with the accredited style, Chinese attacks against Sholokhov during the Cultural Revolution), shows that socialist realism is not simply reducible to the political circumstances which presided at its birth.[2] Moreover, any writing (preface, manifesto, and so on) which announces or codifies after the event a literary undertaking also contains an ideological project. It is useful to recall how Cassirer analyses the "déplacement des motivations" in Boileau's *Art poétique*.[3] The mere linking of socialist realism with matters of political propaganda and ideological education is not sufficient to take away its complexity as a literary fact and to dispense us from reflecting on it.

If the aims of socialist realism merit being called revolutionary, it is not in respect to forms, genres, or even themes which preceded it; it does not break with literary history as a whole, but it proposes to change the relationship which, according to it, any work maintains with some part of reality. Rather than establish a new relationship within the work, it considers it proper to define and perhaps to change what is commonly baptized "reality." Explicitly, socialist realism "demands from the artist a true, historically concrete representation of reality in its revolutionary development. Futhermore, it must contribute to the ideological transformation and to the education of the workers in the spirit of socialism" ("Statuts de l'Association des écrivains soviétiques," *Commune* [September 1932]). At the juncture of the ideological aim (to educate and transform) and the literary project lies "reality." Only a representation on the measure of reality will give the author enough efficacy to act in

[2] Cf. Claude Frioux, "Siniavsky, Daniel et la conscience publique," *Esprit* (Feb. 1967). See also Siniavsky, "Le Réalisme socialiste," *Esprit* (Feb. 1959) (an article published anonymously); Bernard Pingaud, "L'année dernière à Leningrad," *Esprit* (July 1964); and "The Soviet Union and 'The Great Proletarian Revolution' in China," *Survey* (April 1967), pp. 64-80.
[3] Ernest Cassirer, *Philosophy of the Enlightenment*, (Princeton, 1961).

the domain of ideology. But reality in its "revolutionary development," before it becomes the subject of literary works, is the object of a specific, already established science — historical materialism. That is why many formulas underline the fact that the new realism will be revolutionary in proportion to its being scientific: "All revolutionary literature, turned toward the exterior world, necessarily rests on scientific analysis, while reactionary literature escapes into the ideal or the religious" (Fréville).[4] Aragon sounds a like note: "I am speaking of the novelist whose work is the result of a method, and who has scientific regard for reality. This is the only novelist." In other words, socialist realism is science in the novel. And in criticism, according to Judin and Fadeev, it is a "new field" which opens to the writer. The value of this expression must be clearly understood, however. It is not a still little-known sector of reality which the authors, guided by Marxism, could explore at their will in order to show at the end of their personal search, on the one hand, what complex of specific relationships underlies the existence of this reality and, on the other, what relationships the already-known reality enjoys with this new realm. We know that André Breton undertook a task of this kind in his *Vases communicants* and that it was rejected by orthodox Marxists. When socialist realism speaks of reality, it means a reality already elaborated according to models furnished by dialectic materialism. The writer's activity is not autonomous, but derivative. The production of works and literary criticism derives from Marxism, just as techniques may derive from a science.

Yet the general model does not give precise indication of the means to be used. Without studying the works, one can discern a significant gap, already apparent at the level of theoretical requirements, between the model and the necessary procedures for implementation. Thus the question, "Must the writer really know historical materialism?" can receive two kinds of answers. The first indicates a vague link of similarity with science, taking that term in a loose

[4]In order to simplify the notes, the periodical references are merely listed: Aragon: *Commune*, Apr. 1935, Jan. 1936, *Europe*, Mar. 1938, Dec. 1938; Bukharin: *Commune*, Sept.-Oct. 1934; Ehrenburg: *Commune*, July 1935; Fréville: *Commune*, July 1936; Gorky: *Commune*, Sept.-Oct. 1934; Judin and Fadeev: *Commune*, June 1934; Radek: *Commune*, Sept.-Oct. 1934.

sense. For instance, given "a conception of art corresponding to a particular conception of the world" (Aragon), if this conception is socialist, the realism will be too. The second answer is more precise and doubtless also more weighty in consequences; it makes the new literature not just a derivation but a transposition. Thus, it pledges the work either to illustrate a given scientific fact or to seek literary equivalents of scientific exactitude and to move away from its scientific program (or, according to other texts, its philosophical program): "Socialist realism translates dialectic materialism into the language of art" (Bukharin). Where the scientist speaks of waves and electrons, the writer evokes colors; thus, Bukharin goes on to say, the writer must not use the words "base," "value," or "superstructure" to describe society: "He works above all with half-sensory images; the intellectual elements themselves take on an emotional form. Without this essential condition, art in general, and poetry in particular would not be possible." Without this condition a whole mystical prattle, which, since Romanticism, has contrasted intellectual knowledge of the world through science and sensitive intuition of it through art, would be also impossible. Any literary theory which accepts it is necessarily obliged to grant due importance to the idea of creative and mysterious subjectivity, an idea which is the corollary of the following distinction: "Marxism, if it does not bestow genius on the writer, does abolish the fetters of genius" (Fréville). And the writer who is called upon to become an engineer of souls "in the scientific sense of the term" (Aragon) remains an "alchemist."

In the second place, the idea that the author translates the scientific fact into emotions does not lead the socialist realists to admit or even to suggest the value of a concerted study of means of expression. At the outset, the term "engineer of souls" should, according to Aragon, "give its true worth to the technique of writing." As a matter of fact, the authorities put a brake on the research and debates of Russian linguists by deciding that the language differs from the superstructure and by alleging, more justly, that the Russian tongue is not a class product and needs no revolution (that of 1917 affected it very little). Among the writers, an almost general indifference to problems of style testifies to extraordinary compliance with the ideas of the higher-ups. Having accepted Bukharin's opinion according to which "everything that is capable of strengthening the sensory impression can and must find its place in poetic vocabulary, on condition that the metaphor be recognized as such," they are satisfied with the goal formulated by Gorky: "to clothe the most typical facts with brilliant words, precise, and eminently understandable." Literary expression is thus the collective means which allows adornment and communication of a "content" furnished by Marxist theory and practice. Art is in tow of science, and form goes along with content. Such a concept condemns "formal revolutions," those tempests in a teapot. In the name of the only true revolution, that of the content, or content of the revolution , art for art's sake (that old saw), formalism (a more recent enemy, and a fertile one), the Surrealists, Proust, and Joyce, hastily lumped together, have undergone continual repression, an instance of which can be found in Lukács' recent writings.

In the third place, the "content" or "true reality" imposes on the authors diverse and sometimes contradictory imperatives of method. Presentation of a *totality* is all important; the realist cannot accumulate or even juxtapose fragmentary observations; at the same time, this "rich synthesis" (Judin) requires close study of a historical or national, not just geographic, particular: "There is, in France, in 1937, no other road toward socialist realism (which does not grow like a hothouse plant on a pink table) than *French realism"* (Aragon). The writer must both reproduce this complex and moving social totality "just as it is" (all texts insist on this) and suggest the probable direction of its evolution — without, however, risking the epithet of "tendentious." The effect of perspective must be given, but without receding lines. In order not to "inject socialism from the outside," which would bring the method down to the level of propaganda, the author must disappear, either by "organic union with today's conquering socialism" (Judin) or by any other means. This is the ideal: "Realism demands that nothing be interposed between the world and its literary representation" (Fréville).

Jean-Pierre Morel

Clearly enough, the work of art only rarely contains this "content" which it is supposed to have. The real resists the book. By definition, it almost always escapes bourgeois writers — *real* Africa in the case of Leiris, or *real* motives in the case of Mauriac's Thérèse Desqueyroux. The realist critic notes the well-observed elements but especially brings out the fundamental difference between the real (which he knows through science) and the novel and shows the absent or hidden clue which permits putting the writer back on his feet — colonialism with Leiris, money with Mauriac.

It can happen that reality appears partly to escape from a Communist novelist. Then the critic brings out the superficial differences but avers the deep conformity of the book with reality and offers an assurance: "As a *witness* of this epoch, *having known Nizan's models,* or their brothers, I can affirm that what may appear exaggerated in the heroes of his book is still quite gentle and voluntarily toned down by the author from the grotesque and revolting reality" (Aragon, italics mine).

In certain celebrated cases, the concordance between the real and the book of a nonsocialist or even reactionary writer is explained by the fact that genius instead of differentiating itself has molded itself to universal conformity.

Balzac wrote as though taking dictation from his epoch. Nothing came between his attentive eye and the exterior world. "It won't be the author's fault," he writes, "if things speak of themselves . . ." What a definition of realism! His genius triumphs, in spite of his political opinions, thanks to his realist method. (Fréville).

But how, without science, can a method recognize the real before seizing it? In fact it offers itself. Things "speak": in order to explain both the continual nonconformity of the work with the real which overflows it and the existence of works which nevertheless perfectly "reflect" it, one must postulate, in addition to its necessary complex and moving totality, a certain power for revealing itself. The "mirror," which has come quite a way since Saint-Réal, is the spot which the contradictory whole, "the objective tendency of social development," chooses for making its appearance.

Thus in this Romantic-Hegelian path, certain curious texts are easier to understand: conversion to the real, as for example Aragon, who in 1935 presents himself as a convict rehabilitated by realism; the advent of the real in the candid eyes of the Pure: "In order to embrace the world, one must look at it with the eyes of the progressive class which has nothing to hide, nothing to protect, nothing to falsify, — with the eyes of the proletariat" (Fréville); and stage presentation explained as an act of grace:

> When actors offer Shakespeare in our collective farms, the farmers, after the final curtain, promise to increase the crops. Is it because they did not understand Othello, or did the actors introduce a few lines of propaganda? No. The spectators were moved by the play; they felt themselves miraculously growing.
> (Ehrenburg)

Lukács says that no theory, whether it is correct or not, can be useful to an author unless it is translated into "adequate aesthetic categories." We have already seen some of the categories created by this prejudice: expression as ornament, imprecise and enveloping reality, ambiguous "reflections." Their frailty partly explains how critics and writers moved from realism with scientific pretensions to the simple and already traditional designation of a literary school. Moreover, in order to found the new positivity, they went to texts by Marx, Engels, and Lenin which have some sort of relationship with literature — not only to those texts where theoretical elaboration is clear, but to diverse quotations, biographical anecdotes about Marx's "taste" for the classics, rebaptized as "dialectical flair." Such selected passages gave currency to the idea that there was a Marxist or Leninist "literary" point of view — in the sense that one speaks of Jules Lemaître's point of view, for example. In the case of the new doctrinal texts, these are interpreted as answers made by Marx or Lenin to ceaselessly debated questions (although they are undoubtedly asking new ones), and study is made of the way they substituted their criteria for others and furnished new reasons for admiring the "genius" of Balzac (because he depicts the class struggle) or of Tolstoy (because he reflects the 1905 revolution — even if Lenin, in the six articles devoted to this author, limits himself to polite generalities in matters of literary praise). Thus one sees the formation of a chain of writers, parallel to that which links Marx to Stalin, where the "favorite" authors of Marxist theoreticians easily find their place as important links: Shakespeare, Balzac, Zola, Tolstoy, and contemporaries such as Gorky, Rolland, and Barbusse. Moreover, in the future these two chains will be united. "Everything that is best in world literature will follow the broad historical path and will line up under the flag of the literature of Marx, Engels, Lenin and Stalin" (Radek).

Criticism and production are not separated in socialist realism: thus the redistribution of literary values according to the viewpoints of Marx and Lenin is accomplished by a redistribution of models. Marxist literature tries to resemble the great novels of the second half of the nineteenth century (see Lukács' monograph), of which Rolland and Barbusse continue the tradition, or rather it inherits their abundance and substitutes positive and internal appreciation for their external social criticism. This appreciation is also oriented toward the ineluctable perspectives that are proletarian revolution and Communism.

The double concern of this literary theory is centered first on continuity, on the way to guarantee the heritage. The proletariat legitimately appropriates the best part of culture which the bourgeoisie can no longer make fruitful. This part is the great, worldwide, realist tradition, nourished with national traditions which are always the best of the country under consideration: such is the "French realism" which Aragon attempts to rebuild with the aid of the history of painting and literature. Concern is centered second on the content, the essential heritage, a group of themes and means of arranging them. In respect to the past and bourgeois writers, there is a slight topical change among the Russians, but little among the French: it is still the war of 1914 and the pre-war period. Aragon's *Monde réel* is quite close to contemporary cycles by Duhamel and Romains. From the rhetorical viewpoint, the structure and arrangement of fictional material were both worked out before the twentieth century: *Bildungsroman* framework; dramatic, epic tone; multiple and often complex plots; variety and precision of social settings; strong political and social differences (or hierarchic differences in Bek's or Simonov's war novels, for instance); the role of money; a host of characters who are principal or secondary by reason of the degree of character development.

The nineteenth-century novelists, the bourgeois chroniclers of the between-wars period and most of the socialist-realist novelists, thus occupy the same "intellectual area," to use the terms employed by some literary sociologists.[5]

Let us now summarize our findings. Socialist realism, as we have seen, uses a scientific model: historical materialism and an ideological educational function. Its embarrassment in establishing the links between science and literature, however, forces it to seek precarious equilibrium between the scientific methods it claims to use (certainly, if they were really used, they would annihilate the work in favor of information) and at least a partial autonomy, which it wishes to retain in the writer's task. Moreover, it feels the necessity of recognizing this autonomy, but it bases it almost altogether on the outworn distinction between science and art. When it becomes necessary to define the real which is to serve as norm for composition of the work, it hesitates between two representations, one essentially formed by historical materialism, the other more metaphysical. The kind of "realism" which is the object of our investigation thus combines the ideal of a perfect copy and the necessary and often faint effort to attain a goal which is out of reach: "The goal of all great writers was the poetic reproduction of reality; fidelity to reality, the passionate urge toward global, realistic restitution of reality were the specific criteria of literary grandeur for every writer."[6] According to Lukács, Shakespeare, Goethe, Balzac, and Tolstoy are the best

[5]Cf. Barthes, *Le Degré zéro de l'écriture* (Paris, 1953), pp. 99-104.
[6]Lukács, "Introduction aux écrits esthétiques de Marx et d'Engels," *Beitrage* (1956), p. 203. Cf. also *The Meaning of Contemporary Realism* (London, 1962).

examples of this almost mystical devotion demanded by mechanical reproduction of the real.

In truth, if one cannot clearly define the goal of literature according to scientific norms, he must seek in literary history those models which appear to have exactitude and objectivity equivalent to what one expected from science. Socialist realism is then obliged to put together a tradition with which it can claim kinship and from which it can borrow means of constructing or putting together its particular themes.

It is strange that this take-over from the past should create so little difficulty, for has one the right to treat new themes (all reservations having been made on this use of the provisional terms "treatment," "form," "content," and so on) with the help of forms which seem inseparable from "retrograde" ideas (Balzac's and Tolstoy's)? Is it not strange to praise Balzac for his realism *in spite of* his ideology and to condemn Flaubert *despite* his realism, because of the bourgeois mediocrity of his heroes? Are we to understand that in certain cases there is a responsibility of the forms themselves? And why forbid with such severity tendentious representations?

The scientific model serves to impose an unquestionable "reality" without recourse to ideological indoctrination. The literary model "clothes" this reality with the proper forms borrowed from a long tradition but stripped of all the ideological value that they formerly possessed. Everywhere, ideology is absent. This is in fact the best guarantee of its final triumph. But if ideology lets reality speak and argue in its place, is it not because ideology is secretly whispering to reality what it should say?

Among French writers linked with the preceding ones by their momentary political tendencies, one would easily find a discussion or criticism bearing on certain arguable matters: thus, for Gide, "literature does not reflect," and Malraux opposes the idea of conquest to that of inheritance. However, the most definite criticism comes from contemporary texts of Brecht, published but little known.

For him too, realism and truth are linked, but not in a spontaneous disclosure. In a series of choices, choose first of all to write the truth, but not just to write it. The intransitivity of writing is not basic; it is produced by laws which, in any capitalistic society, make writing an object for sale. The artist must decide who will receive this truth:

> Realism means: revealing the mesh of causes in society/ unmasking the dominant viewpoints as viewpoints of those who dominate/ writing from the viewpoint of the class which, for the most urgent difficulties, holds the broadest solutions/ emphasizing the moment of the development/ concrete character and possibility of abstraction.[7]

This definition leads to several other choices. Writing for the German proletariat, at the point it has reached in its struggle, does not mean sentimentally identifying oneself with it or offering it a flattering mirror of its difficulties. Brecht refuses the pathos that certain others feel to be fundamental: "Rejoicing, suffering, loving, hating with the working class, that and only that will give deep sincerity, emotion, artistic influence" (Judin). On the contrary, one should avoid the revolutionary "phrase," the subterfuges of moralism, and the eager justification of the good conscience. Nor does that mean waiting for truth to be revealed to the ingenuous eyes of the proletariat. The "real" is not real in itself: it must be constituted as such from figures and precise information. This choice cannot be made except with solid criteria: "Everyone who writes in this period of complications and great changes must know dialectical materialism, economy, and history."[8] Having acquired this knowledge, one should not change it into "aesthetic" false equivalents, as Bukharin and Lukács propose: "Whoever speaks of population instead of people and of real estate instead of land already is avoiding maintaining a great many lies." Moreover, clarity and frankness are not enough, even for those who think they are "on the right side." The struggle against the rulers imposes "speaking the truth with guile,"

[7]Brecht, "Popolarità e realismo," trans. Paolo Chiarini, in *L'avanguardia e la poetica del realismo* (Bari, 1961).
[8]Brecht, "Cinq difficultés pour écrire la vérité," trans. Armand Jacob, in *Europe* (Jan.-Feb. 1957).

disguising and pretending. Tactical sham — pretending to defend the oppressors, but instead manipulating the code of current meanings either by more apt terms, by changes — "Lenin, threatened by the czar's police, wished to describe the exploitation and oppression of the island of Sakhalin by the Russian bourgeoisie. He substituted Japan for Russia and Korea for Sakhàlin"[9] — or else by recourse to Utopia (More), to miracles (indispensable, for Voltaire, in order to preserve Joan of Arc's honor and show the depravation of a society, even one founded on a religious law), or to rigorous calculations (like Swift concerning the Irish children). One can also alternate tonalities, such as the emphatic and commonplace, or mingle expression and allusion (the famous "Brutus is an honorable man").

That is why, however tempting may be the homonymy, this realism does not immediately merge with that of literary history. The proletariat takes possession of culture "after an expropriation"; it does not just inherit it. And Brecht criticizes those who would be satisfied with style, "With a historically determined fictional form belonging to a historically determined period, let's say that of Balzac and Tolstoy, thus elaborating for realism purely formal or literary criteria."[10] There are just as many realisms as ways of speaking the truth. Each writer must experiment, says Brecht, combine fantasy, humor, and originality, speak clearly in one place and employ fable or parable elsewhere. Agitation and propaganda are as valid "mines of realism" as the poetry of Shelley or the plays of Shakespeare. Concerning tradition, the author should not yield to any "intimidation by the classics"; he will be able to borrow certain forms from them, even certain passages (Brecht's "plagiarisms"), and reject other models. He will not limit himself to any particular school.

In Brecht's case, realism is thus not judged by the conformity to reality of such or such a representation, but by the means of action in reality that this representation reveals or proposes. Let us note that these requirements furnish a certain number of characteristics for a Marxist revolutionary literary theory. For instance, one should

[9]Ibid.
[10]See above, n. 7.

study whether analogous preoccupations underlie Mayakovsky's literary production. Brecht's indications also allow a provisional reclassification of what is usually called "revolutionary literature." It is clear that in France the harvest would be slight: Malraux, on the one hand, and a whole mass of proletarian literature, on the other, would be left outside. On the contrary, Crevel's last works, especially *Les Pieds dans le plat,* deserve more than the facile disdain of aestheticians of all colors. Finally, Brecht's conclusion ("In order to judge literary forms, it is proper to interrogate reality, not aesthetics, not even the aesthetics of realism") does not take away the difficulty. It merely makes it change place.

Must we return to the real which perplexes us in that it can be both that of science and of literature, both the object of a duly constituted knowledge and a simple datum to be reproduced without any change? That would be taking very lightly what Brecht has taught us.

First of all the work does not illustrate an exterior struggle; it is part of the struggle itself. Then, on his ground, the writer must constantly rectify what others say and what he himself thinks; he must also decode, recode, unbaptize, rebaptize. Everything happens as if no meaning were stable and as if it were precisely his duty to bring this out. Everything happens also as if the dearest wish, both of his friends and his enemies, were for all to remain stable and general (for Brecht, an approximate generalization is a lie):

> The essential thing is that one teach a proper way of thinking, a way which seeks in all things and all phenomena the aspect that changes and that one can change. The leaders greatly dislike change. They would like things to remain as they are, for a thousand years if possible.[11]

One recalls Crevel's expression: "to work away at ending immobility." This immobility, at the level of culture and social manifestations, this immobility, into which, according to Brecht, one must bring disorder since it is the outlook of the rulers, is *ideology.* Here we can usefully borrow a definition offered by Louis Althusser:

[11]See above, n. 8.

Jean-Pierre Morel

What is the ideology of a society or of an age except the self-consciousness of that society or age, that is to say any present matter which implies, seeks, and naturally finds spontaneously its form in the shape of consciousness of the self, living the totality of its world in the transparency of its own myths?[12] Using Althusser's works as point of departure, one can characterize ideology with greater precision. First, it is not a datum of bourgeois societies alone. A regime such as that of the U.S.S.R., in full transition between the revolution that it accomplished and the Communist society that it is building, cannot get along without ideology. It is necessary in order to make the citizens understand the long-term aims of their efforts. They must live in it.

Secondly, for those who live in it, ideology is as natural as the air they breathe. What was at first an idea based on certain relations of production (this is no longer apparent without a really scientific criticism of the ideological discourse) loses the notion of its limitations and assumes a natural and boundless appearance. "We always thought this way." The foundation of all questioning cannot itself be called into question. Ideology then appears — or rather is felt — as immediate, spontaneous, and mute. It cannot turn back on itself to question itself, for how can a transparency reflect itself?

What is important here of course is the relation of ideology to the work. Any literary project is an ideological undertaking, even realism which claims to be scientific and which, from Balzac to socialist realism with Zola in between, never had any difficulty in finding scientific models. It is the gap between project and execution (between the ideology and the book) which allows and establishes the book's relationship with the exterior reality which it claims to represent.

"When art reflects life, it uses special mirrors," Brecht has said. Pierre Macherey, after rereading Lenin's articles on Tolstoy, brought forth a conceptual and no longer metaphorical use of the term "mirror": the mirror is neither mechanical reproduction nor instrument of knowledge, but a revealer by its very complexity. It does

---

[12]Althusser, "Le 'Piccolo' Bertolazzi et Brecht," *Esprit* (Dec. 1962).

not reproduce real struggles outside itself but makes their relationships appear. Yet it furnishes a complete and meaningful outlook on a real situation. It "expresses" the situation precisely because it reflects certain aspects and cannot reflect others. (In a sense, every book is built on an absence.) This complex optics, for it is a question of several mirrors subtly arranged, reveals the presence of ideology. One must therefore establish a triple relationship: reality, ideology, work, underlining the capital importance of the last two terms. Macherey has formulated it as follows:

> The work is articulated in relation to reality against the background of which it stands out: not a "natural" reality, an empirical datum: but that elaborated reality in which men (those who write as well as those who read) live, and which is their ideology. It is against the background of this ideology, a tacit and primitive language, that the work is accomplished: not to articulate it, to reveal it, to translate it, to give it explicit form; but to bring into being that absence of words without which there would be nothing to say.[13]

Let us take two examples. Western and Soviet critics both see in Sholokhov's *Cleared Land* the best "picture" of Russian collective farms. In it, oppositions are well dramatized: conflicts among individuals, family rivalries, peasants against former workers, rural people against townsfolk, routine against progress; the picture seems complete. But the "realistic" portraits of certain kulaks are merely illustrations of the party's analyses, presenting them as avid, grasping, brutal, and full of devices, that is to say, presenting them with the moral defects of the "class enemy," very useful in avoiding a differentiation — perhaps difficult — with other peasants, using socioeconomic criteria. All Sholokhov's talent serves more as a political montage than as an ingenious reproduction of reality. There is more: when, in the novel, the peasants disobey and rebel, it is at the instigation of an agitator, a former Cossack officer, who is ready to go to criminal lengths to terrorize friend and foe and who throughout the action, which begins when he arrives at the village, remains invisible and all-

---

[13]Macherey, *Pour une théorie de la production littéraire* (Paris, 1967).

powerful. The book lacks a "real" contradiction: spontaneous opposition of the peasants, even the average or poor ones, against collectivization. The contradiction is not "reflected" but is replaced by an antagonism within the novel: that of the Communists and the Cossack who, in league with other clandestine groups, exploits and feeds the peasants' discontent in order to reconquer Russia sometime in the far future.

The other example is Simonov's novel *The Living and the Dead,* often somewhat critical of the Stalinist regime. The hero is swept, in 1941, into a series of tragic misadventures which could be simply explained by the purges, the panic of defeat, and the general atmosphere of distrust. Does he denounce the humiliating system which allows all manner of suspicion and injustice? No, he realizes that there are good and bad bureaucrats and party members, and he is content to start from scratch in order to regain the confidence which his superiors have unjustly lost in him. Here again, an ideological viewpoint determines the presentation of reality. Everything happens as if this novel, very clear-sighted on certain aspects, suddenly became myopic or blind on others. Thus one is tempted to replace one formula by another and to say that the work "reflects" ideology instead of the real or that it mixes, in unequal quantities, the real (the true) and ideology (the biased or the false). Bourgeois criticism proceeds in just this fashion when it sorts out Soviet works — it was still apparent at the time of Sholokhov's Nobel Prize — the good novels, without ideology, in one category; in the other, the bad ones which "reflect simplistic ideology." Neither of these categories exists.

Ideology is necessary. The blind spot is essential for the Sholokhov novel of which we have just been speaking: the choice of the Cossack Fantômas imposes on the novelist a mystery-book plot and construction. The subject of the novel is the outcome of this intrigue. In the same way, the misfortunes of Simonov's hero can be explained only by dramatic artifice, since the system is not being questioned. The hero loses his party card, or rather a comrade charitably has taken it from him when, wounded and unconscious, he was about to fall into the hands of the Germans and be executed. After that theft, in a logical and diabolical sequence, occur all the errors, recognitions, and sudden changes which furnish the novel's framework — the career of the hero, first Communist, then suspected and humiliated, finally rehabilitated. All representation of reality passes through a certain area of refraction (which one can call "medium" with Hermann Broch or "mediation" with Roland Barthes) revealing the presence of ideology. Barthes justly observes:

> Balzac was able to describe the society of his time, with that realism which Marx admired so much, only from a distance imposed by his reactionary ideology; it was after all his faith and what one could call, from the historical point of view, his error, which took the place of mediation: Balzac was not a realist *in spite of* his theocratism, but really because of it.[14]

But if ideology is found in every work, why is it not "reflected"? And since we have defined it, in accord with Althusser, as a "transparency," how can it have the power of refraction? It is because we have defined it outside the literary domain, everywhere where it exists as the presence, ever accessible and permeable, of social myths. Silent and incontrovertible myths. "Good reading" (religious or otherwise) is that which makes literature an extension of this comfortable shelter. But does "good reading" exist? When one wishes to express, in a literary work, a viewpoint, a vision of the world, a global interpretation of reality, one must make them pass from the state of "consciousness" without problems to the state of exterior object. Balzac constructs not only his characters' physical appearance, clothing, and usual surroundings, but also, in many cases at least, their political and social conscience, literary tastes, and sometimes even their religion. This is what makes them so vivid, so characteristic. To accomplish this, he must cut up his own ideology, show the gaps in it, make the cracks in the throne and altar apparent. It is the same with Sholokhov and Simonov: their ideology determines the manner in which they present reality, but while placing it in their work, they

---

[14]Barthes, *Essais critiques* (Paris, 1966), p. 134. We also call attention to Galvano Della Volpe's important book, *Critica del gusto* (Milan, 1960), which attempts to construct, with Marx, Saussure, Hjelmslev, Carnap, and Wittgenstein as points of departure, a "semantic dialectic materialism." The limits of this article do not permit discussion of his conclusions concerning socialist realism.

oppose it, and it is these contradictions of ideology which will echo those of reality in the book in a relationship which is not mere similarity. From *Cleared Land* on, one can find an ideology which does not consider a political or social adversary as such but recognizes only the traitor and foreign spy. This ideology will show him in quite different fashion after the Moscow trials. When Sholokhov and Simonov use the procedures of the detective or melodramatic novel, which Gorky denounced in 1934 as the worst literary by-products of the "capitalistic world," they are less obedient to considerations of a realistic aesthetic than to the necessity of arranging the parts, secretly scattered, of an ideology which, so long as it is part of a program, remains united, unchangeable, and infinite. Macherey says that a work's cohesion "is only an imagined order, planned where no order exists, and which serves as fictional resolution of ideological conflicts." It is only in the work that one can speak of ideological contradictions, and it is because they break and deform reality that the book can "reproduce" reality and attain the semblance of unity.

Let us conclude. Barthes writes: "It is because socialist realism, in its very aims, does without mediation (at least in the West) that it is asphyxiating itself and dying; it is dying because it refused the thing that hides reality in order to make it more real, which is literature."[14] Perhaps one should add, and which is the ideology included in the literary work, a complex relay between the work and reality, scattering reality because it has itself been shattered as it entered the work. But does socialist realism refuse the ideology included in the work? It does when it condemns tendentious, propagandistic literature. That is not the most important aspect, however. The source of its death is probably in renaming ideology and *calling it reality*. Its norm of reality: a global entity, limitless, smooth, and unbroken, which one must represent *just as it is,* without tearing it apart, without using tendentious presentation (for what is not open to question cannot need any compelling arguments), is precisely the self-awareness of the age. This explains why it is transparent, even in Shakespeare, for the reader from the factory and the collective farm, and why it transforms him in an unexplainable manner. In ideology nothing changes; everything is ineffably tangent. The work is almost on the point of becoming useless.

We see why the scientific model is only an analogy of method. True science drives out ideology. As for the literary model, "realism" in the historic sense of the term, it is important because it seems the most appropriate, the most traditional vehicle of the ideological content and container, the one which runs least risk of dimming or breaking ideology. The value of the fictional discourse is constantly judged on its ideological worth, and this in turn leads to the necessity of narrative techniques in conformity with those of the bourgeois realist, naturalist, and social novels of the nineteenth and early twentieth centuries. Thus, the "real" (read: ideology) demands "realism," and "realism" insures faithfulness to the "real" (read: the permanency of unchanged ideology). Although in practice the good socialist-realist novels are always different from the good intentions of their programs, the ideological circularity is so clear at the program level, and so well masked by abuse of the word "reality," that one can scarcely see how socialist realism by itself could evolve toward something other than what it is predestined to be.

What gives to so-called "revolutionary" writing its reality? This question has been left hanging, and it is not certain whether we can give an answer except by means of new questions. One would have to examine the other side of the Marxist literary doctrine, that of Mayakovsky and Brecht, with its unresolved conflicts, with its not always "well-written" works, either willfully disparate and unbalanced or put together in a way which makes us sense a gap. One would have to extend such a study to the Futurists, to the literary production of the Formalists, and to the Surrealists and begin by *describing* these works in an utterly exterior way; then one would study their functioning and finally how they are attached to an ideology. Perhaps the "revolutionary" work is neither the one that treats the ideological theme of a particular revolution in its historical development nor the one which breaks with tradition, either through its aggressive tone or its apparently new form, and which is hastily named "formal" or "literary" revolution.

Perhaps it is even futile to try to establish a concept of revolutionary literature; would it not only be determined by the history of successive ideological themes? In that case, it would be interesting to study in what way Marxism or Russian Communism are related to precise techniques. Althusser offers the term "décentrement" as the principal technique of the materialist theater, with the purpose of pointing out the gap between the ideologies which are prisoners of themselves and the reality that they cannot attain. All the techniques suggested by Brecht for conveying truth, let us remember, play with these gaps. At the same time, if truth always hinges on the unsaid which is their ideology, are not Brechts' and Mayakovsky's works doubly thrown off center, so to speak? And for that very reason, fragile and vulnerable? Is it for that reason that these authors consider as the normal conclusion for their work its abolition in criticism (revolution being, for Brecht, the supreme criticism) or in struggle ("Meurs mon vers/meurs comme un troupier"), to the point that the most lasting frameworks of traditional reading seem to break up (Mayakovsky said, "No one is the author of my poem" and "I do not know whether one can call so definitely what I have done a *work*")? Is it the impossibility of tearing itself away from the ideology which keeps their work on the edge of emptiness, with that dispersed or even crumbled configuration or that lack of "internal harmony" with which Trotsky himself reproached Mayakovsky? One thing is clear: it is their exemplary disorder, even if not always apparent, which makes us appreciate such works (as also Heartfield's collages, certain texts by Tucholsky, or Crevel's last novel: "And besides, etc., etc. . . continued in the next war"). It is their disorder which makes of them new signs. A new lexicon, and not the old dictionary, even the one capped with Hugo's "bonnet rouge."

Renato Poggioli

The avant-garde and politics*

The problem of the relations of avant-garde and fashion, its public, the intelligentsia, of its artistic and cultural destiny leads naturally to a study of the relation between the avant-garde and politics. Many critics establish this relationship in such a way that the political term is the condition, and the artistic-cultural the conditioned. There is no doubt that a certain political situation can exercise a given influence on art in general, on avant-garde art in particular. All the same, that influence is almost exclusively negative: a regime or society can easily destroy the cultural or artistic condition which it cannot, of itself, bring to life. For example, it is easy to see that the support Fascism originally gave to Futurism (which was almost dead as an avant-garde anyway) was hesitant, Platonic, and short-lived. Certainly that support was noticeably less than the support given the movement when it denied its own heritage and turned into an academy, infinitely less efficacious than the disfavor with which that regime had to ward off any other avant-garde movement. Nazism did not tolerate, indeed it succeeded in abolishing, what it sometimes called "Jewish art," sometimes "degenerate art" (without recalling that it was a Jew, Max Nordau, who transferred the concept from medical pathology to the sphere of art). The same thing happened in Soviet Russia, where Lenin, as against Trotsky, always showed an unreserved antipathy to extremism in art, where avant-gardism died with the suicide of Esenin and was buried with the suicide of Maya-kovsky. Everyone knows how difficult were the life and work of the one Russian artist of our own day who was not part of the crowd or an epigone, the great poet Boris Pasternak.

*Trans. Gerald Fitzgerald from *Teoria dell'arte d'avanguardia* (Bologna, Il Mulino, 1962), to be published by Harvard University Press (Cambridge, 1968) as *The Avant-Garde*, in Mr. Fitzgerald's translation.

Renato Poggioli

The above-mentioned examples seem to lead us to recognize a validity at least relative to the rapport between avant-gardism and the capitalist bourgeoisie; this we shall study in the following chapter, though in practical and social terms rather than ideological or political. Here the connection to be established is, instead, that between the avant-garde and democracy. This means that the avant-garde, like any culture, can only flower in a climate where political liberty triumphs, even if it often assumes a hostile pose toward democratic and liberal society. Avant-garde art is by its nature incapable of surviving not only the persecution but even the protection or the official patronage of a totalitarian state and a collective society, whereas the hostility of public opinion can be useful to it. Having admitted this, we must deny the hypothesis that the relation between avant-garde art (or art generally) and politics can be established a priori. Such a connection can only be determined a posteriori, from the viewpoint of the avant-garde's own political opinions and convictions. These, under a persecuting regime, are often merely a necessary and opportunistic affair; they are almost always questions of genuine sentiment in libertarian regimes, even if the sentiment frequently boils down to mere wishful thinking or caprice. Furthermore, it is in the sphere of political opinion that the avant-garde more often accepts, or submits to, a fashion instead of creating or imposing one. Precisely on this account, the hypothesis (really only an analogy or a symbol) that aesthetic radicalism and social radicalism, revolutionaries in art and revolutionaries in politics, are allied, which empirically seems valid, is theoretically and historically erroneous. This is further demonstrated, to some extent at least, by the relation between Futurism and Fascism, or again by the prevalence of reactionary opinions within so many avant-garde movements at the end of the last and the beginning of the present century.

At issue, if anything, is not so much an alliance as a coincidence, which furthermore could naturally have worked in an opposite ideological direction. From the start, Italian Futurism was also nationalism, as was all the culture of the young generation in that epoch; the Fascism of the epigones of that movement was mere opportunism.

The same thing happened in the ultimate phase of Russian Futurism, which at its beginning was subversive and radical in politics, on the extreme left as the Italian movement was on the extreme right. Such coincidences and analogues of a spiritual kind also determined the Communism of the Surrealists. But the predominantly political phase of Surrealism did not last long, as may be seen from the brief life of the review *Le Surréalisme et la révolution.* If there were among the followers of the movement some like Aragon who abandoned Surrealism for Communism, there were others who resolved the dissension by abandoning Communism and remaining faithful to Surrealism. We must not forget that Italian Futurists and French Surrealists embraced Fascism and Communism, respectively, at least partly out of love of adventure or by attraction to the nihilistic elements contained within those political tendencies. In fact, every avant-garde movement, in one of its phases at least, aspires to realize what the Dadaists called "the demolition job," an ideal of the tabula rasa which spilled over from the individual and artistic level to that of the collective life. *There* is the reason why the coinciding of the ideology of a given avant-garde movement and a given political party is only fleeting and contingent. Only in the case of those avant-gardes flowering in a climate of continuous agitation, as, for example, modern Mexican painting (which one might hesitate to call avant-garde without reservation), does such a coinciding seem to make itself permanent.

In other words, the identification of artistic revolution with the social revolution is now no more than purely rhetorical, an empty commonplace (as seen at the start of this essay). Sometimes it may, though ephemeral, be sincere, a sentimental illusion, as in the case of Blok proclaiming that the new art ought to express "the music of the revolution," as he himself had attempted to do in *The Twelve.* But more often we are dealing with an extremist pose or fashion, as in the case of Mayakovsky's declaring himself "on the left of the 'Left Front' " in order to oppose the group and the review so named. The equivocal survival of the myth of a parallel artistic and political revolution was also favored by the modern concept of culture as spiritual civil war: hence Mayakovsky's postulate that the pen should be put on equal footing with the sword. Besides, from such concepts derive all those terms, often hostile, which aim to delineate the typical psyche of the modern artist, his position and attitude of disdain: rebel and revolutionary, outcast and outlaw, bohemian and *déraciné,* expatriate and émigré, fugitive or *poète maudit* and (why not?) beatnik. It is significant that these pseudo-definitions are used indiscriminately by rightist *and* leftist criticism. It is no less suggestive that the same pseudo-definitions come to be applied, especially in rightist work, to the intelligentsia too; here we must notice that the seriousness and sincerity of the avant-garde's political orientation is in direct proportion to a given group's personal involvement in a genuine intellectual elite. That does not mean that the orientation cannot be of merely marginal and collateral importance — hence the difficulty or impossibility of calling avant-garde movements those cultural currents which are purely ideological or idea-oriented (unconcerned with form), such currents as the French called *unaninisme* and *populisme.*

Actually, as the above terms demonstrate, the only omnipresent or recurring political ideology within the avant-garde is the least political or the most antipolitical of all: libertarianism and anarchism. These we see in the very beginnings of the American left-wing literary avant-garde and in the revivals of more recent times after the disillusionment of Communist or Trotskyite sympathies. The individualistic moment is never absent from avant-gardism, even though it does not destroy the group or sectarian psychology. Sometimes conscious, it produces in such cases the egocentricity and doctrinaire egotism of certain works, organs, or groups. Enough to recall the titles of reviews like *The Egoist,* the names of movements like the Russian Severyanin's egofuturism, the personalism dear to the English cenacle of poets under Henry Treece's leadership, the work called *I* by the poet who dedicated the tragedy *Vladimir Mayakovsky* to himself. Sometimes such individualism is only biographical and psychological, which explains the D'Annunzianism of Marinetti, for example, only an avant-garde caricature of D'Annunzianism properly so called. Sometimes political orthodoxy forces this sentiment to express itself in spurious forms, syncretic and mixed up, as in the Mayakovsky poem, "To a

Cut-Throat," where the poet's personal pride, his certainty that he will personally survive beyond death even into the distant future, fuses with the cult of the anonymous multitude, the future masses.

It is precisely as a function of this theoretical and practical individualism that the recent movement of existentialism shows itself to be avant-garde, even though it appeals to ancient and eternal cultural sources and demonstrates a relative indifference to revolutions in the field of form and technique. From the literary viewpoint its immediate precedent is naturalism; from the ideological viewpoint, expressionism. More mystical than the first, more philosophical than the second, existentialism reveals its avant-garde character precisely through its agonistic and nihilistic tendencies and by its own awareness of how difficult it is for individualistic and anarchistic nostalgia to coexist or survive within the collectivism of modern life.

This difficulty derives from what we might call the untimeliness of anarchistic ideology within contemporary civilization: untimeliness, often felicitously emphasized by leftist critics, who have also best sensed the connection between "culture" and "anarchy" in our time (using that formulation in quite another way from Matthew Arnold's). Perhaps this is why Christopher Caudwell defines the Surrealist, that is, the avant-garde artist most preoccupied with the ego, as "the ultimate bourgeois revolutionary." After the rhetorical question, "And what is the ultimate bourgeois revolutionary in political terms?" he answers lapidarily, "an anarchist." From this untimeliness, which we shall later call "historical alienation," and which at least apparently contradicts the cult of the Zeitgeist, we may derive the conclusion that Sartre, surely a leftist in philosophy as in art, has already reached: the avant-garde unconsciously functions in a reactionary way. Analogously, and conversely, we might with equal facility deduce that the reactionary ideologists to be met often enough in certain zones of avant-gardism are nothing but anarchists, without knowing it. But the problem of the avant-garde's historical function, as much metaculturally as metapolitically, would call for a too lengthy discussion. Apropos of this, and in the limits of this essay, our only remaining

Renato Poggioli

task is the sufficiently modest one of resolving some of the contradictions that seem to derive from the link between culture and anarchy. We recognize that the avant-garde more often consciously adheres to, and superficially sympathizes with, leftist ideologies; we affirm that the anarchistic ideal is congenial to avant-garde psychology. But neither one nor the other serves to deny what was said above concerning the eminently aristocratic nature of avant-gardism — a nature not, in turn, belied by its displays of the plebeian spirit. Thus the withdrawals into individual solitude or into a circle of the few elect, into the quasi-ritualist posture of aristocratic protest, are, like the gestures of plebeian, anarchistic, and terroristic revolt, equally owing to the tortured awareness of the artist's situation in modern society — a situation we shall describe later as "alienation." In the same way, the prevalence of the anarchistic mentality does not contradict the preceding claim that the Communist experiment continues to exercise a particular fascination for the avant-garde mind, even though this experiment is, par excellence, totalitarian and antilibertarian, hostile to any individual exception or idiosyncracy. Besides, as Caudwell succeeded in proving by means of an examination of the reason behind the adherence of many English poets in his generation to Communism, the attraction the Church of Moscow exercises for so many artists, writers, and intellectuals is due precisely to the ambivalence of an unwittingly anarchistic mentality: on one hand, the desire to see realized, in the historical and social dimensions of the present, a destructive impulse; on the other hand, the opposite desire, by which that destruction serves future construction. In other words, this adherence is owed to the extension of antagonistic and nihilistic tendencies into the political field, these tendencies being turned against the whole of bourgeois society rather than against culture alone. In the same way, the activist impulse leads the artist, writer, and intellectualist of the avant-garde to militate in a party of action and agitation, while the agonistic and Futurist impulses induce him to accept the idea of sacrificing his own person, his own movement, and his own mission to the social palingenesis of the future. In other words, avant-garde

Communism is the fruit of an eschatological state of mind, simultaneously messianic and apocalyptic, a thing compatible, psychologically if not ideologically, with the anarchistic spirit. The force of these impulses and the attraction of that fascination are capable of producing a morbid condition of mystical ecstasy, which prevents the avant-garde artist from realizing that he would have neither the reason nor the chance to exist in a Communistic society. That condition prevents self-criticism and self-knowledge. Only a few of those avant-garde artists who, deluded by Moscow, embraced the Trotskyite doctrine of permanent revolution have taken into account that their new, or old, adherence to more or less orthodox socialist ideals was motivated by an obscure anarchistic sentiment rather than by clear Marxist thinking.

Be that as it may, it remains always true that, while ideological sympathies of a Fascist nature seem to negate the avant-garde spirit — or to prevent its growing and developing in any social or political ambience at all — Communist sympathies can favor it, or at least not hurt it, only within a bourgeois and capitalist society. Adherence to Communist ideology does not impede Picasso from freely realizing, with the enthusiastic approbation of a select public, his needs as a creator and innovator: still it is not enough to justify him as an artist in the eyes of that Soviet society to which avant-garde art is anathema, a society that forbids the showing in its own public galleries of those works by the young Picasso which are now state-owned, far-sighted acquisitions of certain collectors of the ancien régime. A totalitarian order opposes avant-garde art not only by official and concrete acts, for example, preventing the import of foreign products of that art or the exhibition of a rare or accidental indigenous product, but also by first of all creating, almost unwillingly, a cultural and spiritual atmosphere which makes the flowering of that art, even when restricted to marginal and private forms, unthinkable even more than materially impossible. When Fascism and Nazism fell, no avant-garde work created in secret and silence, through the years when the spiritual life of two great European nations was suffocated by the tyranny and oppression of those two regimes, came to light. From now on we cannot believe that other master-pieces exist, unless perhaps those once visible and misunderstood. It has been said that every manuscript is a letter in a bottle, but that only means its fate is entrusted to time and fortune. Actually, in the modern world we cannot help doubting the existence of manuscripts closed in chests, paintings hidden in attics, statues stashed away in kitchens. This negative truth, at least as far as avant-garde art is concerned, is even more absolute in the case of Soviet Russia than it was in Fascist Italy or Nazi Germany.

What characterizes a totalitarian state is, in fact, an almost natural incapacity to permit evasions or to admit exceptions; it is not paradoxical to maintain that in Russia today, the Russia of the "thaw," artistic conformity is even more mandatory than moral conformity, perhaps even more than ideological. Aesthetic and formal transgression is certainly more arduous there, if not more hazardous, than political or ethical transgression. The reality of this state of affairs was fully proved in the exemplary case of *Doctor Zhivago*. With that novel, Boris Pasternak, who up until then, especially as a poet, was the last avant-garde artist surviving in Soviet Russia, returned to traditional literary and artistic forms, even prerevolutionary ones, to express a conscientious objection which was not that of an artist but of a man. The only country behind the curtain where residues of aesthetic protest are still displayed is Poland, precisely because that "people's democracy," more than any other, has been constrained to accept compromises with the national and religious spirit. If avant-garde art is not yet totally dead in Poland, this is solely because there culture, at least to some extent, is affected by that pluralism which distinguishes the modern culture of the bourgeois world — a pluralism that suffices to make the new order less totalitarian and monolithic.

Naomi Greene

Antonin Artaud: metaphysical revolutionary

Albert Camus has written that there are fundamentally two types of revolution: one — characterized as revolt — is metaphysical; the other, political. A metaphysical revolutionary rebels against the limitations placed upon him by the very nature of human existence, against the laws governing life and death. Unlike a political revolutionary, involved with the problems of society, he concerns himself with only the most universal and unchanging aspects of human life. His quest is absolute, for he demands not a new or better society, but a radical change in life itself — a transformation of the human condition. In this sense, Sade, Nietzsche, Dostoyevsky, Blake, Rimbaud, and Lautréamont were all metaphysical, or spiritual, revolutionaries. The most desperate, and the most pathetic, metaphysical rebel of recent years was a poet named Antonin Artaud.

Artaud first found himself forced to define the nature of revolution in the 1920s. At that time a member of the Surrealist group, he was shocked when many of his fellow members welcomed Marxist doctrines. Although his own ideas concerning the form a spiritual, or metaphysical, revolution should assume were not yet formulated, he completely rejected the notion that a purely political upheaval could serve any purpose. For this reason, his scorn for the Surrealists who turned to Marxism was unqualified:

> They believe that they can laugh at me when I write about a metamorphosis of the inner state of the soul, as if I had the same vile notion of the soul that they do, and, as if from any absolute viewpoint, it could be of the slightest interest to change the social structure of the world, or to transfer power from the bourgeoisie to the proletariat.[1]

[1]"Ils croient pouvoir se permettre de me railler quand je parle d'une métamorphose des conditions intérieures de l'âme, comme si j'entendais l'âme sous de sens infect sous lequel eux-mêmes l'entendent et comme si du point de vue de l'absolu il pouvait être du moindre intérêt de voir changer l'armature sociale du monde ou de voir passer le pouvoir des mains de la bourgeoisie dans celles du prolétariat" ("A la Grande Nuit ou le Bluff Surréaliste," OC [Gallimard, 1956], 1, 284-85).

Naomi Greene

Political differences served to deepen an existing temperamental cleavage between Artaud and other poets of the group. Unable to share the enthusiasm of an André Breton for life and love, Artaud was emotionally alienated from them; he could not conceive of anything less than an absolute change in life itself that would be capable of solving man's problems.

Artaud was first attracted to the Surrealists because he thought that they shared his desire to penetrate and understand hidden realities in man and the universe. Believing that man's essential character was still to be discovered, Artaud rejected any philosophy presuming to already understand human nature. Years later, he wrote that "The revolt for knowledge, that the Surrealist revolution had striven for, had nothing to do with a revolution that claimed to know man, and that made him a prisoner within the framework of his most bestial needs.[2]

At the time, Artaud was perhaps the only one among the Surrealists to grasp the essential contradiction between the avowed aims of the group and those of Marxism. In *L'Homme révolté,* Camus has clearly shown that the Surrealists' attempt to reconcile Marxist doctrines with their own philosophy was doomed to failure because they were as dedicated to the irrational and the *merveilleux* as the Marxists were to rationality and fact. Artaud's perception of this fundamental contradiction is not surprising, for throughout his life he was horrified by the world of pure fact and matter. Indeed, he constantly sought spiritual and metaphysical realities in which the duality he saw between matter and mind, body and soul, fact and idea, could be reconciled. His desire to find a principle transcending the duality is at the base of his fascination for various mystical doctrines and esoteric religions. Increasingly disillusioned with the dualistic way of thinking that he found in Europe, in 1936 he undertook a trip to Mexico in the hope of finding a people whose metaphysical outlook had not yet been distorted. His writings in and about Mexico delve further into

---

[2]"Cette révolte pour la connaissance, que la révolution surréaliste voulait être, n'avait rien à voir avec une révolution qui prétend déjà connaître l'homme, et le fait prisonnier dans le cadre de ses plus grossières nécessités" ("Surréalisme et Révolution," *Les Tarahumaras* [Arbalète, 1963], p. 177).

the nature of revolution and the necessity for a spiritual transformation of man. He became convinced that until man understood the reality of his role in the cosmos, until he perceived the nature of his metaphysical position, no spiritual revolution would be possible. Although, ideally, man should be directed by a metaphysical philosophy, in Europe men were being repeatedly misled by a series of political parties, each one erecting a philosophical system to justify materialistic aims.

Distinguishing between culture and civilization, Artaud maintained that a culture reflects man's metaphysical outlook, while a civilization is the body of arbitrary forms that social institutions assume. Every true revolution must stem from a cultural or spiritual transformation — a transformation which necessitates a return to the past, to the "great epochs" of history. Artaud loved to envisage a chaotic mythical past of humanity, when the world was being formed and man was still in touch with universal life-forces and gods that were immanent in nature. During these great epochs, natural phenomena embodied metaphysical principles, thereby bridging the dichotomy between idea and fact, between mind and matter. The Nietzschean idea that man can merge, in a Dionysian frenzy, with the oneness of being, or nature, is reflected in Artaud's dream of a mystical union of man and the cosmos in which the individual, as such, is annihilated and becomes one with universal forces. By alienating himself from nature, European man had lost sight of his metaphysical position and no longer functioned in harmony with cosmic forces.

A cultural revolution must be led not by politicians or statesmen but by artists. They alone are able to penetrate and understand the essential harmony that exists between man and nature; only they can awaken man to the true character of his cosmic role. Although different forms of art may coexist in a culture, if artists are in contact with primitive forces, all art forms should reveal man's metaphysical condition. The tragedy is that European artists, lost in the seeming duality of matter and spirit, have lost the capacity to capture and reflect primordial forces. Art in Europe both reflects and helps perpetuate the decadent state of Western culture.

Naomi Greene

Once Artaud introduced this rather romantic conception of the role of art, he raised another vital issue, touching on the nature of language. If the artist is to lead man to a new, metaphysical understanding of himself, he must do so through his particular artistic medium. Artaud, as a poet, had to deal with language, which he felt had to be utterly transformed. He believed that any writer who used language traditionally could not reveal metaphysical truths to man, for ordinary language obscured the spiritual realities of the universe. Europe's cultural decadence was closely related to a linguistic degeneration, in which language had become completely separated from the actual being of things. Words, losing all true meaning, had become mere signs for the objects themselves; as such, they could only distort reality. The duality between mind and matter in Western culture was reflected in the separation of the word and its object.

Seeking a form of language which would not be distinct from its object, Artaud eventually formulated the idea of a physical language in which all ideas and emotions are evoked by physical entities, obviating the necessity for words. Since physical objects suggest, rather than state, ideas and emotions, the possible interpretations of such a language are unlimited. Ideas and sentiments are normally circumscribed by the words expressing them, especially since words, meant for general use and communication, can never exactly correspond to the inner state of each individual. Lacking the words to describe our fundamental states of being, we never become fully aware of our deepest reality. "Therefore I maintain that theoretically words cannot express everything and that because of their predetermined nature, fixed once and for all, they hinder and paralyze thought instead of permitting and aiding its development."[3] Artaud's ideas concerning the relation between a cultural or spiritual transformation of man and a linguistic revolution are clear: in order to achieve a spiritual revolution we must first understand the true nature of our being — an understanding that must be preceded by a radical change in our language.

---

[3]"Car je pose en principe que les mots ne veulent pas tout dire et que par nature et à cause de leur caractère déterminé, fixé une fois pour toutes, ils arrêtent et paralysent la pensée au lieu d'en permettre, et d'en favoriser le développement" ("Le Théâtre et son double," *OC* [Gallimard, 1964], *4*, 132).

Best able at first to envisage a physical language in theatrical terms, Artaud was preoccupied with the stage during the early 1930s. The theater had only to emphasize its nonverbal aspects — sounds, lighting, costumes, decor — to achieve a perfect physical language. This theatrical language could make man aware of primordial forces existing beneath his acquired cultural characteristics. One of the most important of these characteristics, if not the most important, since it shapes the way man thinks, is traditional verbal language. With its new language, the theater could finally show man in his preverbal, prelogical state: "In this theater every creation comes from the stage and find its translation and even its origins in a secret psychical impulse which is the Word before words."[4] Transcending man's social and psychological problems, which form an integral part of his cultural environment, the theater should evoke man's prototypal drives and the universal forces under whose sway he exists. The few concrete suggestions Artaud gives to illustrate how the theater could actually accomplish these ambitious aims were inspired largely by a Balinese theatrical troupe he had seen in Paris. He thought that many of the theatrical techniques employed by the Balinese actors served a metaphysical purpose; their gestures, for example, reflected cosmic motions. The Balinese theater illustrated the relationships that exist between animate and inanimate entities, between man and nature, concerning itself not with the individual self but with a kind of universal life: "The theater must be the equal of life, not of individual life, not of the individual aspect of life in which CHARACTERS triumph, but of a sort of liberated life which sweeps away human individuality, in which man becomes a mere reflection."[5]

Since Artaud's only play, *Les Cenci*, was totally unable to attain the lyrical heights of his theoretical writings, it is not surprising that his experimental group, "Le Théâtre de la Cruauté," failed miserably in 1935. Artaud then turned to Mexico in the hope of finding the key

[4]"Dans ce théâtre toute création vient de la scène, trouve sa traduction et ses origines mêmes dans une impulsion psychique secrète qui est la Parole d'avant les mots" (ibid., p. 72).
[5]"Le théâtre doit s'égaler à la vie, non pas à la vie individuelle, à cet aspect de la vie où triomphent le CARACTERES, mais à une sorte de vie libérée, qui balaye l'individualité humaine et où l'homme n'est plus qu'un reflet" (ibid., p. 139).

to a new language. When, in 1936, he visited the Tarahumara tribe in the mountains of Northern Mexico, he felt that at last he had found this key. Deeply impressed by the physiognomy of the terrain, he saw in the natural configurations, in the rocks and mountains, different "signs." Nature herself had become language and suggested a myriad of ideas and emotions. Here was the primeval, physical language he had so ardently sought: "The country of the Tarahumari is full of signs, forms, and natural effigies which seem to have been born, not by accident, but as if the gods, that can be sensed everywhere here, had wanted to indicate their powers by these strange signatures."[6] For the Tarahumari, idea and being, mind and matter, language and objects, were one and the same. The Indians understood that the basic principles of life are incarnated in material elements and that essential life-forces have a concrete existence. Their language, both natural and physical, was universal since, unlike conventional languages, it revealed fundamental and ultimate realities of existence. Consequently, Artaud's attempt to utterly transform and revolutionize traditional language, to create a new language capable of expressing man's inner reality, ended in a return to the past, a return to the nonverbal language of animistic primitive societies.

Shortly after his return from Mexico toward the end of 1936, Artaud left France for Ireland. There, his already tenuous grip on reality slipped and for the next nine years he was committed to various asylums. Released in 1946, he enjoyed his new-found freedom very briefly, for two years later he was dead. In the course of these last years his ideas concerning spiritual and linguistic revolution underwent a radical change, a change that could have resulted from the mental and physical sufferings he endured or from the terrible realization that his great metaphysical quest had been in vain. In any case, during his grim confinement, he began to focus all of his attention on the human body. The duality between mind and matter that had so long consumed him ceased to exist, as he proclaimed that matter was

---

[6]"Le pays des Tarahumaras est plein de signes, de formes, d'effigies naturelles qui ne semblent point nés du hasard, comme si les dieux, qu'on sent partout ici, avaient voulu signifier leurs pouvoirs dans ces étranges signatures" ("La Montagne des Signes," *Les Tarahumaras*, p. 43).

the source of all, that man was nothing but a body. Violently repudiating all the great metaphysical systems that had formerly fascinated him, he derided with great venom spiritual concepts concerning the soul, God, and metaphysics. The cosmos, with its eternal life-forces, held no more interest for him, as he now impatiently urged not a spiritual revolution but a transformation of the body.

Although proclaiming the absolute superiority of the human body, he could not overcome his lifelong horror of it nor could he manage to divest himself of his former desire to find a spiritual reality beyond the material world. He could resolve this impossible ambiguity only by demanding that the body itself be transformed and purified: he thereby transposed his need for spirituality to the very plane of matter itself. Curiously enough, his affirmation that the body was the sole reality led him to a total refusal of its present state. True reality was attainable only in a pure body; man had first to rid himself of his organs, sexual drives, and bestial instincts. Paradoxically, corporeal transformation was linked to spiritual concepts of immortality, such as resurrection and metempsychosis. Having lost his former belief in an immortal soul and in eternal universal forces, Artaud found himself forced to seek immortality through matter and the body. If man could rid himself of all that is physical, all that is subject to decomposition and decay, he would not die. Man's body decays and dies because it has not purged itself of its animal instincts. True freedom, which is ultimately freedom from death, depends upon man's complete liberation from all that is corporeal:

When you will have given him a body without organs
then you will have delivered him from all his automatic responses
and given him back his true liberty.[7]

No political revolution will be possible until man is transformed physically:

And no political or moral revolution will be possible
as long as man is magnetically held down,

[7]"Lorsque vous lui aurez fait un corps sans organes
alors vous l'aurez délivré de tous ses automatismes
et rendu à sa véritable liberté"
Pour en finir avec le jugement de dieu (Editions K, 1948), p. 40.

by his simplest and most elementary organic and
nervous reactions,

by the sordid influence
of all the suspicious centers of Initiates,
who, cozy in the foot-warmers of their psyches
laugh at revolutions as well as wars,
sure that the anatomical order at the base of
existence and the duration of present society
will no longer be changeable.[8]

Artaud's ideas concerning revolution did not evolve without a
concurrent change in his theories involving language. And, for the
first time, his poetry really illustrated his theories. No longer eager
to find a language uniting being and thought, he sought one that
stemmed from man's physical being. He ceased to reject verbal language and demanded instead that it liberate itself from the control of
the intellect and, in so doing, that it precede any logical, rational
formulation of ideas and emotions. Language was not meant to communicate ideas, which reflect the superficial level of man's being, but
rather to express man's physical presence. In his later poems, he
repeatedly asserts that he has reached a realm prior to thought:

I, the poet, I hear voices which no longer
come from the world of ideas.

For, here where I am, there is no more to
be thought.[9]

He even maintained that this language was for the illiterate, referring
to men who, like himself, rejected rational, discursive language:

But let the swollen words of my life swell up them completely

---

[8]"Et il n'y aura pas de révolution politique ou morale possible
tant que l'homme demeurera magnétiquement tenu,
dans ses réactions organiques et nerveuses les plus élé-
mentaires et les plus simples,
par la sordide influence
de tous les centres douteux d'initiés,
qui, bien au chaud dans les chaufferettes de leur psychisme
se rient aussi bein des révolutions que des guerres,
sûrs que l' ordre anatomique sur lequel est basée
aussi bien l'existence que la durée de la société actuelle
ne saurait plus être changé."
"Le Théâtre et la Science," *Théâtre Populaire,* No. 5 (janvier-février 1954), p. 7.
[9]"Moi poète j'entends des voix qui ne sont plus du
monde des idées.
Car là où je suis il n'y a plus à penser."
"Préambule," *OC, 1,* 11.

alone to live in the abc of writing. It is for the illiterates that I write.[10]

Artaud's cult of spontaneous writing has seen its logical development not only in his own poems, but in the work of writers such as Genet, Henry Miller, and Céline.

Artaud believed that true poetry, unlike discursive language, does not appeal to the intellect, but evokes emotional and physical responses. For him, emotions were largely physical in origin: certain sounds, for example, create various sentiments and feelings. Language could call forth man's most elemental reactions only if the word were used for its sound rather than its rational meaning. Throughout his later writings, Artaud never ceased to stress the importance of the sound of words in poetry.

> All poetic lines have been written primarily to be heard, to be concretized by voices speaking them aloud, and, it is not only that they are clarified by their music and that they can then speak by simple modulations of sounds, sound by sound, but it is that only once removed from the written or printed page, does an authentic line make sense.[11]

In the last few years before his death, Artaud wrote the major poems of his life, such as *Ci-Gît, précédé de la Culture Indienne* and *Artaud le Momo* — poems that are still virtually unknown in France and the United States. They are "sound poems" whose words often convey no meaning until they are spoken or heard aloud. In the short poem "Histoire du Popocatepel," "double vé cé" and "ésse vé pé" make no sense until they are sounded out to give us WC and SVP. Sounds may not even suggest actual words, but may merely awaken ideas or emotions. Deprecating life in the poem "Il fallait d'abord avoir envie de vivre," Artaud wrote,

> larme de larve
>
> larve de larme
>
> de cette langhate,

[10]"Mais que les mots enflés de ma vie s'enflent ensuite tout seuls de vivre dans le b a ba de l'écrit. C'est pour les analphabètes que j'écris" (ibid.).
[11]"Tous les vers ont été écrits pour être entendus d'abord, concrétisés par le haut plein des voix, et ce n'est même pas que leur musique les éclaire et qu'ils puissent alors parler par les modulations simples du son, et son par son, car ce n'est que hors de la page imprimée ou écrite qu'un vers authentique peut prendre sens" ("Sur les Chimères," *Tel Quel*, No. 22 [été 1965], p. 5).

Naomi Greene

thereby intermingling real words with created ones to produce a series of sounds evoking something that is slimy and obscene. Like Joyce, he was fascinated by puns and delighted in those that were, at the same time, erudite and pornographic. A frequent pun concerns the words "Ka" and "Ka Ka." "Kâ," in the ancient Egyptian religion, was the noncorporeal double of the body, conserved in the mummy, while "caca" of course is excrement. Incantatory passages, which reflect his preoccupation with pure sounds as well as his belief in the absolute efficacy and magical value of words, appear very often. Incantation is used in the most precise sense of that word — to exorcise something or someone. In one poem, Artaud uses a number of words containing an anagram of his own name, thereby attempting self-exorcism:

Talachtis talachti tsapoula
koiman koima nara
ara trafund arakulda

The rhythm in this passage, as in all the incantatory sequences, is quite definite and of great importance. These few examples may give some idea of the different ways Artaud experimented with the sounds of words.

It is clear that Artaud's conception of the role language should play in effecting a transformation of man changed radically during the last few years of his life. Before his death, he had completely rejected his former conviction that language could reveal metaphysical truths or influence man's spiritual nature; instead, he asserted that it was directly related to man's physical being, stripped of any nonmaterial quality. Having lost all hope that man could unite with universal forces, he desperately longed for an immortality to be found through a transformation of the human body. Although so many of his earlier ideas underwent a violent reversal, one belief remained constant throughout his life: man's very being had to be altered before any political or social upheaval could be effective. True revolution had to be, first and foremost, metaphysical.

Ludovic Janvier

Literature and the rest of the world*

Incarceration of the writer in literature (even if and especially if he remains silent in it, hides in it) and of literature in itself.

It is easy, probably too easy, merely to read in this attitude the ever successful operation of retreat into words. From one work to another, connecting each to the other at the apex as the most important enterprises of our day, it would appear quite evident that literature is just that for the most exacting writers: a literature cut off from the world and any intent of relationship with the world, but constituting a world. It remains silent about the events of men but naïvely offers itself as an event. It loses sight of any plan for deciphering the structures of the world and proposes instead, parallel to them, a system which borrows from the world the system of words while leaving outside the system of things. But upon reflection, it appears that naïveté, and perhaps seriousness, are not where one looks for them.

Naïveté lies with those who would think it possible to contain within the book the world in which the book is born. An impossible contortion and a decision against nature since the outside cannot here become the inside: the house I build separates me from the outside just as surely as the fact that, born with a skin, I was born separated from the wind, space, and other people. It is from the illusion of the opposite belief that tragedy is born, that tragedy which brings death or murder on all the characters of the "traditional" novel, delegated by the author to seek impossible authenticity, an impossible grasp of the world, or rather of its representative, the ersatz form of the world willed in the book. This outside value, then, judges the hero and suppresses him, the writer making himself the humble agent of this judgment. If the character survives — fairy

*Conclusion of an article on Samuel Beckett: "Le lieu du retrait de la blancheur de l'écho," *Critique* (Février 1967).

tale or rose-water production — it is because this value has recognized him as its own. In both cases, the fictional work — feeble opposition or well-bred compliance — is that moral uselessness, that nothing. Sartre explicitly and abruptly recognized it in remarking the radical qualitative difference between one of his novels and the death of a child, while others, ever boy scouts, expect to rouse the world or bring about revolution. One must go the whole way: it is evident that fiction never has and never will be able to be placed on the same scales as a glance, a death, a love, the weight and the presence of a person. There is a way of taking literature seriously which is harrowing, even dangerous: making it take on the responsibility of history. This angelism leads to the inevitable, the boring tragedy of the good conscience which awakens some morning poisoned by remorse and tortured by helplessness. The dictatorship, acknowledged or not, of the human, of the social, etc., exerts that terror which makes us search in books for a truth when there is only a liberty. Thus one can put in the same boat the *naïfs,* the psychological writers and the psychopathic writers, those who play ladies of good works or small town Don Juans, the convulsionaries and the church pillagers, and finally the civil and political prisoners. And then, one has only to cast a glance at the past: it is not a novel which one bans, or burns, or suppresses when there is danger at home. From *J'accuse* to *La Question,* from *L'Encylopédie* to some clandestine poem, everything proclaims it: only morality is concerned with fiction; history is not interested in it.

Literature that is not naïve passes through refusal to write under the dictation of history, God, or the market. It has too much respect for history to do that. Writing at the dictation of the imaginary, a liberty in form and in words, an invention of liberty, it *creates* history.

Witold Gombrowicz

Journal excerpts

Convinced that Witold Gombrowicz is a writer of great talent — even, we believe, one of the greatest writers of our time — both as novelist and playwright, we present him to our readers in the hope that, their curiosity once aroused, they will be inclined to read more of his work, either in French (most of it has already been translated) or in English (two of his novels have recently come out: Ferdydurke *and* Pornografia; *they will be followed by others). The excerpts of his* Journal *and the "Commentary" on his latest and yet unpublished play,* Operetta, *that we publish here are both directly relevant to the problem raised in this issue.*

Witold Gombrowicz was born in Poland in 1904. A first volume of short stories appeared in Warsaw in 1933. Two years later, a comedy, Yvonne, Princess of Burgundy, *and in 1937, a novel,* Ferdydurke, *were published in Poland.*

In 1939, invited to take a trip to Argentina, he found himself caught in Buenos Aires when the war broke out. To earn his living he worked in a bank but continued to write (a play, The Wedding; *three novels,* Trans-atlantic, Pornografia, Cosmos; *and his* Journal).

In 1957, the more liberal Gomulka government allowed the publication of his works, with the exception of his Journal. *Enthusiastically received, they were soon found dangerous by the regime, which censured them again.*

Gradually, however, Gombrowicz' works were translated throughout western Europe, and his plays produced with much success in France, Germany, Sweden, Switzerland. In 1963, the Ford Foundation invited him to spend a year in Berlin. A year

Witold Gombrowicz

*later, he settled in France, on the Riviera, where he presently
lives. We hope the International Publishers Prize that he received
this year will contribute further to establish the long overdue
reputation of this exceptional writer.*

J. E.

1956

Saturday

Why, then — with, on my right, capitalism, whose stifled cynicism I know well, and on my left, the most humane revolution in the
world — why am I unable to join with the Communists? And yet I
want to create an art that is truly my own, and such art requires
noble and fervent blood: art and rebellion are almost equivalent. I
am a revolutionary because I am an artist; indeed, to the extent that
I am an artist, this whole thousand-year process studded with the
greatest names — Rabelais or Montaigne, Lautréamont or Cervantes
— has never been anything but an unremitting and burning call to
rebellion, sometimes uttered in a low voice and sometimes rising to a
sharp outcry. How is it, then, that the position I take — I, who went
into literature under the sign of rebellion and provocation, as they
did, and who understands admirably that writing is an act of passion
— how is it that my position happens to be on the other side of the
barricade?

What reasons could have thus made me betray my vocation?
Let us look into them. Is it that I consider the program of this revolution a utopia and refuse to believe that the eternal, immutable nature
of injustice can ever change? For a century now, and almost blindly,
art has been aiming at such reform. Why, then, must I be opposed to
it — and today, when I myself am so much more aware than they are
of the fact that mankind is in the process of moving irrepressibly, that
history is accelerating: we are no longer walking but flying toward
the future. Never has the term "immutability" been so out of date.
But would my resistance to Marxism perhaps be based on absolute
causes? God? abstract Reason? No, that rock has slipped; I can no
longer use it as a support; all absolutes are mixed in with Matter, and

Thought, by way of a dialectical movement, has become impure for me; it is dependent on Existence. Would I then be opposed out of mere pity? considering the boundless woe? the mountains of corpses for which any proletarian revolution is responsible? Not at all! Though a small child, I was schooled in the ideas of Schopenhauer and Nietzsche; I'm a child who knows how to say: After all, what is the suffering of ten million slaves? or even a veritable charnel house of a hundred million corpses? If one were to resurrect all the victims that history has tirelessly put through its mill, that it has tortured to this day, what an endless procession! Anyway, had I forgotten? Isn't the very essence of life tragic?

Consequently, since he has realized that suffering is inevitable, man should at least be able to give some human meaning to his suffering! How is it possible to resist a revolution that finally gives us a Meaning: our very own?

Monday

Long ago, some twenty years back, I was a "landowner"; I belonged to one of the higher classes of society. And today? Today, completely destitute, I make my living by writing. An independent intellectual, entirely free of any shackles, an artist whose work as well as his economic motivation are far more likely to be fully understood on the other side of the barrier. Were I to settle over there, in Poland, what support I would get! I would be helped everywhere, in everything; for me as an individual and for my glory, it would be more than perfect. Could it be some love for the past, then, that still holds me here? Nay, I am a specialist of freedom, and the school of exile has merely increased that which has been essential to me since birth: the bitter joy of leaving what has left me. If there is a man free of prejudices, it is myself.

I am, of course, molded by the world of yesteryear. But which of you, dear Communists, is not a child of the past? If the Revolution consists in conquering one's inherited consciousness, why would I not succeed in it as well as you? I, who am aware of the dialectic that is able to remove the Mind's autonomy?

Witold Gombrowicz

Tuesday

Here I should like to complete the foregoing: my vision of reality is not far removed from that of the Communists. To begin with, my universe is devoid of God. In this universe men *create one another.* I see man as dependent on man; I see him in a perpetual relationship of creation with others, penetrating "the* others," who prompt his most "personal" feelings. That is how things happen in *Ferdydurke* and in *Le Mariage.*

There is more. Being an artist, I have always tried to enhance that "interhuman sphere" which, in my *Mariage,* for example, takes on the dimensions of a creative Force — much higher than a mere individual consciousness: a prevailing higher Force, the only Divinity that is accessible to us. This is so; why is it so? Because it is *between* men that the Form which determines us — each one, as an individual — is born. I myself am one voice in the orchestra, one which must harmonize with the whole, find its true place in the symphony, or like the dancer who cares less about his own dance than the desire for it to integrate him into the dance of the others. And neither my thinking nor my feeling are really free or really personal: I think and I feel "for" men, so as to rhyme with them; and if I deform myself, it is because of the supreme necessity: to harmonize with other men, with the others, in Form.

I have, for example, applied this thought to art, trying to demonstrate (in, among others, my essay *Contre les Poètes* and in my reflections on painting in Chapter III, above) that it is very naïve to believe that our admiration for a work of art springs from ourselves: in great part, such admiration originates not *in* men but *between* men, and everything happens as if we mutually forced one another to admire, whereas, "personally," none of us is really taken and none of us admires.

Consequently, however, I find that we can have no thought or feeling that is truly authentic or that is entirely our "own." To my mind, a kind of artifice, a kind of lie (which has an effect even on our innermost reactions), is the true element of the human being subject to the "interhuman." Why, then, does the artifice and the lie of the man under the sway of Communism repel me to such a degree? What is it that keeps me from acknowledging that everything is happening as it should?

One further and last observation. I am generally considered an artistocratic writer — and I have nothing against that. Yet what writer has felt more violently than I the dependence of the Higher on the Lower? Who has gone as far as I in the feeling that Creation, beauty, vitality, and all the Passion, all the poetry, of the world is situated precisely at the point at which the Higher, the elder, the most mature, is under the sway of the Lower, the Younger, the Junior? Yes: all that is deeply personal to me (to the extent that it can be personal to me), and it is an experience that should — and with what ardor — unite me with the Revolution.

Why, then, has it not done so?

Friday

Let us note straightaway that they [the Polish writers of today — that is, of 1956] have had two major experiences: the War and the Revolution. It is only to the extent that these two tremendous experiences have really gotten into their blood that they may be, become, represent something, that they may create. For they have actually ceased to be the men of 1939 — yes, they are made according to the 1956 pattern. If, having lost the other reality, they have not fully digested the new one, if they *are* not — intensely enough — either one or the other, what, then, are they? Nothing.

It would seem to me that they have not really lived their lives.

They have not lived the war. In these periodicals [the weeklies *Nowa Kultura, Zycie Litervackie, Przeglad, Kulturalny,* and *Po Prostu*] Adolf Rudnicki[1] is quoted. He is supposed to have said that Polish letters of the postwar period were unable to really exhaust, get to the bottom of, the war themes as a whole and that we are far from having expressed the whole human element that could be extracted

---

[1]Adolf Rudnicki (1912-   ): novelist and publicist, one of the most prominent of the postwar period. Before 1939 he wrote *Les Rats* and *L'Eté.* Of Jewish extraction, he published, after the Liberation, poignant tales of Warsaw in flames and of the ghetto (*La Mer morte et la mer vivante* and *La Fuite de Iasnaya Poliana*). As an essayist, he periodically published very sharp *Feuillets bleus.*

from these abysses of hell. Certainly not much has been drawn from them, to be sure. But can one exploit hell?

These writers — among others and above all, Adolf Rudnicki — have undertaken to speak of tortured bodies in the belief that the abysses of suffering would furnish them with a truth, an ethics, or at least some new knowledge about the limitations that are our own. But they have hardly contributed any new elements — fruitful or creative. A Tadeusz Borowski, for example, has revealed that our baseness knows no limits, that all of us, such as we are, are vile. Fine, but if everyone is vile, no one is! The adjective is degrading only when it serves to distinguish a man from his fellowman. Listening to them, one would think that the culture of aesthetes is nothing but sorry scum. Ah! the splendid revelation, antediluvian and childish to boot. In thus describing the inhuman element in question, they urged, as good moralizers (like Andrzejewski),[2] more human feelings. Pious sermons of this type change nothing whatever either in the preacher or in the listener. Embarrassing, if anything, is the contrast between the mountains of bloody bodies and the feeble commentary which, dripping with exclamation marks, was in fact incapable of inventing anything better than the *pia desiderata* already contained in the declarations of the Holy Father: "men should be not wicked but good." In his *madeleine,* his maid Françoise, and his princes, Proust was able to find far more than all these good spirits could in the chain of crematories which, for years, have covered Europe with their smoke. Nor is it surprising that this acrid smoke ultimately served as incense for the new Dictatorship, and it is with this incense — forgetting the smoke from the camps in Siberia — that they set about exalting the Stalin regime, to which they owed the Liberation.

No, I don't find that the impotence of these artists confronted with the war is at all shameful: on the contrary, it was predictable. After all, how is it that the soldier who goes off to war, fights at the front, sees the most frightful atrocities, and becomes an atrocity himself finally returns home as if nothing had happened? exactly the same

[2]Jerzy Andrzejewski (1909-   ): Catholic novelist, author of *Cendre et diamant* (Fr. trans.) and *Les Portes du Paradis* (Fr. trans.).

as before he had left? Because some doses are too strong: one's organism rejects them. And if, during this postwar period, I were president of their Writers' Union, I should recommend the greatest caution to those who would venture to deal with such diabolical subjects — yes, the greatest caution or else exceptional wiles. To come back to Proust — if this novelist drew so very much from his aristocrats, it was because he moved among them with ease, and there was no reason for him to be terrified by his *madeleine;* but four million murdered Jews is a Himalaya! The Polish naïveté which consists in thinking that only the summits are fruitful in discoveries must be abolished. No, on the summits you find only snow, freezing drifts, ice, and bare rock. But what a multitude of things may be seen in our own little gardens! When, pen in hand, you approach these Himalayas of suffering endured by millions and millions, you are gripped by respect, by fear, by horror; indeed, your pen begins to tremble and your stammering lips cannot help but moan. Yet moaning has still never constituted literature — neither the emptiness proposed to us by Borowski nor the "conscience" of Abbé Andrzejewski.

All this, of course, is concerned with more than just literature. The average Polish intellectual was not able to *live* the war either. Under such conditions, the only fitting solution would be to give up, to not try and live the war — an impossible experience to really live — but rather to consider the question of knowing why an experience of that caliber remains *inaccessible* to us. The Pole in no way "felt" the war. All he was able to feel was indeed that one is unable to feel it (by feel, I mean drain to the very dregs) and that no sooner was peace made than another dimension had returned — the normal dimension. Thus stated, the problem has at least the distinction of saving such writers, in peacetime, from becoming ossified as much on a moral as on an intellectual and sentimental level. If ever they learned to know precisely how much their natures can accommodate, they would find it easier to recover their balance.

However, their attitude with regard to the war was distorted by the following criterion: it was a "great" experience! therefore a great emotion and a great lesson must be drawn from it! And anyone who does

Witold Gombrowicz

not succeed is vile. Since none of them managed to succeed, all of them felt vile and all of them fell prey to thoughtlessness. Why didn't anyone tell them: be well assured that war is not a jot more horrible than what goes on in your little garden on a beautiful summer's day. If you really know what goes on in the universe, and in life, why are you appalled by so many atrocities? And if you don't know, why do you want, at all costs, to gain a working knowledge of it precisely in connection with war?

No, there is no cynicism in these observations: I want only to emphasize the fact that access to certain phenomena cannot be gained by taking the most direct shortcut: it may be gained solely by way of the whole universe and by way of human nature — through what is most essential in both.

They did not experience the Revolution. Indeed, what elements — formulated elements — did the war cause to enter their consciousness? In truth, almost nothing: a few detached thoughts on "atrocity," a touch of pathos, halting and puffed up with morality.

The end of hostilities found these writers staggered, dazed, played out. If they happened to be still capable of a common effort, it was because they clung to anything at all for the sole purpose of enduring, holding on, moving; the instinct for struggling and living tossed them about like corks, like people who have been "knocked out." And it was precisely into that inner emptiness of theirs that the Marxist doctrine burst: I imagine that it came upon them before they were completely themselves again — I mean, back to their prewar mentality. And if they were unable to experience the Revolution, it was because there was nothing within them to prepare them for experiencing it! For Marxism did not make its way progressively into Poland: it was more as if a cage had been brought down over the heads of hooded falcons or as if a naked man had been dressed in a suit.

. . .

Sunday

As I read their publications, I become annoyed at seeing that all these scribblers are a pretty sad bunch, even on the level of art.

Despite all the upheavals of the Revolution, which really shook the foundations of their existence, in the columns of their literary reviews nothing has changed. The whole universe collapsed, to be sure, but their little artistic world has remained in good shape — unchanged.
. . .

How is one to tolerate, for example, that the poet Wyspianski[3] be proclaimed our national bard when, in reality, there are not even a hundred Poles in the nation who have some knowledge of his works? Why declare that our great Romantics delight us, seeing that they don't appeal to anyone? that the poet Kasprowicz[4] continues to live on among you, when his name — assuming that you still remember it — survives only thanks to library catalogs? Isn't it fair to state this type of question with regard to a country in which the meaning and social role of art have star billing? And yet the questions I state here are still considered obscene and indecent! Supposing that one of the old country's publications had dared to reprint my study *Contre les Poètes*[5] (published in Paris in *Kultura*): the text would have proved to be among the most authentically revolutionary of them all; yet the Revolution is yours, you who should have taken it in hand ages ago! Yes! you should have accosted art with brutality! violently demolished all the myths about it! revised and recast, from top to bottom, daddy's style, the threadbare, down-at-the-heels, obsolete language used by that group of acolytes and glossarists! verified the foundations of the old style in order to substantiate its very essence! Only then would we have gone a few steps forward. In your confusion, however, you ask me how to go about it? Nothing is simpler. Only you must stop lying and declaring that "art delights us," and say — because this is true — that while art may indeed sometimes delight us, it is in fact people, above all, who mutually force one another to be delighted by art. But then, you ask again, why do they do it? How? And for what

---

[3]Stanislas Wyspianski (1869-1907): one of the greatest Polish playwrights since the Romantic poets. A visionary writer and painter, he was an innovator in the theater, and his plays, particularly *Les Noces* (1901), have never been dropped from the repertoire. He translated *Le Cid* into Polish.
[4]Jan Kasprowicz (1860-1926): a poet of peasant origin, author of *Au Monde qui meurt* (1902) and *Le Livre des pauvres* (1916). Professor at the University of Lvov, he translated the Greek tragedies as well as most of the nineteenth-century European poets.
[5]See Gombrowicz, *Journal, 1953-1956* (Paris, 1964), p. 368.

purpose? For my part, I have already spoken about this elsewhere, but mind you, the mere fact of stating the question in this way is beginning to draw you out of the enchanted circle of adorations, fictitious values, and anachronistic liturgy.

Isn't it true that your Revolution has created a favorable climate for authentic realism? Isn't that kind of realism consistent with the very spirit of Marxism? (I am obviously referring here, not to the amazing aesthetic theory of realism preached by all the would-be Marxists, but to the Marxist spirit itself.) Yes, consistent with Marxism, for such a perfectly dialectical conception shows you the event and the artistic experience as something that originates *between* men. A realism of this stamp would have been a great success with the Poles: by separating us from the West, it would have given rise to our own conception of art; it would have led us to an aesthetics far more consistent not only with our lives but with our natures.

What did Poland do instead? Nothing at all.

Translated from the French by June Guicharnaud

Witold Gombrowicz

Operetta

Characters

Master Fior	the Priest
Prince Himalay	the President
Princess Himalay	the General
Count Charm	the Marquise
Baron Firulet	the Professor
Albertinette	Count Hufnagel
Albertinette's parents	Ladislas, the valet
the scoundrels	valets, guests

Commentary

The texts of contemporary plays have become less and less suitable for reading. They have become increasingly like scores that take on life only when they reach the stage, when they are performed as spectacles.

There is yet another difficulty involved in the reading of this "Operetta." I have always been entranced by the form of operetta, which, in my opinion, is one of the most successful forms the theater has produced. While opera is something awkward, irremediably doomed to pretension, operetta, in its divine idiocy, in its heavenly sclerosis, takes wing thanks to song, dance, gesture, and mask and seems to me to be perfect theater, perfectly theatrical. It is not surprising, then, that I yielded to temptation . . . .

But how is one to fill the puppet-show emptiness of operetta with real drama? For, as we know, the work of an artist is eternally dedicated to reconciling contradictions, opposites — and the reason that I am tackling so frivolous a form is to provide it with seriousness and suffering. Therefore, while one aspect of this operetta must, from beginning to end, be nothing but operetta, untouchable and sovereign in its standards as operetta, it must also present the touching drama of humanity. No one would believe the amount of energy that has been swallowed up in giving dramatic structure to this bit of foolishness. To incorporate a certain passion, a certain drama, and a certain pathos into an operetta, without in any way infringing on its sacred stupidity, is truly a problem — and a real whopper!

The colossal idiocy of operetta, on a par with the colossal pathos of history — an operetta mask covering the face of a humanity steeped in blood because of some ridiculous sorrow — would doubtless be the best mise-en-scène for *Operetta,* not only in the theater but also in the reader's imagination.

Plot

Act I: *Before the First World War — around 1910*

The social lion and blasé reveler Count Charm, son of Prince Himalay, is planning to seduce dainty Albertinette. But how is he to meet Albertinette "without having been introduced to her"? Charm evolves the following plot: a scoundrel, a young thief and wastrel, who has been brought in for the purpose, will approach Albertinette as she sleeps on a bench and will pinch something from her — a purse or a locket. At this point Charm will catch the scoundrel and thus, without breaking the rules of "good form," may introduce himself to the maiden.

But what happens? In her sleep Albertinette has felt the scoundrel and dreams of a light touch not of theft, but of love — which was aimed not at her locket, but at her body. Henceforth this girl, excited and enraptured, will dream of nakedness and will continue to sleep all the time in order that she may go on feeling the denuding contact.

Curses! For Charm, a count dressed from head to foot, feels ashamed of nakedness, adores clothing! He does not want to use his nakedness to seduce her, but rather the elegance of his manners, of his suits! His desire is not to undress her but, indeed, to dress her — at the most expensive couturiers and milliners . . . .

But who arrives straight from Paris on a visit to Himalay Castle?

The famous Fior in person, universal master and dictator of men's and women's fashion! There is to be a great ball in the castle, with a fashion show during which the master will introduce his latest creations. Thus, while Albertinette dreams of nakedness, High Fashion, Chic, and Finery begin to reign supreme under the guidance of Fior!

The master, however, is undecided and apprehensive: What fashion should he decree, what shape should he initiate, with the fast-moving times so vague, decadent, and ominous, and since no one has any idea where history is leading?

Hufnagel, count and squire, offers his advice. Let us invite the guests to collaborate, he says. Let us have a masquerade, and those who want to take part in a fashion tournament will wear bags over whatever garments they have fashioned. When a signal is given, the bags will fall, the jury will give awards for the best creations, and Fior, inspired by these ideas, will decree the fashion for the next few years.

Curses! For Hufnagel is neither Hufnagel nor a count nor a squire! No, he is Joseph, the Prince's former steward, who in the past had been fired and has become a political agitator and revolutionary activist! Ha, ha, ha! Brought into the castle under that assumed name by the Marxist Professor, the masked terrorist, under the pretext of the masked ball, wants to permeate the castle with a more bloody Fashion — a more terrifying Costume. He wants to sow the seeds of rebellion among the flunkys, who until now, had polished and brushed the boots. He wants Revolution! . . .

Act II: *The Ball at Himalay Castle*

The guests who are to take part in the competitive show of New Fashion arrive in their bags.

Charm brings Albertinette. Weighed down by her clothing (for Charm, instead of undressing her, dresses her) and still captivated by the thief's touch, she sleeps all the time and dreams of nakedness — even invokes nakedness in her sleep.

This drives Charm and his rival, Firulet, to distraction. Charm came to the ball with his scoundrel on a leash — to keep an eye on him? — so that the scoundrel would be up to no tricks? Or could he

Witold Gombrowicz

be jealous of the thief's touch when free, or perhaps tempted and excited by the idea that the scoundrel would poke about all over with his thief's fingers? . . . Firulet, the rival, also has a scoundrel on a leash. Unable to answer dreaming Albertinette's appeal, Charm and Firulet make fun of each other, and a tragic desire for self-destruction leads them to a duel. Finally, when the ball is at its most glorious, when the dress and masks are most dazzling, the desperate rivals let the scoundrels off their leashes: may they really have a fling, may they steal, may they poke into everything!

Chaos. Panic. The scoundrels steal right and left, while the guests, not knowing who is touching and tickling them, squeal and go wild! In the midst of this complete loss of manners, in the midst of this debacle of costumes, Hufnagel, the squire-terrorist, gallops in at the head of the flunkys — it's the Revolution!

Act III: *The Ruins of Himalay Castle*
The Revolution.

The wind of history . . . . Quite a long time has passed. It is after both World Wars, after the Revolution.

Man's clothing has gone to pieces . . . . In a high wind, through flashes of lightning, appear the strangest disguises: the Prince — a lamp; the Priest — a woman; a Nazi uniform; an antigas mask . . . . Everyone is hiding behind a mask, and no one knows any longer who's who . . . .

Hufnagel, the squire at the head of the squadron of flunkys, gallops about chasing the Fascists and the bourgeois.

Master Fior, at a loss, dumbfounded, tries to get his bearings at this new Fashion Show.

The trial of the arrested Fascists begins. Fior vainly demands normal legal procedure. Storm! Storm! The wind muffles, blows . . . .

But what's that? Ah, what's that?! Charm and Firulet appear, chasing butterflies, and behind them, a coffin carried by two undertakers. They tell their sad story: at that terrific ball, Albertinette disappeared, and only the abundant remains of her wardrobe were found! And so did the scoundrels disappear. Convinced that Albertinette had been stripped, raped, and murdered, Charm and Firulet went out into the big world with the coffin, in order to bury the naked body of Albertinette.

At this point everyone lays his own defeats and sufferings in the coffin. But what's that? Ah, what's that?! When finally Master Fior, cursing the Clothing of man, and Fashion, and Masks, at the height of despair, lays the holy, ordinary, eternally ungraspable human Nakedness in the coffin, out of the coffin, naked, rises Albertinette!

How did she get into the coffin? Who hid her there?

The two undertakers throw off their masks: they are the ones who had abducted Albertinette from the ball, undressed her, and hid her in the coffin . . . .

Eternally young nakedness — eternally naked youth — eternally young nakedness — eternally naked youth . . . .

Note on the acting and the mise-en-scène

Music, verses, dances, sets, and costumes, in the classic style of the old-fashioned Viennese operetta. Easy, old-fashioned melodies.

But gradually the whirlwind of history takes hold of *Operetta* and gets madder and madder.

The storm effects — wind, thunder — which are more or less rhetorical at the beginning, change into a real storm in the second and especially in the third act. The Shakespearean scenes of the third act must be touching and tragic.

The contrast between clothing and nakedness is the main motif of *Operetta*. A dream of the nakedness of man imprisoned in the strangest and most frightful clothing . . . .

Translated from the French by June Guicharnaud

Jonathan Spence

On Chinese revolutionary literature

Recent Chinese literature may be classified as "revolutionary literature" — at least in the sense that the Chinese people have been living
a revolution off and on for nearly sixty years and have been using
literature in their attempt to grapple with the complexities of their
own experience. The general problem of definition is a tricky one,
however, and since the Chinese Communist regime is now fundamentally reevaluating its own past (as we shall see below), this essay
makes no claim to be more than a sketchy introduction to a complicated field, an attempt to put a few prominent names in some kind
of framework.

Chinese revolutionary literature is little known in the West. This
is not solely because China has not been very widely studied or
because its language poses such a formidable barrier. There are, after
all, scores of monographs on twentieth-century Chinese history written in English, and there are numerous translations of modern Chinese
novels and short stories. There may in fact be another surprisingly
simple reason for our ignorance: the quality of most of the works that
make up the canon of Chinese revolutionary literature is just not high
enough to interest Western readers who have been reared on a richer
diet. As C. T. Hsia, whose anti-Communistic but thorough *A History
of Modern Chinese Fiction, 1917-1957* (New Haven, Yale University
Press, 1961) is the best general survey of the field yet written, puts it
with some asperity:

> A literature is to be judged not by its intentions but by its actual
> performance: its intelligence and wisdom, its sensibility and style.
> And by this test the majority of modern Chinese writers, like
> engagé writers everywhere, are seen to suffer from a moral
> obtuseness, a lack of style and ambition, a conformity of vision

and opinion, which are the obvious debilities of too much cultural uniformity or literary cliquism. (p. 506)

If one of the reasons for our unfamiliarity with modern Chinese literature is its low level of quality, we have to confront another problem, namely, the reason for that reason. For on balance we would have expected the quality to be extraordinarily high. The Chinese were blessed with a long literary tradition. Members of the upper class grew up with books and competed in examinations for the degrees that brought bureaucratic office. Poetry and essays were read and written both for edification and amusement. The written word had a particular sanctity, holding together men separated from direct communication by time, distance, or dialect. One would have thought that this shared literary experience might be a springboard from which to leap into the baffling complexities of twentieth-century China, that political turmoil would strengthen and enrich the writer, that the clash of past and present would be a perpetual challenge and inspiration.

Why did this not happen? One answer has occurred to me, an answer that might also be of some use in drawing cross-cultural generalizations about revolutionary literary experience. It is possible that, just as the enforcement of spurious clarities limits endeavor and leads to the banal sterilities of much "socialist realism," so also great revolutionary literature cannot develop when the stress, the challenge, the discontinuity, and the excitement become *too* great. In other words, that maximization of literary potential only occurs when there are certain genuine clarities, a clarity of context and of issues. Both were lacking in early twentieth-century China, and before they could be attained the spurious clarities were being enforced.

The context was blurred, not only politically, but even linguistically. The written language of the bureaucratic and educated elite which had dominated imperial China was rejected by the new writers because its complexity was a barrier to mass literacy and the attainment of a broad reading public. In adapting the colloquial diction of the Peking area (*pai-hua*) as a means of readily accessible literary expression the new writers were being truly revolutionary; it is essential to remember that by so doing they were not just playing stylistic games. They were cutting themselves off almost entirely from their own literary heritage and forcing themselves to start from scratch. This decision, with all its dangers, they took knowingly though sometimes sadly, and the pathos of this rejection has been brilliantly captured by Lu Hsun, the one writer of undeniable genius in modern China. In a story dated March 1919[1] Lu Hsun wrote of a failed and impoverished classical scholar, K'ung I-chi, who had been reduced to stealing books to keep himself in wine and had become the butt of the wits of the local tavern. K'ung is also the surname of Confucius, a point that no Chinese reader would have missed. At the conclusion of the story K'ung I-chi returns to the tavern after a long absence. His legs have been broken in a savage beating he received from a member of the local gentry who had caught him stealing, though naturally K'ung tries to hide the true cause from his interlocuters:

"I fell," said K'ung in a low voice. "I broke them in a fall." His eyes pleaded with the tavern keeper to let the matter drop. By now several people had gathered round, and they all laughed. I warmed the wine, carried it over, and set it on the threshold. He produced four coppers from his ragged coat pocket, and placed them in my hand. As he did so I saw that his hands were covered with mud — he must have crawled here on them. Presently he finished the wine and, amid the laughter and comments of the others, slowly dragged himself off by his hands.

A long time went by after that without our seeing K'ung again. At the end of the year, when the tavern keeper took down the board, he said, "K'ung I-chi still owes nineteen coppers!" At the Dragon Boat Festival the next year, he said the same thing again. But when the Mid-Autumn Festival came, he did not mention it. And another New Year came round without our seeing any more of him.

---

[1]That is, just before the May 4th student riots that gave their name to the literary revolution. Cf. Chow Tse-tsung, *The May Fourth Movement* (Cambridge, Harvard University Press, 1960).

Nor have I ever seen him since — probably K'ung I-chi is really dead.[2]

C. T. Hsia comments that this story "has an economy and restraint characteristic of some of Hemingway's Nick Adams stories" (p. 34). Others may catch in it echoes of the ending of Fitzgerald's *Tender Is the Night*. In either case, a point is made: for critical parallels to Lu Hsun we look to Europe or even to America of the twenties rather than to any facet of the Chinese tradition. Having rejected their own tradition the Chinese writers had turned to Western sources of inspiration, avidly reading translations of Zola, Maupassant, Chekhov, Gogol, and Dickens, absorbing in the process a Western literary sensitivity that only a great writer could bend back into his own culture. Few succeeded, and the history of Chinese fiction is strewn with imitative failures.

Rejection of their own past, adoption of a new set of values, search for new style, and a grappling with Western modes of sensitivity, all these made the literary context baffling. Perhaps, though, all these obstacles could have been surmounted and some powerful new synthesis arrived at if there had been some clarity in the political context, if the writers had achieved either a sense of where they were going or of where they wanted to go.

But the Chinese Revolution was untidy, without geographical focus, without a clear beginning, and without foreseeable end. From 1911, when the Manchu Ch'ing dynasty was overthrown, to 1949, when the Communists inaugurated the Chinese People's Republic, the country was in turmoil. There were successive "constitutional governments," warlord regimes, the Kuomintang Nationalist party, the Communist Soviets, and the Japanese invasion. Crisis followed crisis: to name just a few, each of which had major repercussions, there were the Japanese 21 Demands of 1915, the May 4th movement of 1919, the May 30th movement of 1925, the Shanghai purge of 1927, the Mukden Incident of 1931, the Fukien Rebellion in 1933, the Marco Polo Bridge Incident in 1937, the New 4th Army Incident of

[2]*Selected Stories of Lu Hsun* (Peking, Foreign Languages Press, 1960), pp. 45-46.

Jonathan Spence

1941, and the full-scale civil war after the Japanese surrender and the failure of the Marshall mission. Intellectuals and writers, tossed by political and military storms, searched in vain for some group or program that might offer stability. For many the Communist party came to be the only hope.

Things had seemed so simple when the Manchus were still on the throne. If the old corrupt regime and its sycophantic officials reared through a degrading examination system could be obliterated, then the Chinese could breathe again and advance to a new life. As Liang Ch'i-ch'ao, doyen of the radical journalists, put it at the turn of the century:

> What then is the path by which we may be saved from danger and seek progress? . . . We must take the obsolete and effeminate system of studies and sweep it away and expose it and say good-by to it; we must make it impossible for those tens of thousands of bookwormish, parrotlike, jellyfishlike, doglike scholars to shake their pens, wag their tongues, elaborate their style, work over their compositions, in support of the robbers of the people. Only then can we have new ears and eyes and really go forward.[3]

But others were less confident. In his novel *The Travels of Lao Ts'an,* written between 1904 and 1907, Liu T'ieh-yün warned against the deceptively simple program of the revolutionaries:

> Most of them are eloquent and embroider everything they say. Like those jealous women who destroy the whole house, they preach what seems like a reasonable sounding doctrine, but anyone can see that the house will be destroyed by them. In short, the arguments of the southern revolutionaries have such surprisingly brilliant and attractive features that it is clear all morality will be twisted and destroyed by them.[4]

In 1919 Liang Ch'i-ch'ao's particular demons had been overthrown, but the constitutional experiment had failed in turn and China had not found peace or a new order. Nevertheless there could still be manifestos, and there was still faith in the curative powers of

[3]Liu T'ieh-yün, *The Travels of Lao Ts'an,* trans. Harold Shadick (Ithaca, Cornell University Press, 1966), p. viii.
[4]Ibid., pp. 126-27.

youth in alliance with the forces of Western science and democracy. As Ch'en Tu-hsiu, editor of the magazine *New Youth,* wrote in 1919 in answer to his critics:

> We plead not guilty. We have committed the alleged crimes only because we supported the two gentlemen, Mr. Democracy and Mr. Science. In order to advocate Mr. Democracy, we are obliged to oppose traditional arts and traditional religion; and in order to advocate both Mr. Democracy and Mr. Science, we are compelled to oppose the cult of the "national quintessence" and ancient literature. Let us then ponder dispassionately: has this magazine committed any crimes other than advocating Mr. Democracy and Mr. Science? If not, please do not solely reprove this magazine; the only way for you to be heroic and to solve the problem fundamentally is to oppose the two gentlemen, Mr. Democracy and Mr. Science.[5]

Such optimism was not sustained. Ch'en Tu-hsiu himself joined the Chinese Communist Party and became secretary of the Central Committee. By 1928 the satirist Lao She was uncomfortably aware of the irresponsibility, cruelty, and cowardice of youth in the mass, as he showed in his powerful description of a university after a student riot:

> Outside the President's office lay a strand of rope: the President had been tied up and beaten. In the hallway were five or six satin slippers: the teachers had escaped barefoot. Pinned against the door-frame of an office by a three-inch-long nail was an ear with its blood already congealed: it had been lopped off the head of a faithful, prudent (his crime!) supply clerk of twenty years' standing. On the green near the hothouse was a patch of blood that had turned black-purple: it had poured forth from the nostrils of a gardener whose income was ten dollars per month.[6]

In the 1930s, far from being allowed to brood over the experiences of the previous decades in peace, Chinese writers were caught

[5]Chow Tse-tsung, *May Fourth Movement,* p. 59.
[6]Hsia, *Modern Chinese Fiction,* p. 171.

Jonathan Spence

in the growing rigors of the Communist-Kuomintang struggle, a struggle that continued even during the "United Front" period of resistance to the Japanese. This process with its combination of heartaches and growing didacticism is well described by C. T. Hsia and there is no sense in retracing the ground, but it is worth looking briefly at some of the problems writers faced in this period.

The life of the critic and essayist Hu Feng is a good example.[7] He was born into a poor Hupeh family in 1903 but managed to get to high school in Nanking in 1923, where he joined the Communist Youth League. He went to Japan for further study in 1928, staying there until 1933 when he was expelled for his involvement in a leftist demonstration. In 1934 he joined the League of Left Wing Writers in Shanghai and became a disciple of Lu Hsun. During the Japanese War he lived in Kuomintang controlled areas, but he remained in China in 1949 and participated in Communist government literary movements. During the early 1950s criticism of him mounted, until in 1955 and 1956 he became the target of a national campaign of criticism spearheaded by Chou Yang and was finally arrested and imprisoned.

The trouble with Hu Feng was that, in a world increasingly broken into hostile camps each demanding total obedience, he remained independent and pugnacious, insisting on the writer's need to choose his own subject matter. He described himself both as a "revolutionary writer" and as a man "not satisfied with the present"; in 1946 he summarized his credo thus:

Even when one discovers that his feelings are opposite to what is popular at the time, he should not hesitate to express himself. At first he may not be understood. But his isolation will pass . . . . Because what is genuinely true to one person, will definitely be true to millions.[8]

These brave words, however, were issued from a beleaguered position, for in 1942, in his lecture on "Reform in Learning, the Party, and Literature," Mao Tse-tung had put the writers squarely in their place,

[7]Besides C. T. Hsia, cf. also Merle Goldman, "Hu Feng's Conflict with the Communist Literary Authorities," *China Quarterly, 12* (Oct.-Dec. 1962), 102-37.
[8]Ibid., p. 113.

221

urging them to leave their desks and concentrate on the effort to gain a truly proletarian consciousness:

> You can open and close a book at will; this is the easiest thing in the world to do, a great deal easier than it is for the cook to prepare a meal, and much easier than it is for the cook to slaughter a pig . . . (Laughter) he slaughters him . . . the pig squeals. (Laughter) A book placed on a desk cannot run, nor can it squeal. (Laughter) You can dispose of it in any manner you wish. Is there anything easier to do? Therefore, I advise those of you who have only book knowledge and as yet no contact with reality, and those who have had few practical experiences, to realize their own shortcomings and make their attitudes a bit more humble.[9]

Though there have been fluctuations in the tightness of party control of literature, particularly in the "Hundred Flowers Movement" of 1957 and in the early 1960s, there has never really been a time since 1942 that the intellectual owing allegiance to Communist China has been able to escape this Maoist dictum and indulge his individuality. Yet at the same time writers have persevered with the novel and the short story, forms permeated with Western (not traditional Chinese) sensitivity, and have found it hard to conform to the limitations implicit in Mao's statement. Chou Yang, long-time foe of both Lu Hsun and Hu Feng and deputy minister of culture and a senior official in the propaganda department, summed up their predicament in the *Literary Gazette* in March 1958, admitting his common background with the strugglers:

> We couldn't liberate ourselves from the hold of individualism . . . . The masterpieces of nineteenth-century European literature habitually described the conflicts between individual and society, the anarchistic rebellion of isolated, defiant individuals against the detested society; this had left a strong impression upon our brain. We once fervently welcomed Ibsen, took to heart his famous saying "The strongest man upon earth is he who stands

[9]Boyd Compton, trans., *Mao's China, Party Reform Documents, 1942-44* (Seattle, University of Washington Press, 1966), pp. 16-17.

most alone." Many of us embarked on the revolutionary path via the individualistic detour, and joined the revolution with the individualistic knapsack upon our back.[10]

Chou Yang's loyalty to Mao had always been unquestioned. He was known in the West as "Mao's literary commissar." Most observers were therefore genuinely surprised when in the summer of 1966 he became one of the first prominent victims of the Great Proletarian Cultural Revolution. He was denounced at mass meetings as "the big red umbrella covering all monsters" and a statement in *Red Flag* for July 1, 1966, ran: "For 24 years Chou Yang and company have consistently refused to carry out Comrade Mao Tse-tung's line on literature and art and stubbornly adhered to the bourgeois revisionist black line on literature and art."[11] What is the significance of this? One scholar of Chinese literature has observed bluntly: "After years of bitter conflict with the writers, Mao appears to have concluded that it is not only writers but literature itself that is subversive."[12] If by literature is meant the novel and the short story (and a good deal of poetry), this judgment may very well be correct. Chinese revolutionary literature has failed to impress Western critics, but it has equally failed to come to terms with the demands of a "proletarian culture" because it could not rid itself of its Western shackles. In the final event Chou Yang, urbane and well read, is no more use to the present regime than his former intellectual victims. The Chinese writers, at sea in a world that had neither clarity of issues nor clarity of context, had never been allowed to find a middle-ground in which their spirits could expand; instead they were plunged straight into a world of totally circumscribed issues and context, which also adversely affected their creativity.

The Chinese revolution has not ended; we have that on the authority of Peking. It may be, indeed, that Chinese revolutionary literature has not even begun. What has been called Chinese revolutionary literature — literature produced in the first half-century of the

[10]Hsia, *Modern Chinese Fiction*, pp. 347-48.
[11]Merle Goldman, "The Fall of Chou Yang," *China Quarterly*, 27 (July-Sept. 1966), 132-48, quotation on p. 132.
[12]Ibid., p. 143.

Chinese revolution — may simply have been individualistic bourgeois posturing. Certainly something new is now in the air — an ultimate synthesis of dance, music, and lyrics, drawn from the folk songs and folktales of traditional China, blended with the true streams of a proletarian consciousness, girding itself for the final triumphant confrontation with the world of imperialism. This revolutionary literature, it is believed, will truly spring from the people, but to give correct guidance the People's Liberation Army has taken over much of the supervision. New works in this genre are "The Dance of the Lumbermen," "Iron Man Wang," "Three Power Lines Come to the Countryside," and "We Dare To Make the Sun and Moon Shine in New Skies"; there is also "In Praise of Heroes in a Sea of Fire" presented by the cultural troupe of the Navy political department, "In Praise of the Red Guards," and the drama "The Congo River Roars." Remembering the passage from the August 8, 1966, decision of the Central Committee of the Chinese Communist Party concerning the Great Proletarian Cultural Revolution — "In the great proletarian cultural revolution, the only method is for the masses to liberate themselves, and any method of doing things on their behalf must not be used"[13] — and holding it constantly before us, the best thing we can do at this stage is to let Peking speak for itself.

An entirely new spirit lights up Peking's stage in the present upsurge of the great proletarian cultural revolution. Imbued with strong proletarian sentiments, revolutionary art workers sing the praises of our most respected and beloved leader Chairman Mao, of heroes armed with the invincible thinking of Mao Tse-tung, of the great victory of the great proletarian cultural revolution, and of the lofty ideals of communism, in fresh and beautiful language.

Recently, amateur artists from the ranks of workers, peasants and soldiers, and many cultural groups in the capital have taken up their pens to write, and have performed many revolutionary songs and militant dances. They sing the praises of the revolu-

[13]*China Quarterly,* 28 (Oct.-Dec. 1966), p. 160.

tionary spirit of the awakened African people in the struggle against U.S. imperialism, or reflect the firm revolutionary will of the Chinese people. The rays of a new epoch shine on Peking's stage.[14]

This new revolutionary literature is now in full swing, and, crucially, it has finally passed from the hands of professional companies to the hands of the workers themselves. The first play in the pure new genre was "The Rising Sun,"[15] six acts, written, sung, and acted in 1966 by the workers and their families from the Taching oilfield. These proletarians were "The first among workers, peasants and soldiers to present on the stage a full-length modern drama on such a scale." The play itself is "the stirring story of how the family members of the workers of Taching oilfield, nurtured on the thinking of Mao Tse-tung, get organized to engage in collective productive labor and take the road of the revolution" and was reportedly performed 133 times before 220,000 theatergoers in Peking. A review adds that "the success of the play of these ordinary working people was a resounding slap in the face of the bourgeois 'experts' and 'authorities.' "

We may rest assured that these bourgeois experts and authorities are not merely American and European academics; they are also the cultural spokesmen for the Soviet Union and all Eastern European Communist countries (with the sole exception of Albania). The Chinese statement implies, in effect, that there has as yet been no true revolutionary literature anywhere outside China. The claim is bold and unambiguous. The Taching oilfield acting troupe become, in this context, a cultural commune.

---

[14]*China Pictorial*, No. 1 (1967), p. 52.
[15]For the following summaries and quotations cf. the review of "The Rising Sun" in *China Reconstructs*, *15*, No. 9 (Sept. 1966), 22-25.

Lawrence W. Chisolm

Lu Hsun and revolution in modern China

Lu Hsun's "Diary of a Madman" is news that stays news, which is the kind of revolutionary literature that matters. It was the first story written in modern vernacular Chinese, and its appearance in May 1918 in *New Youth,* the leading journal of China's modernizing intelligentsia, opened a new era in Chinese literature. It also announced the emergence from scholarly seclusion of Chou Shu-jen (1881-1936), using a new pen name, Lu Hsun, formed by adding his mother's family name Lu to Hsun, taken from a name he signed to an essay of 1907.

Lu Hsun, like the madman in his famous story, insisted on penetrating the surfaces of pious words to find out what was really happening. His report of what he discovered presented symbolically in this first story raises questions at the outset about the organizing structures of his imaginative world and about the relation of that world to his life and to the course of revolutionary change in China. Why, for example, do images of enclosure and cannibalism introduced in this story recur throughout his best writing? What connections exist between his personal history and the shifting conditions of Chinese culture? What kinds of changes were taking place at the time?

In China connections between perspective and action have been made clear by the vast scale of revolutionary change. It has been evident from the beginning that problems of creating a new written language and new forms of expression could not be separated from problems of reshaping social structures and reordering China's relation to world life. In this respect the continuing Chinese revolution is peculiarly modern, widely relevant despite its extreme contrasts between tradition and innovation and its compression of cultural changes into a comparatively short span of time. This modern kind of revolution is not so much a matter of dramatic events clustered around a central political stage but rather a question of underlying processes, in this case what Harold Lasswell calls "the permanent revolution of modernizing intellectuals," a revolution which assumes a permanently changing world and which casts in leading roles men who work with symbols that fuel change and that render change intelligible. One of the aims of writers and artists of all sorts during this permanent world-wide revolution has been to create new shapes, to structure new kinds of social space, and to chart journeys of the inner mind.

Yet China's triple revolution in conceptual, social, and inter-national relationships allows no easy historical analogy. Models for analyzing change when derived from Western experience tend to over-look the unique trajectories of Chinese events and to scant the author-ity and resources of China's traditional culture. In the case of literary revolutionaries, Chinese situations are apt to be too readily assimilated into those of Western intellectuals, but the scope and pace of Chinese intellectuals' readjustments in outlook since 1900 are enough to set them apart. They have had to survive and think in a whirlwind, all of them — Lu Hsun's generation, the older men who led the way, and the younger men who came after. As they fought against the habits of the old order, they were forced at the same time to consider how world developments might lead toward a new order at once Chinese and modern.

What this involved can be suggested in brief summary. They had to come to terms somehow with the entire tradition of Western thought largely unmediated by any Chinese predecessors, and this novel conceptual framework was itself continuously expanding throughout the period at a rate which left Western intellectuals them-selves lagging far behind. For Chinese thinkers this meant assimilating Western theory and technology while at the same time creating media for communication with a public hopefully literate and participant — all in an atmosphere of mounting anti-Western nationalism and in a social setting continuously wracked by civil wars, foreign invasion, and fratricidal ideological struggles. This whole enterprise, it is worth emphasizing, remained embedded in a culture rich in its models of continuity and opposition, a culture conveyed in a written language powerfully conservative by virtue of its restricted access. Chairman Mao's recent Great Cultural Revolution, like all China's modern revolutions, has been cultural in the thoroughgoing sense of transforming basic human outlooks — a process begun in earnest fifty years ago.

Lu Hsun, as it turns out, was involved in nearly every phase of cultural revolution, often close to the center of action. The turns of his life match the turns of China's history, and his writings derive much of their power from the web of connections he spins between private and public conditions and events. In fact all his writing is historical in its focus on Chinese conditions and autobiographical in its repeated efforts to rethink connections between individual life and a changing China. Problems of historical interpretation are enormous, and in the case of Lu Hsun appraisal is complicated by his posthumous rebirth as a legendary figure, Revolutionary Hero as Writer: "Fierce-browed, I coolly defy a thousand pointing fingers;/ Head-bowed, like a willing ox I serve the children."[1]

Fortunately the man back of both the Hero and the ghost remains available through his writings and in the fully documented record of his life. The figure is properly complex, and historical controversy should increase. Lu Hsun might well have lived to admire Mao in many ways, but the Nietzschean spirit of his youth would as likely have persisted. If Lu Hsun resembles, as he does, Mao's fierce yet willing ox, a beast of burden serving the children, he is also a troubler of the herd like Nietzsche's Zarathustra, urging man on to metamorphosis from beast of burden into lion and, finally, into child — creator of new values.

Lu Hsun's education in connecting private and public events and in distinguishing illusions from facts began in late childhood. Born in Shaohsing city in the coastal province of Chekiang in 1881 he grew up in a gentry family of modest wealth, the eldest of three sons of a gentleman-scholar and a self-taught literate countrywoman. His

---

[1]Lines are from Lu Hsun's poem, *"Tzu-ch'ao"* ("Self-mockery"), in *Chi Wai Chi (Collection Outside the Collection)*, in *Lu Hsun Ch'uan Chi (Lu Hsun's Complete Works)* (20 vols. Shanghai, 1938), 7, 510. Translation is from the official English version in Mao Tse-tung, *Talks At the Yenan Forum on Literature and Art* (3d ed., rev. trans., Peking, 1962), p. 41.

Lawrence W. Chisolm

traditional Confucian training was sharply and permanently interrupted by a series of family disasters. In 1893 his grandfather, an honored official in Peking, was disgraced; and the family fortunes were exhausted in negotiations for clemency. Meanwhile, Lu Hsun's father had fallen ill. Despite herbalist treatments which led Lu Hsun back and forth from doctor to pawnshop to pharmacy for three years or more, his father died. The mother now widowed — a serious plight —became a "poor relation" along with her young sons. "I believe those who sink from prosperity to poverty," Lu Hsun later declared, "will probably learn what the world is really like."

These personal family troubles became identified in Lu Hsun's mind with more general national problems as he managed to continue his education by government scholarship in Nanking at the new schools for Western learning — first at the Naval Academy and then at the School of Railways and Mines where he learned some German. Events of that time, notably the reform failures of 1898 and Western suppression of the Boxers, made Lu Hsun and many of his fellow students keenly aware of the weakness of China and the impotence of the Manchu court. In Nanking Lu Hsun discovered Western medical books and was impressed by Huxley's *Evolution and Ethics* in Yen Fu's translation. The way toward understanding Western power seemed to lie through Japan, whose rising position was due, Lu Hsun surmised, to an intellectual reformation begun with the introduction of Western medicine. Again government scholarships opened the way for study in Japan, where for eight years (1902-09) Lu Hsun explored the intellectual world outside the great wall of Chinese culture.

At first China's reformation seemed a matter of physical health. "I dreamed a beautiful dream," he recalled, "that on my return to China I would cure patients like my father, who had been mistakenly treated, while if war broke out I would serve as an army doctor, at the same time strengthening my countrymen's belief in reform."[2] The dream of curing China's ills by making the Chinese

[2]"Preface" (1922) to *Na Han, Ch'uan Chi, 1,* 271. This and subsequent translations rely on versions by Wang Chi-chen and by Gladys and Hsien-yi Yang (see Bibliographic note).

physically healthy was shattered by Japan's quick victory over Russia and the all too evident passivity of the Chinese constrained to be spectators at their own dismemberment. The limitations of reform through medicine were brought home to Lu Hsun while studying at Sendai Medical School. As the only Chinese student there, he seems to have been treated with a special condescension, alternately protective, envious, and dominating, maintained by the Japanese toward the representative of a culture once eminent but now weak and subordinate. The ironies of Lu Hsun's personal situation and the plight of his countrymen were connected dramatically one day when he was watching lantern slides of the Russo-Japanese War shown at the end of a medical lecture.

> I suddenly encountered Chinese faces on the screen. One of them was bound, surrounded by others, all of strong build but with stupid and vacant expressions. According to the caption, the one who was bound was a spy for the Russians and was about to be beheaded by the Japanese military as a warning to the populace; the crowd around him were there to enjoy the show.[3]

Lu Hsun left for Tokyo without finishing the school year, now determined to work for a reformation of Chinese spirit through the power of literature.

This new dream of a literary vanguard of change sustained Lu Hsun up to the Revolution of 1911 and revived his ambitions later on, but in its first phase, as a dream of anti-Manchu revolt leading to the reform of China, it proved to be another illusion. Yet the philosophical views which Lu Hsun formulated in these early years — especially his speculations about the writer's role in social change — established a measure for later assessments of self and society. As a hopeful revolutionary (Lu Hsun joined an anti-Manchu society in 1908), he turned enthusiastically to such Promethean literary rebels as Byron, Mickiewicz, and Petofi — men in love with freedom and, he declared, not tame like the common herd but wild "like zebras." Among philosophers Lu Hsun singled out Nietzsche's outcries against

[3]Ibid., p. 271.

hypocrisy and habit and cited Stirner's libertarian insistence on each man's unique and continual self-reconstruction. These particular principles had the added advantage, important psychologically, of revealing the shortcomings of Western society as well as providing intellectual instruments for the reform of China.

Like other reflective and hopeful men all over the world, Lu Hsun, from his vantage in Tokyo, felt the intellectual attraction of the idea of evolutionary progress; it seemed to offer a set of concepts which could give order and meaning to world life. For a while he believed in this organizing vision of human development, and something of this faith may have survived the repeated shocks in the years which followed. To young literary rebels looking out from Japan it seemed that the past in China would have to give way to a future which might well be better. With high hopes Lu Hsun and some friends planned to launch a new journal to be called *New Life,* and with his brother he planned to publish a series of translations from Western literature to add to the range of models available to Chinese writers. But *New Life* perished for lack of funds before it was born, and the first cosmopolitanizing volume of short stories (most of them by Slavic writers and translated from Japanese versions into classical Chinese) sold only twenty-one copies in the first six months, and the second volume twenty. It was evident that the eldest son's responsibilities to his family could no longer be put off. Unsuccessful in medicine and literature Lu Hsun returned to Shaohsing in 1909 and a conventional job teaching school.

Although his personal hopes for a literary career seemed to have died with *New Life,* his hopes for revolutionary change in China were stirred anew by the Wuchang uprising of October 10, 1911, and the subsequent collapse of the Manchus, the end, as it turned out, of two millennia of imperial rule. The Revolution brought new faces and new hopes to Shaohsing, but it soon became apparent that in Shaohsing, as elsewhere, very little had really changed, that results would be a long time coming. Lu Hsun recalled how after the Wuchang success a "revolutionary" government organized by the old-style gentry emerged in Shaohsing, to be replaced shortly by a new Military

Governor who came from Hangchow with his troops and "in less than ten days most of his men in the yamen [administrative building], who had arrived in cotton clothes, were wearing fur-lined gowns though it was not yet cold." Lu Hsun was appointed principal of the Normal School, but before long he left town just ahead of soldiers' bayonets because the Governor had been criticized too bluntly in the name of a newly free press by some ardent young innocents who had prevailed on Lu Hsun to act as their sponsor.

Lu Hsun returned to Shaohsing again only on rare visits. He obtained a minor post in Peking in the Education Ministry of the new Republic and withdrew as much as possible from public participation, indulging his scholarly interest in early Chinese literature. Once again, personal disappointments, this time as a writer-reformer, were felt to be closely related to the more general frustrations of the Chinese scene. As Lu Hsun watched from his quiet study in Peking, Yuan Shih-k'ai's imperial pretensions focused and dissolved; warlord factions vied violently for the center of the stage; the disillusions of Shaohsing were repeated again and again on a larger scale. Under the circumstances Lu Hsun's scholarly retreat can be considered a conventional public act as well as a sign of private disappointment: his withdrawal echoes traditional Chinese forms of protest against deteriorating standards of public life. Even Mao Tse-tung after brief service with a revolutionary army in 1911 seems to have hung back, his schooling in Changsha somewhat prolonged. Not until 1917 did the forces of intellectual revolution begin to gather in Peking.

In retrospect Lu Hsun's emergence in 1918 from his antique reveries seems only natural, part of the intellectual ferment of the May 4th period, whose span coincided closely with his most creative period. His new reform activities as writer, teacher, and editor were made possible by cultural changes catalyzed by student protests in May 1919 against Japan's humiliating new gains won at Versailles. A new Chinese intelligentsia was emerging, a broad group of literate people (estimated at ten million by 1918) whose education included some modern learning. The cultural revolution stemmed specifically

Lawrence W. Chisolm

from the reorganization of Peking's National University under Ts'ai
Yuan-p'ei in 1917 and from the proliferation of literary and intellectual journals of all sorts led by Ch'en Tu-hsiu's militant *New
Youth*. Geographically, Peking was the center, its population nearly
doubling from 1919 to 1923, its parade of warlord factions a reminder
of political fragmentation and social disorder. Ironically, warlord dis-
ruptions seem to have encouraged intellectual adventuring by block-
ing centralization of authority and by loosening the bonds of consensus.

Very little was stirring, however, early in 1918 when Lu Hsun
took up a new career as a vernacular (*pai-hua*) writer. It was at the
special urging of an old friend who was discouraged at the heavy
silence which greeted the calls for revolution crying out from the
pages of *New Youth*. (This was Ch'ien Hsuan-t'ung, advocate of
swift and total latinization of Chinese script, already driven to con-
cocting angry letters to *New Youth* attacking his own views in hopes
of controversy.) The campaign to create a modern literature written
in the language of common speech *(pai-hua)* had been launched offi-
cially the year before by Hu Shih and others, and *New Youth* had
just begun in January to publish all its articles in the vernacular style.
Lu Hsun was reluctant to emerge, remembering past failures — and
he was approaching forty — but the new spirit at Peking University and
the prospect of a literature at once Chinese and modern stirred his
hopes. His first story, *"K'uang-jen Jih Chi"* ("Diary of a Madman"),
as noted earlier, opened a new chapter in China's literary history.

In the famous preface to *Na Han (Cries in Battle)*, Lu Hsun's
first volume of stories, he recalled how he resolved his doubts in a
query to his friend:

> "Suppose there is an iron room with absolutely no window or
> door and impossible to break down. Suppose there are many
> people fast asleep in the room slowly suffocating to death. But
> they will pass directly from sleep to death with none of the fears
> and sorrows of approaching death. Now you start shouting and
> you wake up the few people who are not so fast asleep and
> make them suffer the agonies of inescapable death. Do you think

you are doing them a kindness?" "Even if only a few should
wake up," came the reply, "you cannot say there is absolutely no
hope of breaking down the iron room."[4]

The metaphor establishes a balance weighted toward death which persists in many of his stories, and the imagery of illusions as forms of
stifling enclosure points to a darkened skepticism.

Lu Hsun's skepticism is fundamental. The only certainty which
he offers is the certainty of change. Many of his finest stories describe
how "you can't go home again," how new experience makes the old
accustomed ways no longer comforting, in fact no longer possible.
His most complex characters are men uprooted and made wanderers
not only by the forces of change but by their own honesty and sensibility. There is little nostalgia for the past in Lu Hsun's fictive world.
Nor does he sentimentalize the common people. At best they live by
habit, evading unpleasant facts by dreams; at worst they are cruel
and credulous, their illusions murderous. Although they are bound
together by custom and circumstances, their gestures of human solidarity consist often of abusing those who are weak and ridiculing
whatever is new.

Lu Hsun's sensitive and often scholarly wanderers, by contrast,
feel at home nowhere but keep going, surviving somehow for a while,
their imaginations alive to contrasts: flowers in the snow, light and
darkness, the peppery and the bland, stasis and motion. Even despair
becomes a kind of vanity: in the end it is survival that matters and
the only hope, if it can be called that, the road itself. To the voyager
reflecting back on childhood as he floats down the river, hope is not
something absolute which either exists or does not; it is "like the
roads that travelers make across the face of the earth where there
were none before." Although the past revisited by the voyager in *"Ku
Hsiang"* ("My Old Home") cannot be recaptured, it survives as an
image connecting the past with the future.

If it was not clear to Lu Hsun where the roads of change were
leading, some kind of common language was clearly needed to name
the routes and identify the landscape of change — which is what his

4Ibid., p. 274.

best writing achieved. One man alone would not likely survive the journey, and lives without felt connections with one another were as good as dead. The need to name new kinds of human relationships and new forms of consciousness was perhaps more urgent in China than elsewhere because the persisting force of outmoded names caused much confusion. All Lu Hsun's writing is about China and directed at China — even his translations aim to enlarge Chinese consciousness — his mission, to help create forms of written expression through which he and his countrymen might understand their situations, might name their personal and common plights and joys, so that they would no longer be cut off from one another by walls of silence and indifference.

This concern animates his writing as a recurrent theme and also defines the achievements of his style. Through his best work he released the newly literate into a world complexly imagined yet disciplined so as to heighten perception, neither blurring the mind's newly opened eyes with sentimental plots nor dazzling with eccentric impressions. His chosen instrument was a supple vernacular, clear and economical, a style strong enough to assimilate both classical phrases and foreign ideas, using them to particular effect, embedding the old and the new in the flow of orderly modern consciousness. His short stories introduced the form to Chinese writing and set standards for all who followed; his prose poems combined classical with vernacular in new forms; and in his regular social commentary he developed an influential new style of *tsa wen,* terse pithy essays aimed at specific targets and adaptable across a wide range from satire and polemics to personal impressions and random reflections of all sorts.

The inner world which sustained Lu Hsun's best imaginative work collapsed after 1926 for reasons which may never be fully understood. The mounting violence of revolution and the sufferings of his personal friends and students shocked him deeply. And the killings and quarrels among the young may well have destroyed his waning hopes for the future. The first heavy blow came on March 18, 1926, when a group of student petitioners were savagely attacked by the soldiers of warlord "President" Tuan Chi-jui; among the forty-seven killed were two young girl students of Lu Hsun's at the Women's Normal College. When he first heard the news, he could not believe his own countrymen could commit such horrors: although habitually ready to think the worst, he had "never dreamed of such a thing."

His life endangered by his continued protests, he fled Peking, heading south and east toward the centers of political radicalism, his travels symbolizing his countrymen's continuing searches and the opening of a new revolutionary phase. As the Kuomintang's Northern Expedition swept toward victory in the summer of 1926, Lu Hsun moved to Amoy and then to Canton, observing the rising fury of factions among students, noting how slander was replacing argument, how impatience flared toward violence. He finally left in September 1927, arriving in Shanghai soon after mass executions there, and hearing a few weeks later from friends in Canton about massacres on all sides. "The revolutionaries are killed by the counter-revolutionaries. The counter-revolutionaries are killed by the revolutionaries," he wrote at the time.

> The non-revolutionaries are sometimes taken for revolutionaries and killed by counter-revolutionaries, sometimes taken for counter-revolutionaries and killed by revolutionaries, and sometimes killed by either revolutionaries or counter-revolutionaries for no apparent reason at all. . . . Revolution, r-e-v-o-l-u-t-i-o-n, REVOLUTION."[5]

Sickened by fratricidal killings and increasing government suppression of criticism and dissent, Lu Hsun moved more completely into the opposition, drawn further toward the left politically by every oppressive act of the right. Although taking a leading public role in the League of Chinese Left-Wing Writers, he did not join the Communist party and remained scornful of "writing under other people's orders." The idea of "revolutionary literature" seemed something of a contradiction in terms to Lu Hsun. During real revolution there is no leisure for literature, he surmised, and when leisure exists, literature cannot be made by blueprint out of such abstractions as "the masses."

[5]*Erh I Chi (That's All), Ch'uan Chi, 3,* 511.

Lawrence W. Chisolm

The idea of "revolutionary love" struck him as equally unreal. "I think there is only non-revolutionary love," he wrote in a letter. "With sex as with food, there can be temporary selection but not permanent involvement."[6] Rather than bowing to a new set of abstract pieties literary men might better range freely over the world's literature in the cosmopolitan spirit of the great days of T'ang. In the end, the flowering of literature in China would depend on writers who had broad education and independent spirit. At the moment, however, China needed men willing to struggle against enemies pressing in from all sides.

What makes Lu Hsun important, finally, is the quality of his mind. At issue is not so much his explicit social commentary, or his literary and political arguments, or his scholarly work in Chinese literary history or in voluminous translations. At issue are the clues that Lu Hsun may offer as to what is involved in an individual's sequential attempts at reintegrating a set of changing cultural situations and, more specifically, how that experience can be organized into symbolic structures, structures capable of identifying particular human lives as trajectories across scenes whose elements change at variable rates and capable, at the same time, of organizing the web of mutual implications among people within cultural frameworks variably shared. This is a somewhat abstract way of describing one of the crucial achievements of writers during the permanent revolutions of worldwide modernization.

For the moment, consider only the particular revolution that Lu Hsun reimagined in his stories and reminiscences — the Revolution of 1911. This was the crucial cultural event in his own public and private life, and the progressive versions of the event in his writings help identify the process of his imagination, especially the versions in *"Ah Q Cheng Chuan"* ("The Real Story of Ah Q" — 1921) and *"Fan Ai-nung"* (1926).

Ah Q, Lu Hsun's most famous character, was almost immediately taken into the Chinese language as a symbol of "Ah Q-ism," a set of

[6]Quoted and translated in Harriet C. Mills, "Lu Hsun and the Communist Party," *China Quarterly, 1* (Oct.-Dec. 1960), 23, from Hsu Kuang-p'ing, ed., *Lu Hsun Shu Chien (Lu Hsun's Letters)*.

typical Chinese deficiencies: self-deceptions which turn defeats into victories, shallow opportunism responsive to the appearances of power, a pervasive vagueness helpful in evading facts. Ah Q's special gift, it seems, is the ability to forget almost immediately any experience which might damage his latest pleasing illusion — so goes a standard analysis. But Ah Q has other qualities which complicate interpretations of his progress toward death by execution for revolutionary crimes he did not commit during a revolution which did not happen. For example, he is alert to power but not obsequious; he is active rather than passive; and his honesty gets him into as much trouble as his fantasy — in fact, his honesty is what finally kills him. Ah Q totally lacks any past, even a name, and as the story unfolds it becomes evident that he is continually reinvented by others, that he is largely comprised of other people's shifting images of him. Equally striking is the fact that he never learns from experience because he has no continuous interior life of his own. Words fuddle him, especially fragments of old Confucian homilies, and leave him dependent for connection with the world on scattered cues imprinted by threats and ridicule and by animal pain and pleasure. Only when he recognizes that he is on his way to death does he comprehend his feelings and ignore the expectations of the crowd. This nameless man is killed by forces from the past in the name of changes which are unreal partly because left unnamed. But it is also because Ah Q has no past that he dies; in a sense, he has no future because he has no connection to any past, and some kind of continuity remains necessary even in the most extreme situations. Whatever resources one brings to life must somehow survive from the past into the future.

Lu Hsun's own reminiscences, most of them written in 1926 after he was uprooted from Peking, suggest the importance of such survivals out of the past. In naming his connections with people and places that had mattered to him, he was engaged in the kind of reconstruction of inner life more familiar in the modern West where autobiography is now seen as a promising prelude to further cognitive and creative growth. In Lu Hsun's case these autobiographical sketches signaled the close of his public imaginings, and he did not return to writing reminiscence again until near the end of his life. The bridge that he sought to build from the past into the future may have been barred by the discontinuities of the present in 1927 and 1928.

Among the reminiscences written in 1926 is the story of his friendship with Fan Ai-nung. The story pivots on the Revolution of 1911, and in this last reimagined version of the event, Lu Hsun faces the implications most directly. He recalls how he first met Fan Ai-nung in Japan when they both were young students plotting against the Manchu court; how they quarreled at the time; how they met unexpectedly later in Shaohsing and became friends; how with the coming of the Revolution their hopes for China rose, especially Fan Ai-nung's; how their spirits fell swiftly when the old order continued; how Lu Hsun moved on to Peking and how Fan Ai-nung could find no place to go; how Lu Hsun finally heard the news of his friend's suicide. As the story develops, Lu Hsun's emotional relationship to Fan Ai-nung and their hopes for China become fused with the plight of China and the problem of locating responsibility, generally and personally, for the failure of these hopes.

The reminiscence opens with the assassination of a Manchu governor and the execution of two Chinese revolutionaries, a man and a woman; it closes with Fan Ai-nung's death and the unnamed future of his only daughter. As Lu Hsun looks back, his initial rudeness to Fan Ai-nung in Tokyo and his misconstruals of his friend's behavior are revealed as due to Lu Hsun's own pride and condescension, to his own selfish preoccupations which later insulate him from his friend's despairing situation and which contribute directly to Fan's death. Lu Hsun is finally revealed as an assassin connected irrevocably to his victim, to other assassins — Chinese, Manchu, Japanese — to China, and to the very hopes, his own and Fan's, which he, Lu Hsun, has helped to kill. But the effect of this work of high art, achieved by directing the full force of irony onto himself, is to communicate a sense of the potentially integrating power of the imagination when disciplined into full awareness. The reader, drawn into this process of progressive self-awareness by a style of understatement, comes to fully feel and imagine what he had only suspected at first: that Fan

Ai-nung is China and Lu Hsun is also China, that the web of mutual implication between them really was and now is, and that Lu Hsun hoped that the same kind of failures would not recur and at the same time felt that they would, inevitably so.

Lu Hsun's sense of the extremity of China's situation and the terrors latent in hopelessness found imaginative integration in recurring images of cannibalism. His first vernacular story hinged on traditional cannibal acts: the central delusion-which-is-truth is the madman's discovery in a book of China's history that although words like "benevolence" and "righteousness" were scrawled over every page, hidden between the lines everywhere were the words *"Ch'ih jen"* ("Eat men"). The theme recurs in Lu Hsun's recollections of Fan Ai-nung: the Chinese patriot from Shaohsing who assassinates the Manchu governor has his heart torn out by his captors, then fried and eaten. In Lu Hsun's symbolic world cannibal acts represent ultimate violent human paradoxes.

Other kinds of death imagery cluster around cannibalism. Images of enclosure — rooms and boxes which hem in, walls which bar the way, ice which is freezing fire, circles which constrict — contribute to a sense of expectancies blocked, of breath stifled, of forces pressing inward toward crises of contained violence, powerfully implosive and apocalyptic in the aggregate. This enclosure imagery intensifies the symbolic implosiveness of cannibal acts imagined as breaking into the core enclosures of the human body.

Several paradoxes converge. Although cannibal acts break through walls which isolate man from man, such acts simultaneously separate man from man: cannibalism simultaneously connects and sunders, nurtures and destroys. In the imagery of group relationships, human nurture, when imagined as a cannibalistic sequence, provides a symbolic model of "partial modernization" applicable to a China "Westernized" in the nineteenth century and, in the process, sliced up like a melon, with the added cut that the slicing was said to be for China's own good — benevolent cannibalism.

Cannibalism can also be considered as symbolizing the terrors of cultural change and suggesting the proper limits of rates of change.

Lawrence W. Chisolm

New forms which replace old ones too rapidly, which destroy the old completely in the name of the new, are cannibalistic. When the new devours the old, the future is destroying parts of itself which require a nurturing relation to the past in order to survive. This is one of the paradoxes of Ah Q, who was killed by the past because he had no past; it is part of the plight of Lu Hsun's fictional wanderers whose connections with both past and future have been ruptured by rapid change. The paradox is present in creating new forms of written language: as vernacular style displaces and destroys Chinese classical forms, it destroys some of the qualities of conception it needs — latinization breaks even more completely.

Lu Hsun's responses to a series of extreme situations in China's history led his imagination toward comparable symbolic forms, in this case, paradoxes appropriately violent. Toward the end of his life he was driven to fight with a fierceness often thought of as "revolutionary." What made him a revolutionary writer whose news stays news was a symbolic imagination which nurtured continuity as it recognized overwhelming changes and which held on to individual life while sensing universal destruction.

Bibliographic note
All stories discussed above may be read in English translations in *Selected Works of Lu Hsun,* trans. Yang Hsien-yi and Gladys Yang (4 vols. Peking, 1956-60), which includes a biographical sketch of Lu Hsun by Feng Hsueh-feng. See also *Ah Q And Others: Selected Stories of Lusin,* trans. Wang Chi-chen (New York, 1941), and Wang Chi-chen, "Lusin: A Chronological Record 1881-1936," *China Institute Bulletin, 3* (January 1939), 99-125. C. T. Hsia, *A History of Modern Chinese Fiction 1917-1957* (New Haven and London, 1961) offers a summary account with bibliographies.

Contributors

ROLAND BARTHES, author of *Le degré zéro de l'écriture, Essais critiques, Sur Racine,* and, most recently, the "semiological" study *Système de la mode,* teaches at l'Ecole Pratique des Hautes Etudes . . . MICHEL BEAUJOUR is Associate Professor of French at N.Y.U., an editor of *L'Herne,* and writes frequently on Dada and Surrealism . . . JEAN MARC BLANCHARD, lately a student at l'Ecole Normale Supérieure, teaches at Columbia and is writing a dissertation on "The Myth of Action" in the modern French novel . . . MAURICE BLANCHOT, novelist and critic, author of *La part du feu, Faux pas, Le livre à venir* . . . A Yale Fellow in East Asian Studies LAWRENCE CHISOLM is author of *Fenollosa: the Far East and American Culture,* and presently at work on a biography of Lu Hsun . . . On WITOLD GOMBROWICZ see the introduction to his pieces in this issue . . . RICHARD GREEMAN is engaged in translating the first three novels of Victor Serge, teaches at Columbia, and is a member of the National Editorial Board of *News and Letters* . . . NAOMI GREENE, who is preparing a dissertation on Artaud for N.Y.U., has begun teaching this year at the University of California at Santa Barbara . . . MICHAEL HOLQUIST teaches Slavic at Yale, and is studying the fantastic genre in realist fiction . . . ROMAN JAKOBSON is Professor of Linguistics at Harvard . . . LUDOVIC JANVIER is author of *Pour Samuel Beckett* . . . RICHARD KLEIN studies and teaches French at Yale, and is writing a dissertation on Baudelaire . . . A sometime *normalien* who has also taught at Yale, JEAN PIERRE MOREL is a specialist in Franco-Russian literary relations . . . Until his death in 1963, RENATO POGGIOLI was Reisinger professor of Slavic and Comparative Literature at Harvard; his publications included *The Phoenix and the Spider,* a study of Russian poets, and *Teoria dell'arte d'avanguardia,* which will soon be published by Harvard University Press

Contributors

in English translation . . . ANTONIO REGALADO, who teaches
Spanish at N.Y.U., is author of a recent book on Galdòs . . . On
VICTOR SERGE, novelist and revolutionary who participated in
the 1917 Revolution and was later exiled by Stalin, see the details
furnished by Richard Greeman's article . . . JONATHAN SPENCE,
Assistant Professor of History at Yale and frequent commentator
on Chinese politics, is author of *Ts'ao Yin and the K'ang-hsi Em-
peror, Bondservant and Master.*